GCSE
Applied Business

Dave Hall ✪ Rob Jones ✪ Carlo Raffo ✪ Dave Gray

Edited by Ian Chambers & Jackie Dickinson

 Causeway Press

Cover design by Caroline Waring-Collins
Image provided by Getty Images
Graphics by Caroline Waring-Collins, Anneli Jameson and Tim Button
Cartoons by Alan Fraser
Photography by Andrew Allen and Dave Gray
Page design by Caroline Waring-Collins
Reader - Mike Kidson

Every effort has been made to locate the copyright holders of material reproduced in this book. Any errors and omissions brought to the attention of the publishers are regretted and will be credited in subsequent printings.

British Library Cataloguing in Publication Data
A catalogue record of this book is available from the British Library

ISBN 1-902796-62-4

Causeway Press Limited
PO Box 13, Ormskirk, Lancashire, L39 5HP
© Dave Hall, Rob Jones, Carlo Raffo, Dave Gray, Ian Chambers, Jackie Dickinson
First impression 2003

Design and page origination by Caroline Waring-Collins and Anneli Jameson (Waring Collins Limited)
Printed and bound by Scotprint, Haddington, Scotland

Acknowledgements

The publisher and authors would like to thank the following for the use of photographs and other material in this book.

Acknowledgements
Amazon.com p64, Angela Lubrano/PAL/Topham p92, Boots p22, BT p57, Cooperative Bank p73, Corel pp56(b),80(tl),89,111,136(br),219, Egg p44, Dana Petroleum plc p24 (tr), Digital Stock pp39,56(t),62,114,191, Digital Vision pp12(bl),32(bl),35,41,42,43,44(c),45(r),46,84(r),91,92(tl),100(tr),116(t),124,169,187,201(tr),209,203, Ford pp70,78,100(tl),120, Fyffes p4, HSBC p234, IPC p82(b), JD Wetherspoon plc p73, Lloyds TSB p234, Michael Crabtree/Reuters/Popperfoto p120(br), NatWest pp226,234, Northern Foods plc p40(tr), PhotoBiz p223, PhotoDisc pp8(l),12(br),20(r),24(tl,cr,bl),29,30,31,32(tl,br),36(t),38(l),44(l,r),45(l),56,60,67,73,76,81,87,88,92,93,95, 97,104(tr,br),107,108,112,117(r),129,135,136(bl),147(r),148(t),151,152(bl,br),156,160(tl),163,167,168,172(br),175,176(b), 177(r),188,200(tl),204,212,215,216,228,231,232,235, Play.com p164, Powergen plc 172(tl), Range Cooker Group p73, Rex Features p96, Rexam plc p40(tl), Suma p19, Stockbyte pp4,7,8(r,b),16,24(cr,bl),36(b),47,48,59,63, 68(t,b),69,71,75,79,84(tl),100(bl,br),104(br),116(c,b),117(l),138,139,140,142,147(l),148(b),152(t),160(br),172(tr,bl),176(t, 177(l),179,183,184,186,189,200(tr,b),201(tl,b),211,207,208,220,226,227, Tesco p65, The Realeat Company Ltd p82(c), Thistle Hotels plc p40(b), Topham/PA pp121,123, Topham/Pressnet p99, Topham/ProSport pp12(t),176(tl), Topham/Universal Pictorial Press pp80(br),217, Towers Business Park p20(l), Unilever plc p51.

All other material is acknowledged at source.

Preface

GCSE Applied Business is designed for students, teachers and lecturers who are following the **GCSE Applied Business (Double Award) qualification**. It is organised into 4 page sections which mirror the specifications of all awarding bodies. This allows users of the book to follow the course easily, whilst allowing flexibility of course construction.

Features
○ Designed in full colour. This helps the understanding of important ideas and diagrams.
○ Contains 58 short, accessible 4 page sections, allowing easy access to topics.
○ Comprehensive coverage of the specifications of all awarding bodies. This allows students, teachers and lecturers to find the part of the book relevant to their learning and teaching easily.
○ Each 4 page section begins with a series of case studies to introduce the topic area simply.
○ The 4 page sections in Units 1 & 2 end with a portfolio practice question. This helps students to develop the skills required to produce a successful portfolio for internal assessment. Sections in Unit 3 end with a practice examination-type question.
○ The book highlights and defines important key terms. Together they make up a dictionary of Business Studies.
○ Each unit has a set of short questions to help understanding.
Also available to complement this book.
○ **GCSE Applied Business Portfolio Book** - an essential companion to **GCSE Applied Business**, which gives guidance on the skills required to produce a portfolio for internal assessment.
○ **GCSE Applied Business Teachers' Guide** - a photocopiable guide for teachers which contains suggested answers to all questions in the students' books and important support material.

Contents

1 Business aims and objectives

Getting started...

All businesses have aims and objectives. These are what a business wants to achieve. Some businesses just want to survive. Others want to grow. Some might want their sales to double next year. Think about the following businesses.

Case 1 *Dibjacks*

Caitlin Dibble has just left college where she studied design and fashion. She has set up a business called Dibjacks, making and selling jackets and tops. At the moment she still lives with her parents, but she wants to make enough money to become independent. Her main concern in the first twelve months is to stay in business. She needs to make and sell 500 products to cover the business's costs, such as materials for the tops and jackets and her wages.

Case 2 *Fyffes*

Fyffes manufactures and distributes fresh produce, such as fruit and vegetables. It aims to 'meet the demands of customers by supplying the widest range of products to the highest standard of service from state of the art facilities, using the latest technologies, communications and distribution services'.

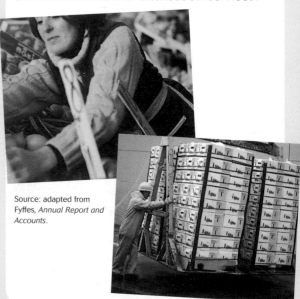

Source: adapted from Fyffes, *Annual Report and Accounts*.

Case 3 *Timestrut*

Mumtaaz Aziz runs a fast growing business called Timestrut. The business supplies schools with teachers to cover for permanent staff who are absent. Mumtaaz already has a lot of teachers on her books. But next year she is trying to increase this by 20 per cent so she will make more profit.

What are:
(a) Dibjacks
(b) Fyffes
(c) Timestrut
trying to achieve?

What are the aims and objectives of business?

Aims

BUSINESS AIMS are general statements about what a business intends to do. Examples of the aims of businesses are shown in Figure 1.

Figure 1 *The aims of businesses*

Profits Most businesses aim to make profits. Some businesses try to make as much profit as possible. They are known as PROFIT MAXIMISERS. Others just try to make a satisfactory profit. The choice will depend on the views of the owners of the business.

Survival Sometimes the main aim is to 'stay in business'. New businesses are often risky because someone setting up for the first time may lack experience. It also takes time to build up regular customers. So, at first, a new business might be happy just to survive.

Survival might also be an aim if a business has problems such as low sales. This can happen if the economy is in a RECESSION. Other businesses might aim to grow by expanding their sales or profits as quickly as possible.

Maximising sales or quality Some businesses aim to maximise sales. This can put the business in a strong position in its market. Managers often aim for sales to grow so that they can be paid higher salaries.

Some businesses try to maximise the quality of their products and how they are made. This should lead to fewer production faults and better products. If customers are satisfied with the product, this should improve the reputation of the business.

Providing products to the community Some businesses aim to provide goods and services that people in the local area need. A hairdressing salon or a local bus service are examples. Other businesses provide goods or services for all people in a country, such as electricity. Some businesses sell their goods worldwide, such as Coca-Cola.

Providing a competitive service Many businesses try to offer a better service than their rivals. This is often the case in very competitive markets, such as supermarkets or mobile phone companies. They might try to offer a wider variety of products or make it easier for customers to buy them.

Offering a charitable, voluntary or community service Some organisations are non-profit making, such as Oxfam. They aim to sell products and donate the money to worthy and needy causes, such as helping children, older people or those in countries with low incomes. Others offer voluntary services, such as help for the homeless, or local community services, such as transport for the disabled.

Being environmentally friendly Some businesses are concerned about their impact on the environment. They try to protect the environment by keeping pollution or waste to a minimum. Or they might help to build parks or gardens in the local area.

Objectives

BUSINESS OBJECTIVES are the goals that a business wants to achieve. Objectives are more precise than aims and can be measured. To meet its objectives a business may set a TARGET. This shows the amount it wants to achieve and the time in which it wants to achieve it. Examples of a business's objectives are shown in Figure 2.

Objectives can be used to judge whether a business has achieved its aims. A business that has cut smoke emissions by 10 per cent may decide it is becoming more environmentally friendly. A business that has failed to increase profit by 10 per cent over two years might decide that it has not achieved satisfactory profits.

Figure 2 *The objectives of businesses*

Selling more than competitors A business might want to sell more than other businesses. It might want sales of £10 million a year compared to a rival's sales of £3 million. Or it might want to sell to 30 per cent of all customers when its closest rival sells to only 10 per cent.

Reducing costs A business might want to reduce its costs. It might have a target to cut costs by 5 per cent over the next two years. Or it might want to reduce its costs from £100,000 a year to £80,000 a year.

Providing more services A business might want its sales to grow. It might want sales to increase by 10 per cent next year or by 30 per cent over the next 5 years.

Producing new goods and services A sportswear business might want to sell a new style of trainers in the next year. It might carry on selling its older styles or stop selling them altogether. The introduction of broadband for the Internet is an example of a new service. But it will take a number of years for it to be sold in all areas.

Improving a product An objective might be to produce a better product. This might be a product that operates better, such as a faster computer. Or it might be a safer product, such as a child's car seat. Or it might be a healthier product, such as a pudding with reduced fat.

key terms

- **Business aim** - *a general statement of what a business intends to do.*
- **Business objective** - *a precise and measurable goal of a business.*
- **Profit maximisers** - *businesses that aim to make the greatest amount of profit possible.*
- **Recession** – *usually when spending by customers is falling and business profits are low.*
- **Target** – *the amount a business want to achieve in a certain period of time.*

key terms key terms key terms key terms key terms

Quick quiz

1 True or false? All businesses aim to make a profit.

2 Fill in the missing words. **Competitors   Survive   Sales**

(a) A business that maximises ...... might be able to pay its managers more.

(b) New businesses might try just to ...... for the first few years.

(c) Businesses in markets where there is a great deal of competition aim to offer a better service than their ....

3 A precise goal that a business seeks to achieve is called an ....

4 State whether the following are business aims or objectives.

(a) To maximise profits.

(b) To be an environmentally friendly business.

(c) To increase sales by 12 per cent over the next twelve months.

(d) To provide a service that is needed by local residents.

(e) To sell a computer game with more realistic graphics.

5 A hairdressing business wants to provide a high quality service. Last year it failed to send any of its new employees for training. Do you think it has achieved its aim?

Portfolio practice

Fisco Supplies

Fisco Supplies makes and supplies safety clothing and equipment to the building industry. Since the business started, 10 years ago, it has been successful in meeting all its aims and objectives.

Senior managers and directors of the company are meeting soon to agree the aims and objectives for the coming year. Certain factors are likely to influence them.

✪ The development team has produced a new lightweight safety helmet. Tests suggest that this new product would be very successful. The business plans to introduce it next year.

✪ Trading conditions have been difficult. The construction industry has been in recession, so there has been a reduction in demand for clothing and equipment from construction businesses.

✪ Competition has increased. A similar business has set up recently. It has persuaded some of Fisco's customers to buy its products by offering discounts for large orders. Fisco has lost 10 per cent of its sales to the new business, but hopes to regain half in the coming year.

✪ In the past, Fisco Supplies has donated money to a community group to help with the building of a local community centre. It has been in discussions about offering a further £10,000 next year.

✪ The owners of Fisco Supplies are concerned that profits have been falling over the last three years. They do not want to see profits falling again this year.

1. Describe what has happened to the:
   (a) trading conditions;
   (b) profits;
   (c) competition
   of the business
   recently. (3 marks)

2. Identify:
   (a) two possible aims
   (b) two possible objectives
   that Fisco Supplies might have during the coming year. (4 marks)

3 How might:
   (a) the change in trading conditions and
   (b) changes in competition affect the aims and objectives of the business in future? (8 marks)

2 Business ownership - sole traders and partnerships

Getting started...

Different businesses have different types of owners. A sole trader owns the business alone. A partnership is owned by two or more people.

Case 1 Hudson Guitars

Tyrone Hudson owns his own business repairing electric guitars. Tyrone says 'I can choose the hours that I work. I can leave early to play in my band in the evening. Or I can stay late if I have some urgent work on.' He works very hard and knows that he doesn't have to share the money he makes with anyone else.

(a) Are (i) Hudson Guitars, (ii) L&S Accountants and (iii) Grainger Designs sole traders or partnerships?

(b) Why do you think that they decided to go into business as a sole trader or a partnership?

Case 2 L&S Accountants

Lisa Albright and Sasha Crystal run an accountancy business. They set up together after completing their accounting qualifications. One of the strengths of the business is that they are good at different things. Lisa likes working with figures and giving advice to small businesses. Sasha works with some of their larger clients on financial planning. Last year the business needed a new computer. They each put in some money to pay for it.

Case 3 Grainger Designs

Molly Grainger is a website designer. She set up her own business just a few months after leaving a large design company. She likes working for herself. 'It's great not being hassled by a boss. But it's a bit frightening knowing that I have to take all the responsibility myself. I'm sure that I can get work from some of the customers I used to design websites for in my old job because they always liked my ideas.'

What are the main features of sole traders and partnerships?

Legal status

Sole traders Most businesses in the UK are SOLE TRADERS. A sole trader is a business owned by just one person. Sometimes other employees are taken on to work for the business, but they are not owners. Sole traders are often small businesses in areas such as plumbing, carpentry, agriculture and retailing.

Partnership In an ORDINARY PARTNERSHIP, between 2 and 20 people can own the business. Partnerships are often found in businesses such as legal services, accountancy, surveying and information technology.

Use of profits

Sole traders There is only one owner. So that person takes all the profits of the business.

Partnerships Sometimes partners sign a DEED OF PARTNERSHIP. This shows how the business will be run and how the profits will be shared. If there is no deed, the law says that profits must be shared equally between the partners.

Liability of owners

Liability is about who is legally responsible for the debts of a business.

Sole traders Sole traders have UNLIMITED LIABILITY. This means that the owner is liable for **all** debts of the business. In UK law there is no difference between a sole trader's private money and the business's money. So if there is not enough money within a business to pay off its debts, the owner's personal money might have to be used to settle them. In some cases, personal possessions, such as a house, might have to be sold to raise money to settle debts.

Partnerships Partners in ordinary partnerships have unlimited liability, like sole traders. They have to pay the business's debts even if this means using their own money or selling their own possessions.

But there are two other types of partnership where partners can have LIMITED LIABILITY. They are only liable for the money they have put into the business. If the partnership does not have enough money to pay its debts, their private money or possessions cannot be taken. These partnerships can have more than 20 partners.
- In **limited partnerships**, some partners can invest money in the business, but they are not actively involved in its running. They are called **sleeping partners**. Sleeping partners have limited liability.
- In a **limited liability partnership**, all the partners have limited liability.

Advantages

Sole traders
- They are easy to set up and run. The business might only need to fill in tax forms.
- The owner is the only person in control, so decisions can be made without asking others.
- The owner keeps all the profits and doesn't need to share them with anyone else.

Partnerships
- They are easy to set up and run. Partners may sign a deed of partnership.
- The burden of running the business is shared.
- Partners can be given responsibility for different parts of the business.
- Partners may bring different skills to the business.
- Two or more people might be able to put more money into the business than one person.

Problems

Sole traders

- ✪ Sole traders have unlimited liability for the debts of the business.
- ✪ There is no one else to rely upon. If a sole trader takes time off ill, the work will not be done and sales might be lost.
- ✪ Sole traders often work long hours and do most of the work themselves. This can lead to stress and strain.
- ✪ Sole traders can find it hard to raise the money to expand. They may have to use up their savings or sell their property. Banks may not lend them money.
- ✪ The business may have to close completely if a sole trader dies.

Partnerships

- ✪ Partners may disagree. This can cause delays in making decisions. Sometimes disagreements might even cause the partnership to collapse.
- ✪ Partners in most partnerships have unlimited liability. They are liable for any debts of the business.
- ✪ If one partner leaves a partnership, the business ends. A new business then has to be formed.

key terms

- ✪ **Deed of partnership** – *a legal contract between partners, stating how the partnership will be run and how the profits will be shared.*
- ✪ **Limited liability** – *where the owners of the business are not responsible for paying off all its debts. If the business has debts, only the money they have put into the business can be used to settle them, not the owners' personal money.*
- ✪ **Ordinary partnership** - *a business owned by between 2 and 20 people, all with unlimited liability.*
- ✪ **Sole trader** - *a business owned by one person.*
- ✪ **Unlimited liability** - *where the owners are responsible to pay off any debts of a business.*

key terms key terms key terms key terms key terms k

Quick quiz

1 List three types of business where sole traders are likely to be commonly found.

2 Complete the sentence.

Partners may sign a .... which shows how profits will be shared.

3 Choose the correct answer a, b, c or d.

The number of partners in an ordinary partnership can be between:

(a) 1 and 10   **(b)** 20 and 200   **(c)** 1 and 20   **(d)** 2 and 20.

4 True or false?

(a) Unlimited liability means that the owners of the business are liable for all the debts of the business.

(b) Sole traders do not have unlimited liability.

5 How do the following examples illustrate the problems of sole traders and partnerships?

(a) Johnsons Partnership has decided to buy a new office building, but the owners cannot agree where it should be.

(b) Lee Healy, a plumber, has been off sick for 3 days and has lost £500 worth of work.

(c) Karrick, a decorating business, has just lost a job painting a factory because the job was too big for the owner. She did not have enough money in the business to hire the equipment she needed to do the work.

Portfolio practice

Rover Madness

Tim Hill started a car sales business called Rover Madness with his sister Grace and his brother Alan. The business is a partnership, with each partner having unlimited liability. Each partner put some money into the business to give it a good start.

Rover Madness sells second-hand Land Rovers. They are bought from military suppliers at home and abroad. Tim has built up many good contacts and knows how to get the vehicles at the lowest price. He is also a good salesperson. Grace is in charge of promotion and accounts. Alan is an experienced mechanic. He can sort out problems on most Land Rovers, even really old ones.

In the first few years of trading things went well and the business was very profitable. In the third year they were able to spend £40,000 buying up stocks of vehicles. They also took £10,000 each as a bonus.

But by the fourth year Tim was having second thoughts. He wasn't happy with Alan's idea that they should buy more vehicles from abroad. On top of this, he and Grace felt that Alan was not pulling his weight in the business. Alan often left early to play squash and was missing customers who called on their way home from work.

Tim was thinking about leaving the partnership. He would then set up either as a sole trader or in partnership with his sister.

1. What does unlimited liability mean for Tim, Grace and Alan? (2 marks)
2. Explain the (a) advantages (4 marks) and (b) disadvantages (4 marks) of a partnership for Tim, Grace and Alan.
3. If Tim left the partnership, would you advise him to set up as a sole trader or in partnership with his sister? Give your reasons. (8 marks)

Business ownership - limited companies

Getting started...

Limited companies have different features from partnerships and sole traders. They have different types of owners and they are set up and run differently. They raise money in different ways. Think about the following limited companies.

Case 1 Manchester United plc

Alan Radford's dad bought him some shares in Manchester United Football Club for his birthday. Alan was over the moon about this. He was now one of the owners. But he didn't realise he was just one of many people who owned shares in the club. Alan was a bit concerned about being an owner. But his dad said, 'Don't worry. You can only lose what you put into a limited company.' On 31 January 2003, the club's shares were being bought and sold for 116.50p on the stock exchange.

Source: adapted in part from the *Financial Times*, 31.1.2003.

Case 2 Maddox plc

Maddox plc is a large company that makes glass products. An annual meeting will be held soon. At the meeting thousands of shareholders who own the company will get a chance to vote for directors to run the business on their behalf. Some of the directors have said, 'If we are re-elected, we plan to double the company's turnover within 5 years.' The shareholders will expect a reward if the business does so well.

Case 3 The Repair Place Ltd

Charlie Hills, his brother Ged, and his cousin Intzar, own a car repair company. It rebuilds car bodies after road accidents. They want to expand by building another workshop. But they don't want to borrow the money from the bank. Charlie has asked if anyone from the family wants to buy shares in the company and become an owner. Some of their relatives are interested. But the relatives want to look at the accounts held at Companies' House to see how well the business is doing.

(a) What features of limited companies are shown in these case studies?

What are the main features of limited companies?

Owners

Limited companies are owned by SHAREHOLDERS. These are people who own SHARES in the company. Shares are the parts into which the value of the company is divided. So if a business is valued at £100 million and there are 200 million shares, each share will be worth 50 pence.

All shareholders have **limited liability**. They are only liable for the amount they have put into the business. If a company closes down, shareholders can only lose the money they have invested. They will not be liable for anything else.

Control

Limited companies are owned by their shareholders. Large limited companies might have thousands of shareholders. So each shareholder has little direct control over the running of the business. Because of this, each year shareholders vote for directors at an Annual General Meeting (AGM) to represent their interests. Directors decide on company policy and appoint managers to run the company on a day-to-day basis.

In smaller limited companies, the directors and managers who run the business are often the shareholders as well.

Setting up

By law, all limited companies must register with the REGISTRAR OF COMPANIES at Companies House. They must also produce a number of documents about the business, such as:
- a memorandum of association, giving details including the name, address, activity and shares of the company;
- articles of association, giving details of the voting rights of shareholders, how profits will be shared and what directors will do.

A certification of incorporation will then be given to the company, so that it can start trading. Each year, the company must send a copy of its accounts to Companies House. These can be inspected by anyone.

Annual Reports and Accounts of public limited companies

Use of profits

The profits of companies are used in two ways.
- ✪ Some of the profits are kept back or **retained** by the business for spending in future years.
- ✪ Sometimes profits are given or **distributed** to shareholders. This payment is called a **dividend**.

Advantages and disadvantages of limited companies

Limited companies can raise extra finance by issuing shares. This can help a business to grow. Unlike a bank loan, the money does not have to be paid back. Shareholders might expect a share of the profits if the business is doing well.

The accounts of limited companies are available for everyone to see at Companies House. So rivals can find out the profit or sales a company has made in a year. Limited companies are more complicated to set up than sole traders or partnerships. They must also follow certain rules when selling shares.

Private and public limited companies

There are differences between PRIVATE LIMITED COMPANIES and PUBLIC LIMITED COMPANIES.

- ✪ **Name.** Private limited companies add Ltd after their name, for example Selecta Tyre Ltd. Public limited companies add plc, for example Unilever plc.
- ✪ **Share capital.** By law, a plc must have at least £50,000 worth of shares to trade before it can set up. A private limited company can be set up with just £2 worth of shares.
- ✪ **Buying and selling shares.** Shares in a plc can be traded on a STOCK EXCHANGE or the Alternative Investment Market (AIM). Anyone can buy the shares of a plc if there is someone willing to sell them. This usually means that there are large numbers of shareholders. In a private limited company, shares are bought and sold from the shareholders. They can only be sold if the majority of shareholders agree. This usually means that there are only a small number of shareholders in a limited company. A private limited company cannot sell shares to the general public.

PizzaExpress PLC
ANNUAL REPORT 1999

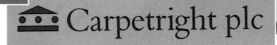
Carpetright plc

key terms

Quick quiz

1 Complete the following sentence.
A plc is also known as a ....

2 Choose the correct answer a, b, c, d.
A public limited company must have at least the following value in shares before it can start up.
(a) £50,000. **(b)** £5,000.
(c) £15. **(d)** £125,000.

3 True or false?
By law a private limited company must be registered with the Registrar of Companies.

4 State which of the following are public limited companies and which are private limited companies.
(a) Alliance and Leicester plc.
(b) McNulty and Sons Ltd.
(c) Mars Ltd.
(d) British American Tobacco plc.

5 True or false?
The shares of a private limited company are traded openly on a stock exchange.

6 State two disadvantages of a limited company.

Portfolio practice

Astra Zeneca

Astra Zeneca plc is one of the world's leading pharmaceutical companies. It invents and manufactures a range of medicines. These include medicines designed to fight cancer and infections and control pain.

Astra Zeneca spends over £7 million every day researching and developing new medicines. Its headquarters are in the UK, but it sells products in over 100 countries and manufactures medicines in 20 countries. In total it employs 54,000 people and in 2001 sold £11.4 billion of goods.

In 2003 it launched a new medicine designed to treat cancer. On the London Stock Exchange Astra Zeneca is one of the leading 100 companies with over 4 million shares traded at over £20 each.
The business is run by a highly experienced team of senior directors and managers.
Source: adapted from www.astrazeneca.com

1. Who owns Astra Zeneca? (2 marks)
2. Who runs Astra Zeneca? (2 marks)
3. Which type of limited company is Astra Zeneca? Give at least two reasons for your answer. (3 marks)
4. How might Astra Zeneca finance its huge investment in new medicines? (4 marks)
5. Explain why people might want to become shareholders in Astra Zeneca. (5 marks)

Getting started...

Co-operatives, public sector businesses and franchises are different types of business ownership. They each have unique features.

Case 1 *Pizza deliveries*

Josh Madeley hated his job in the pizza restaurant and thought his talents were being wasted. A relative left him £20,000, so Josh decided to use this money to set up his own business. The problem was that he had no idea what sort of business. Then he saw an advert in the local newspaper which gave him the answer. The advert said that he could buy into an existing business which specialised in take-aways and home delivery pizzas. For a fee, he could use the business's name and ideas. The business was well known and would provide plenty of training and support. Josh would be setting up as part of a franchise.

Case 2 *Software designers*

Some IT teachers developed a software programme to help young people who were learning how to use spreadsheets and databases. They wanted to set up a business to make and sell the product. They wanted this business to benefit the school they worked at, so they set up a business where they all had an equal say in how it should be run. Although they could have shared the profits amongst themselves, they agreed to put the money back into the school. As one of the teachers said: 'We didn't come into teaching to make lots of money. We wanted to make a real difference to people's lives'. The teachers were hoping to set up a co-operative.

Case 3 *Railways*

In 2002 there was growing concern about the state of Britain's railways following a series of accidents. Some rail passengers suggested that the businesses running the railways were more interested in profits than safety. There was also criticism that these businesses would not admit responsibility when things went wrong. The rail passengers argued that the government should take over part of the rail industry. It would then become a public sector business. They felt that this would result in fewer accidents, better organisation and better planning of the UK's railways.

Source: adapted from various newspaper articles, 2002.

(a) For each of the cases, state the main features of the businesses that could be set up.

What are the main features of franchises, co-operatives and public sector businesses?

Franchises

A FRANCHISE can be a good way to set up a new business because it reduces the risk for the person starting the business. The new business is set up using the name of another business. Examples of franchises include Benetton, The Body Shop, Burger King, Domino's Pizza, Kentucky Fried Chicken (KFC) and McDonald's.

In a franchise, the FRANCHISOR is a larger, established business which allows a smaller, new business, to use its name, business ideas and image. The franchisor will charge the smaller business, the FRANCHISEE, a fee to do this. The franchisee keeps any profits its business makes. Usually the franchisor will give training and support to its franchisees.

Figure 1 *How a franchise operates*

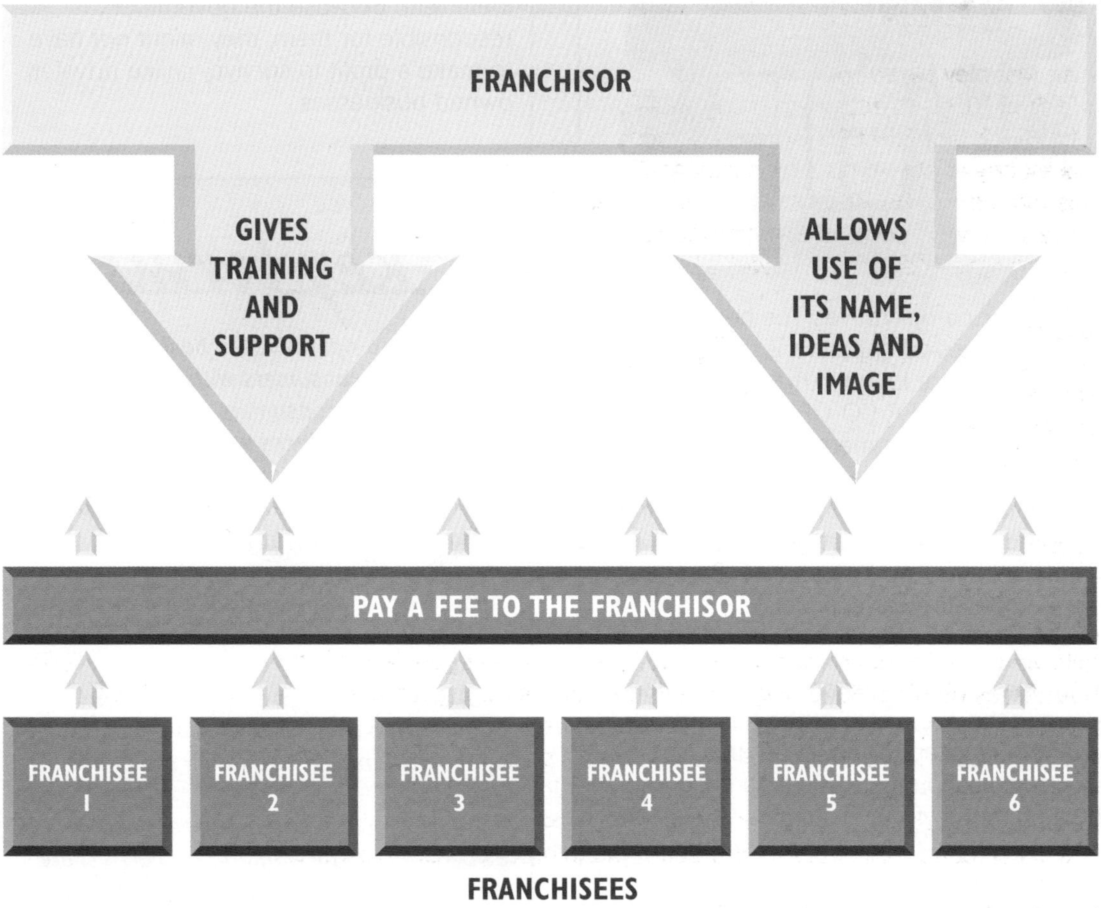

FRANCHISOR

GIVES TRAINING AND SUPPORT

ALLOWS USE OF ITS NAME, IDEAS AND IMAGE

PAY A FEE TO THE FRANCHISOR

| FRANCHISEE 1 | FRANCHISEE 2 | FRANCHISEE 3 | FRANCHISEE 4 | FRANCHISEE 5 | FRANCHISEE 6 |

FRANCHISEES

Co-operatives

There are two main types of co-operative.

Worker co-operatives This is when a group of people who work in and run a business share the decisions and the profits. In a WORKER CO-OPERATIVE, the jobs are usually shared around, so that everyone has a variety of different jobs to perform.

One of the advantages of a worker co-operative is that there is little conflict between owners and workers. This is because the owners are also the workers and decisions are shared. Profits are also shared equally.

But shared decision making can also be a problem because it is very time consuming. Successful worker co-operatives often find ways of sharing decisions without it taking too long. Worker co-operatives might also find it difficult to recruit the best workers. Top managers often want high salaries which worker co-operatives will not pay because they believe everyone should be paid equally for doing the same work.

Consumer co-operatives The best example of a consumer co-operative is the 'co-op' stores which are found in many towns and cities. CONSUMER CO-OPERATIVES are set up to prevent consumers being exploited by the high prices charged by shops. Consumer co-operatives are owned by their customers and profits are shared out amongst them. The Co-operative Bank and the Co-operative travel agents are examples of consumer co-operatives in the UK.

Their main advantages are that customers share in the ownership of the business and are not exploited for profit. But this type of business has found it difficult to raise enough money from customers to expand and modernise to be able to compete with larger supermarkets.

Public sector businesses

PUBLIC SECTOR BUSINESSES are those which are owned and controlled by the government. They are paid for out of money from taxes or licenses. Because public sector businesses are not usually concerned with making a profit, they are sometimes called organisations rather than businesses. Examples include the British Broadcasting Corporation (BBC) and the Royal Mail.

The government often owns and runs organisations because they are vital to the country. For example, British Gas, British Telecom and British Coal were owned by the government in the past. They were sold to private buyers during the 1980s and 1990s.

Their main advantage is that the government can run them in the public interest. For example, it can make sure that there are daily deliveries by the Royal Mail all over the country. But these organisations have often been criticised as slow and inefficient. Because the government is responsible for them, they might not have to make a profit to survive, unlike privately owned businesses.

key terms

Consumer co-operative – a business that is owned by its consumers with profits shared amongst those consumers.
Franchise – a business which allows another business to use its name and image.
Franchisee – a smaller, new business which is using the name and image of a larger, established business.
Franchisor – a larger, established business which allows a smaller, new business to use its name and image.
Public sector business – a business or organisation which is owned and controlled by the government and run in the public interest.
Worker co-operative – a business that is owned and run by workers, who also share the profits and decisions.

uick quiz

1 True or false?

A franchise is when a smaller business allows a larger business to trade using its name and image.

2 Complete the sentence.

A ...... is a large business which allows another to use its name and image.

3 Give three examples of businesses which operate franchises.

4 State one main advantage of worker co-operatives as a form of business ownership.

5 Give two examples of consumer co-operatives.

6 Who owns public sector businesses?

7 Which of the following are public sector businesses or organisations?

(a) British Gas.　　　**(c)** The Royal Mail.

(b) BBC.　　　**(d)** Sainsbury's.

Portfolio practice

Suma

Suma is a wholesale business, based in Halifax, specialising in healthfoods and wholefoods. It prides itself on providing environmentally friendly products. It buys them from growers and manufacturers, stores them in its warehouses and then distributes them to shops, schools, prisons, hospitals and supermarkets.

Suma's managers are elected by the workers. The wages are equal for managers and workers and the business is owned by those who work for it.

Decisions are made democratically, so everyone who works at Suma has the chance to contribute to decision making. This caused Suma lots of problems in the past. At one time, the business used to close for one afternoon every week while the workers argued endlessly about decisions. It was not unusual for decisions taken one week to be changed the next.

In the 1990s Suma introduced a system of electing managers who took responsibility for making decisions. This solved many of the problems caused by the arguments and disagreements. Today Suma is a multi-million pound company with 70 employees.

It has 7,000 product lines and its own fleet of vehicles.

Source: adapted from www.suma.co.uk

1. Describe how decisions are made and wages are paid at Suma. (2 marks)
2. Would you call Suma a worker or consumer co-operative? Explain your answer. (3 marks)
3. Which main disadvantage of worker co-operatives is referred to in this case? (4 marks)
4. Do you think it likely that the government would want to own and control Suma? (3 marks)
5. Why might a new business wishing to start up in the wholesale trade choose to become a franchisee? (6 marks)

5 Business location

Getting started...

Business location is about **where** a business is situated. Is it in a town centre, on an industrial estate, near to a motorway or in the countryside? Why are businesses located in certain places? Think about the locations of the following businesses.

Case 1 *Cerys Evans' chip shop*

FISH & CHIPS

PART TIME HELP WANTED

I opened my chip shop here because it's on the edge of a big housing estate. The shop is opposite a couple of pubs and there's a factory along the street. The rent and business rates are cheap. And there are plenty of people on the estate who want part-time jobs.

Case 2 *Peter's Pottery*

My business is in 'The Potteries' in Staffordshire. Pottery has been made here for hundreds of years. Businesses came to the area for the clay used to make pots. So, many people have pottery skills. Like me, some have trained in pottery-making at local colleges. Because we get a lot of tourists, nearly all my pottery is sold to nearby gift shops.

Case 3 *Abbey National*

Abbey National located its offices at Towers Business Park, Manchester. The business park has lots of office space and is surrounded by green fields and trees. It is also close to local shops and restaurants.

What factors have affected the location of:
(a) Cerys Evans' Chip Shop
(b) Peter's Pottery
(c) Abbey National's offices
(d) Tariq's Paper Mill?

Case 4 *Tariq's Paper Mill*

RAIL TERMINAL

MOTORWAY M305

Tariq's Papers

My family's business makes paper. We sell it to printers all over the UK. We built the paper mill here because it's next to a motorway and near to a railway. We got a grant to locate here because we were taking on so many workers.

What factors affect business location?

Transport

A business might locate near to transport links. This makes moving goods easier, quicker and cheaper. Examples are:

❂ a delivery business next to a motorway;
❂ a UK business that sells to Europe setting up in the South, near to the Channel Tunnel;
❂ a business making heavy products next to a railway goods depot;
❂ a USA business that sells to Europe setting up in the UK.

The cost of premises or land

The cost of premises, such as shops or factories, can affect location. A business may set up in an area where there:

❂ are premises to buy or rent at low prices, sometimes in a business park, in a shopping centre or on an industrial estate;
❂ are low BUSINESS RATES that have to be paid to the local authority;
❂ is cheap land to buy, or room to expand;
❂ is land to build on, such as BROWNFIELD SITES, which have been cleared of buildings, or GREENFIELD SITES, which have not been built on before.

Businesses may set up on an industrial estate where there are premises to buy or rent

The cost of labour

LABOUR COSTS are what it costs a business to hire workers, for example their wages. A business may locate where workers' wages are low. Examples are:

❂ clothing businesses setting up factories in Bangladesh;
❂ electronics companies setting up in Malaysia.

In the UK, wages are often higher in London than in other areas. Some businesses have moved out of London to reduce their wage costs.

Financial help

A business may move to an area if it is given money, such as a grant. The government and the European Union (EU) help businesses to set up in areas which have problems. These might be areas where people have low earnings. Or there might be high unemployment.

Figure 1 shows areas in the UK where businesses might be given money from EU funds to locate.

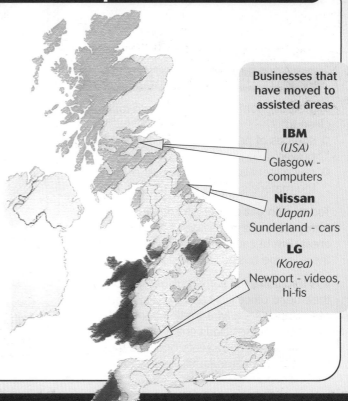

Businesses that have moved to assisted areas

IBM
(USA)
Glasgow - computers

Nissan
(Japan)
Sunderland - cars

LG
(Korea)
Newport - videos, hi-fis

Figure 1 *Assisted areas in the UK*

● *Areas where income per head of the population is less than 75% of the EU average.*

● *Areas of high unemployment and rural and industrial decline.*

● *Fairly high unemployment, help only to small and medium sized businesses.*

Near to customers and businesses

Some businesses have to be near to their **customers**. Hairdressers need to be near to people, as their customers will not travel far to get their hair cut.

Some businesses set up near to **competitors** who sell similar products. Shoe shops or estate agents are often found in the same street so that customers who shop around can visit them easily. Other businesses set up away from competitors so they have no competition, such as newsagents.

Some businesses set up near to **suppliers** who provide parts or materials. This can save delivery time. Also, working together they are able to reduce costs.

Similar shops may be located on the same street

History and tradition

In the past, some businesses were located close to:
- ✪ sources of power, such as coal or water power;
- ✪ raw materials, so that the cost of moving the materials would be kept low.

Today, with gas and electricity and cheaper transport, there is less need to locate in such areas. But because they have always been there, some businesses stay in an area.

It is traditional for some businesses to have their head offices in London. This is because of its importance as a trading centre. Also, some businesses traditionally stay in the same area for many years because they are owned by the same family.

Sales techniques

Some products are sold direct to customers.

- ✪ Mail order companies send out catalogues. Customers write, fax, phone or email orders for goods, which are sent to their home.
- ✪ More and more products are sold through the Internet. Customers look at the products on the computer screen and then send an order to the business.

These businesses are free to locate in many different areas. They are often called FOOTLOOSE BUSINESSES.

Skills

Businesses might locate in areas where workers have the skills they need. Examples are:
- ✪ carpet production in Kidderminster and Bradford;
- ✪ computer chip production in 'Silicon Valley' between London and Bristol, in the area called the 'M4 corridor';
- ✪ shoe making in Northampton;
- ✪ aeroplane building in Preston.

Local colleges and universities often run courses in these areas to teach these skills.

key terms

Brownfield sites - *areas that have been cleared of old buildings.*
Business rates - *charges on factories and shops that have to be paid to the local authority.*
Footloose businesses - *businesses that are free to locate in any area.*
Greenfield sites - *areas that have not been built on before, such as farmland.*
Labour costs - *the amount a business has to pay to hire workers, for example their wages.*

Quick quiz

1. True or false? An area of land which has been cleared of old factories is called a greenfield site.

2. Complete the sentence. Charges made by local government on shops and factories are called ....

3. Fit these missing words.

   Grant   Unemployment   EU

   Finance, such as a ...... , might be given from ...... funds to help businesses locate in areas with high ....

4. What is a footloose business?

5. A business might set up in an area where wages are low to cut its:

   (a) time   **(b)** labour costs   **(c)** sales   **(d)** factory size.

6. Match the location factors (a)-(c) to the examples (i)-(iii).

Location factors	**Examples**
(a) Near to customers.	**(i)** Head offices in London.
(b) Tradition.	**(ii)** A delivery business.
(c) Transport.	**(iii)** A hairdressers.

Portfolio practice

PEX

PEX is a company that makes parts for computers. It sells most of its parts to businesses in Europe. Its present factory is near Newcastle, close to the main A1 road. The factory is quite small, with no room to expand. PEX wants to move and must choose between sites at East Kilbride and Basingstoke.

East Kilbride, near Glasgow, Scotland
It's in 'Silicon Glen', close to electronics companies like Seiko and IBM. There are factories available to rent. The factories are 25-30km from Glasgow Airport, 15km from Glasgow port and 10km from the M74 Motorway. Unemployment in the area is 4% and grants are given to businesses that take on workers.

Basingstoke, south-west of London
It's next to the M3 Motorway, 25km from 'Silicon Valley' and 50km from Heathrow Airport. Also it's only 50km from the South coast of England and the port of Southampton. There are no grants and a new factory would need to be built. But there is cheap land available to buy. Unemployment in the area is 1%.

1. Describe the location of PEX's present factory. (3 marks)
2. Identify the advantages and disadvantages for PEX of moving to East Kilbride. (6 marks)
3. Should PEX move to East Kilbride or Basingstoke? Give reasons for your answer. (7 marks)

6 Business activity

Getting started...

Businesses are involved in a huge range of activities. Look at the business activities below.

Case 1

Case 2

Case 3

Case 4

Case 5
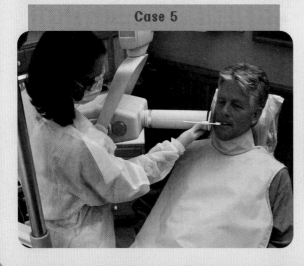

Case 6

(a) Describe the business activities taking place in each case.

What activities are businesses involved in?

Businesses processing raw materials

Some businesses produce RAW MATERIALS. They are also called RAW GOODS. These are natural resources such as wheat, coffee beans, timber and oil. They are needed to make other goods and services. For example, coffee beans are used to make instant coffee. The following are examples of business activities that involve producing raw materials.

✪ Farming – growing crops such as barley, and rearing animals, such as sheep and cows.

✪ Mining and quarrying – extracting raw materials from the earth, such as coal, tin and stone.

✪ Fishing – harvesting fish from the sea and fresh water.

✪ Oil and gas – extracting oil and gas by using oil wells and gas platforms.

Businesses manufacturing goods

RAW MATERIALS → **MANUFACTURING** → **PRODUCT**

Figure 1

Manufacturing businesses often start with raw materials and turn them into other GOODS. Goods are physical products, such as cars, radios and machinery, that can be seen and touched. For example, breakfast cereal MANUFACTURERS like Kellogg's, Nabisco and Nestlé begin with raw materials such as wheat, oats, sugar and barley. From these they can make Corn Flakes, Weetabix, Shredded Wheat and Cheerios. This is shown in Figure 1.

There are two main types of manufactured goods.

Consumer goods CONSUMER GOODS are goods that are for consumers to use. Examples include books, televisions, washing machines and processed foods, such as baked beans and microwave chips.

Capital goods CAPITAL GOODS are goods that are used to produce other goods. Examples include forklift trucks, machinery and cranes.

Businesses providing services

SERVICES are products which are not physical and which cannot be touched or kept, such as taking a holiday abroad or going to the cinema to see a film. When a consumer receives a service, there is nothing physical to keep. Filmgoers pay for the experience of watching the movie on a large screen with surround sound, from a comfortable seat. But they can't take the film home.

There are three main types of service.

Client services CLIENT SERVICES are services that are tailored to meet the needs of particular individuals or groups of consumers. Examples include sports and entertainment, health care and financial services such as banking and Internet access.

Retail services RETAIL SERVICES are services that involve the selling of goods. Examples include shops, mail order businesses and website based sales.

Other services These include a range of services which do not fit into the above two categories. For example:
- transport services, such as taxis, trains and planes;
- communication services for consumers, such as mobile phone networks.

Changes in business activity

Business activities are constantly changing as consumers and the world around them also change. One of the main changes in the UK is that service businesses have increased in importance over the last twenty to thirty years. But, at the same time, businesses providing raw materials and manufacturing goods have declined. One of the reasons for this change has been technological developments such as the invention of mobile phones and the creation of the Internet. They have allowed many new service businesses to set up and grow quickly.

There are certain ways in which changes in business activity can be measured.

The level of consumer spending on different goods and services Consumers today spend a much higher proportion of their incomes on services than they did twenty five years ago.

The number of people employed in different activities There has been a huge increase in the number of people employed in service businesses. At the same time, the number of people employed in producing goods and raw materials has declined.

The value of goods and services produced by businesses The value of the services provided by service businesses has grown by huge amounts over the last twenty five years.

key terms

Capital goods - goods that are used to produce other goods.
Client services - services that are tailored to meet the needs of particular individuals or groups of consumers.
Consumer goods - goods that are intended for use by consumers.
Goods - physical products that can be seen and touched.

Manufacturers – businesses that make goods.
Raw materials/raw goods – natural resources that are used to make other goods and services.
Retail services – services that involve the selling of goods.
Services – products which are not physical and which cannot be touched.

Quick quiz

1 Complete the sentence.
Raw materials are also known as ....

2 What is the difference between capital goods and consumer goods?

3 Which of the following are examples of goods?
(a) A visit to a swimming pool. **(b)** A can of cola.
(c) An afternoon watching Manchester City. **(d)** A new computer game.

4 Which of the following are examples of services?
(a) A plane journey from Bristol to Milan. **(b)** A carton of popcorn.
(c) A night in a hotel. **(d)** A new DVD.

5 True or false?
The number of people employed to manufacture goods in the UK has increased in the last 25 years.

Portfolio practice

Legoland

Legoland is a theme park in Windsor, Berkshire. It is owned by the Lego Group and is based on the popular children's building toy, Lego. It contains models made from over 32 million Lego plastic bricks. In 2002, the number of visitors to the park was estimated to be 1.63 million a year. This was a 9.5 per cent increase over the year before.

The theme park is split into different themed areas. It offers a variety of other entertainment for visitors, such as rides, shops, and food and drink for sale. When people book, they can also reserve a hotel in the area with their park tickets. The park also holds events and concerts. In July 2003, Atomic Kitten played there.

Source: adapted from www.lego.com, www.lego.com/legolandnew/windsor and www.bbc.co.uk/1/hi/business

1. What type of activity is each business engaged in? (2 marks)
2. What are the differences in the activities of the two businesses? (6 marks)
3. Explain how the information shown in Figure 2 might affect Legoland. (9 marks)

Nestlé

Nestlé is a well-known public limited company. It makes a variety of products including:
✪ drinks such as Nescafé coffee and Perrier water;
✪ chocolate, such as KitKat and Smarties;
✪ milk products and ice cream;
✪ dried food, such as Buitoni pasta.

KitKats are manufactured at a factory in York. 50,000 tonnes were produced in 2002.

Source: adapted from Nestlé, Annual report and Accounts, www.thisisyork.co.uk/york/archive/2002/05/28/york_news_local5ZM.html

Figure 2 *Visits to the UK by overseas residents*

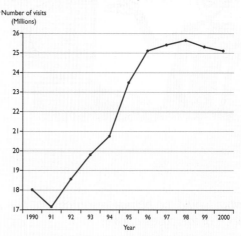

Source: adapted from *Annual Abstract of Statistics*, 2002, ONS.

7 Human resources

Getting started...

Businesses want to recruit the best employees. They also need to make sure that their employees work effectively and safely. The responsibility for these tasks often rests with the human resources department. Human resources staff specialise in dealing with the people who work in the business. They handle such things as recruitment, training, retirement, redundancies and working conditions. Think about the following cases.

Case 1 *Production manager*

I NEED NEW STAFF FOR MY DEPARTMENT. HOW MANY WILL I NEED? HOW SHOULD I FIND THEM AND WHAT DO I NEED TO DO NEXT?

Case 2 *Till operator*

I THINK THAT WE NEED MORE REGULAR BREAKS; AND I REALLY THINK THAT WE NEED MORE CHAIRS. MY BACK'S KILLING ME BY THE END OF THE DAY.

Case 3 *Computer operator*

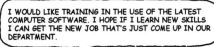

I WOULD LIKE TRAINING IN THE USE OF THE LATEST COMPUTER SOFTWARE. I HOPE IF I LEARN NEW SKILLS I CAN GET THE NEW JOB THAT'S JUST COME UP IN OUR DEPARTMENT.

Case 4 *Trade union official*

WE NEED TO NEGOTIATE HIGHER WAGES.

(a) What would the human resources staff be responsible for doing in each of the cases above?

What are the tasks and responsibilities of human resources staff in a business?

Recruitment, retention and dismissal

Employees with the right skills have to be RECRUITED and selected if a business wants to be successful. One of the main tasks of the human resources staff in a business is to find suitable employees.

The business will then want to keep its employees, particularly if they are good. The reason for this is that good employees are costly to replace. So the business may offer good pay and conditions, or the chance of promotion, in order to RETAIN its employees.

Human resources staff are also responsible for DISMISSING employees who are not doing their job properly. For example, employees might break the company's rules or the conditions that they agreed upon when they first started work. They also make staff REDUNDANT if the job is no longer needed.

Working conditions

The human resources department is responsible for setting and organising employees' working conditions. This might include:
- ✪ time spent at work - the hours in a day or week, weeks in a year and holidays;
- ✪ organising the work - the number and length of breaks, and any flexitime;
- ✪ whether employees work alone or in teams;
- ✪ pay and benefits - wages, salaries, overtime and pension contributions.

Training, development and promotion

Successful businesses will train their employees. Human resources staff are usually responsible for organising this TRAINING. Businesses face many changes, such as new legislation, new technology or new working methods. This means that employees have to be flexible and alter the way that they do things in order to cope with the changes. Training helps employees to do this. It also gives employees new skills that may help them to get promoted.

Training is often organised by the human resources department to help employees gain new skills

Negotiations with trade unions or other representative organisations

Trade unions represent the interests of their members in the workplace. To prevent disagreements, businesses usually consult trade unions and other staff associations before making changes to employees' pay or work conditions. Human resources staff usually negotiate on behalf of the business. The two sides try to reach an agreement that both the employer and the employees will accept.

Health and safety

Human resources are responsible for health and safety both inside and outside a business. Businesses must provide their employees with a safe working environment and protect them against accidents, injuries and illness. These can result in absences and lost production. Businesses must also protect people outside who might be affected by the business's activities, for example, people living near a chemical or industrial plant.

Effects on other people working in the business

The human resources department provides a service to other areas of the business. For example, if employees in the finance department were not happy with their pay, human resources would be responsible for sorting out the problem. This would be done by working with the managers in the finance department or talking to organisations that represent the employees.

Human resources are also responsible for making sure that a business offers equal opportunities and that there is no discrimination on the grounds of sex, race or disability. They also make sure that the business does not break any laws about discrimination.

key terms

Dismissal – where employees are no longer employed by the business because they have broken their agreed working conditions and arrangements.

Recruitment – finding employees to fill job vacancies.

Redundancy – where employees are no longer employed by the business because the job they were doing has ceased to exist.

Retention – keeping staff employed in a business so that they don't leave to take another job.

Training – teaching new or existing employees so that they learn new skills or develop their existing skills further.

Quick quiz

1. Fill in the missing words in the following paragraphs.

Promoted
Dismiss
Recruited
Trained
Conditions
Laws
Trade union
Retained
People
Human resources
Safe

The ...... department is involved with ...... in a business. Workers must be ...... when there are vacancies. But any new worker will need to be ...... to do their job and shown how the business operates. This will make them more effective. Workers who work well might be ...... by the business.

Workers expect their place of work to be .... They also expect working ...... to conform to health and safety .... Workers who have a complaint might ask their ...... to talk to employers about their situation.

A business might ...... a worker who breaks company rules or their working agreements. They also need to find ways to motivate employers so they are ...... in the business.

Portfolio practice

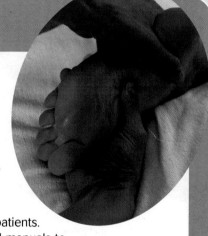

Human resources at Ryan's Reflexology Remedies

Anne Maculey set up a reflexology business in Exeter called Ryan's Reflexology Remedies. Reflexology is the massage of the feet to help with bad backs, poor circulation and headaches. The business was an instant success. It now has 5 surgeries in the South of England.

Each surgery has a senior and junior reflexologist and a receptionist. Anne has a website offering online support to patients. She also has a catalogue mail order business selling oils and manuals to help with reflexology. This is done through a warehouse which has 10 packers, 2 administrators and an IT specialist.

There are lots of health and safety issues to be dealt with at the warehouse. Employees at the surgeries have also been complaining about differences in their levels of pay and a lack of training. They have discussed these issues with their union representative.
The staff are finding it hard to cope with greater demand. New employees will need to be recruited for the warehouse, to help with the website and in the surgeries. All these employees will need to be trained.

In the main office, there is a human resources manager and an administrator. Anne has just employed another manager to cope with the expansion of the business.

1. Identify three issues that are the responsibility of the business's human resources department. (3 marks)
2. Identify two human resources problems that the business has and explain how they could affect the business. (6 marks)
3. Explain how the human resources department might be able to solve the business's problems. (9 marks)

8 Finance

Getting started...

An important part of management is controlling the money coming into, and going out of, the business. As a business grows, this job becomes even more important. This is because the amounts of money involved get larger and the business has more to lose. Large firms often have a separate finance department to manage their finances. Look at the activities taking place in the finance departments of the businesses below.

Case 1 *Harrison Insurance*

Sam Hardwick works in the finance department of Harrison Insurance. The company employs 2,400 staff and Sam's job is to calculate the staff's wages. The computer does this automatically after Sam has typed in information from employees' time sheets. Sam also deals with enquiries about wages from staff.

Case 2 *Welland Engineering*

Welland Engineering makes sheet metal products. When a new order is received, Gina Matthews calculates the cost of making it. She presents her calculations on a cost sheet. The cost sheet below has been produced for an order of 1,000 components. It shows that the order will cost Welland Engineering £1,300 to make.

Cost sheet - 1,000 components	£
Labour 20hrs at £10 per hr	£200
Steel (sheets) 100 x £2.50	£250
Rivets 10,000 x 1p	£100
Overheads	£500
Other costs	£250
Total costs	**£1,300**

Case 3 *Balham Plant Hire*

Balham Plant Hire hires out excavators, fork lift trucks, hydraulic breakers, tipper wagons, and other machinery. Many of its customers have accounts and pay monthly. Trevor McDade is employed in the finance department to keep a check on what each customer owes. He also has to chase payments when they are overdue.

(a) Describe the jobs being done in the finance department of each business.

What activities are carried out in a finance department?

The roles in the finance department

Senior accountant

The senior accountant is the head of the finance department and is responsible for preparing accounts, recruiting and supporting staff, reporting to the board and handling the department's budget. The senior accountant might also be involved in financial decision-making.

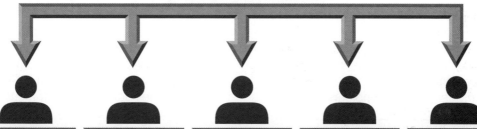

Sales ledger clerk	Purchases ledger clerk	Payroll clerk	Cashier	Credit controller
The sales ledger clerk deals with customer accounts and records the details of all sales transactions. The sales ledger clerk also deals with enquiries about customer accounts.	The purchases ledger clerk records all transactions relating to purchases from suppliers. The clerk enters details of purchases onto the computer system and speaks to suppliers when there are enquiries.	The payroll clerk's job is to calculate staff wages. The take home pay for each worker must be calculated by subtracting tax and other deductions from GROSS PAY. The clerk will also deal with queries.	The cashier is responsible for all banking and cash transactions. The cashier may check bank statements to see if they agree with entries in the bookkeeping system. The cashier might also be responsible for the PETTY CASH system, which staff can use to buy small items such as stamps.	Businesses sometimes make CREDIT SALES. This is where they allow customers to take goods now and pay at a later date. When a business gives credit to customers, the CREDIT CONTROLLER must make sure that customers pay when payment is due. The controller may chase late payers and is likely to work closely with the sales ledger clerk.

Recording business transactions

The finance department is responsible for controlling the money in a business. Businesses must keep a record of their BUSINESS TRANSACTIONS such as buying resources, selling products, borrowing from the bank and paying tax. The job of recording all these transactions is called BOOKKEEPING. If a record of transactions is kept, it is easier to keep a check on the money coming into, and going out of, the business. Records of transactions are also used to produce ACCOUNTS. These are statements that show important financial information about a business.

Obtaining capital and resources

As well as paying for the resources that the business buys, the finance department will be involved in raising finance. For example it might have to:
- prepare documents and reports for a bank before getting a loan;
- deal with administrative matters when issuing shares;
- communicate with potential investors;
- pay dividends to shareholders.

key terms

Accounts – statements that give important financial information about a business.
Bookkeeping – a system of recording details of business transactions.
Business transactions – any purchase or sale that affects the finances of a business.
Cost accountant – an accountant that specialises in calculating the costs of business activities.
Credit controller – the person responsible for monitoring customer accounts and chasing overdue payments.
Credit sales – selling goods and allowing a period of time before payment is due.
Financial accountant – an accountant that prepares accounts from bookkeeping records.
Gross pay – a worker's pay before deductions such as tax and National Insurance contributions.
Management accountant – an accountant that produces and uses financial information to help in business decision-making.
Petty cash – money used by a business to make small payments.

Types of accountant

- In large businesses, FINANCIAL ACCOUNTANTS control bookkeeping and prepare final accounts, such as the profit and loss account. They may also calculate how much tax the business has to pay.
- MANAGEMENT ACCOUNTANTS provide information to help a business make decisions. They may be involved in forecasting and controlling costs.
- COST ACCOUNTANTS provide cost information. For example, they might calculate the cost of making a new product or building a new factory.

Finance and other departments

The work of the finance department affects other departments in the business. For example:
- the credit controller may tell the sales department that a customer cannot receive any more goods until payment has been received;
- the cost accountant may provide cost information for the production department showing that a new machine would improve efficiency;
- departments may be told to stop spending for a while because the firm is heavily overdrawn at the bank. This is shown in Figure 1.

Figure 1

MEMO

To: All department heads
From: Senior Accountant
Date: 13.5.02

Please stop all non-essential spending until 1.6.02.

Quick quiz

① True or false?
(a) The sale of an old machine is a business transaction.
(b) Accounts are the books in which transactions are recorded.
(c) A 50p postage stamp might be paid from petty cash.

② Which of these would deal with customer transactions?
(a) Senior accountant.
(b) Sales ledger clerk.
(c) Purchases ledger clerk.
(d) Payroll clerk.

③ Which of these prepares accounts?
(a) Financial accountant.
(b) Management accountant.
(c) Turf accountant.
(d) Cost accountant.

④ The credit controller might work closely with which of the following?
(a) Sales ledger clerk.
(b) Purchases ledger clerk.
(c) Payroll clerk.
(d) Purchasing officer.

⑤ State two tasks that the cashier might perform.

Portfolio practice

Linden Motor Parts

Linden Motor Parts is a large distributor of motor car parts in the South West. It buys parts from manufacturers in the motor industry. The staff in the finance department are:
✪ Rahila, the senior accountant;
✪ Scott, the credit controller and cashier;
✪ Stefan, the sales ledger clerk;
✪ Brenda, the payroll clerk;
✪ Katie, the purchases ledger clerk.

One afternoon, when they return from lunch, the following tasks have to be done.
1. A customer has complained about an error on her account.
2. A supplier who is waiting in reception wants a cheque payment.
3. Ten purchases need to be entered onto the computer system.

1. What is Rahila's role in the department? (2 marks)
2. Explain which members of the department will deal with the above three tasks. (6 marks)
3. Using examples, explain how the work done in Linden's finance department might affect other departments in the business. (7 marks)

9 Administration and IT support

Getting started...

To run smoothly, a business must make sure that it has good support services. Support services help other areas of the business. They provide such things as technical help, help to organise meetings, cleaning services, and help to communicate with employees and those outside the business. Support services are often part of the administration and IT support department in a business. Think about about an airline company.

Case 3
Managing director

'Can someone organise the meeting and make sure that some drinks are provided?'

Case 1
Booking staff

'I have to check the latest flight times, but my computer has just crashed.'

Case 4
Public relations manager

'We must reply to this customer's complaint within 4 days. That's the company's policy.'

Case 2
Personnel manager

'This letter has to be word processed and then sent to all employees.'

Case 5
Quality controller

'This plane needs to fly out again in one hour. We must make sure it is clean and does not have any problems.'

(a) What type of administration and IT support might be given in each case?

(b) What might happen if administration and IT support was not given?

What are the different jobs in administration and IT support?

The role of administration

Employees in administration and IT support don't usually produce anything to sell to customers. They provide a service to other employees to make sure they give the best service to their customers. Without these services, businesses might:

✪ not have records of meetings or transactions;

✪ not type and send out letters on time;

✪ not have clean and tidy offices;

✪ not have reliable computer systems.

So it is vital for businesses to have good administration and IT support services. The types of support given are shown in Figure 1.

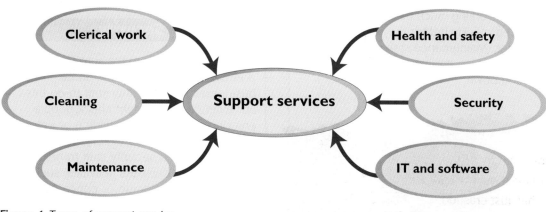

Figure 1 *Types of support service*

Clerical work

Clerical work involves many activities. Some of the most common are shown in Figure 2. Administration and IT support staff provide these types of service to other functions in the business. As developments in technology have advanced, many of these tasks are now undertaken using IT because with more information being stored on computers and accessible to more people, there is now less need to have detailed central filing systems. Often files are received and sent electronically. Businesses now tend to organise their files by using a database or keeping them on a central server or store.

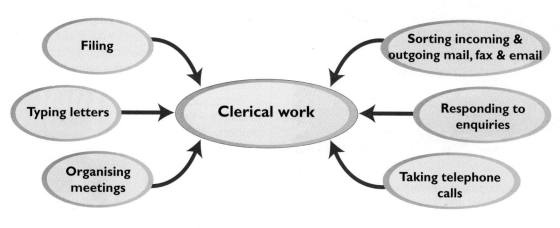

Figure 2 *Examples of clerical work*

Cleaning and maintenance

Businesses need to keep their premises clean so that they:

- ✪ meet health and safety laws;
- ✪ create good working conditions;
- ✪ make a good impression on visitors and clients.

In some businesses, such as hospitals, chemical manufacturing and computer disk production, a clean environment is essential.

Sometimes business equipment, such as a lift, stops working. Such problems have to be solved quickly before they cause any difficulties. Maintenance staff repair faults and also service equipment to avoid it breaking down.

Health and safety

Businesses must meet health and safety rules and regulations. This is often the job of administration support staff. For example, they may draw up the business's health and safety policy. This will include procedures for recording accidents or injuries that occur in the workplace. They will also make sure that all the staff are aware of health and safety practices and that they understand fire drills.

Security

Businesses need to make sure that their premises and staff are safe. Some businesses have security staff to do this. For example, they might check people entering or leaving the building or entering a dangerous area of a factory. Some businesses need security staff to help them carry out their business activities, such as door staff at a nightclub or concert arena.

Businesses may also have security staff to guard the building at night. They are responsible for ensuring that equipment and machinery are safe from damage or theft.

Software and communications

One of the most important roles of IT staff is to support the use of software in the business, such as word-processing, payrolls, accounts and databases. They make sure that these programmes are working correctly so that employees can carry out their jobs. They also make sure that electronic communication systems, such as email, the business website and electronic transfers systems, such as faxes are working properly. As the use of IT has grown, many businesses now have a separate IT department or use online support from software producers.

Some business have cleaning services to keep offices organised and tidy

Quick quiz

(1) What type of activities in a business might be classified as clerical?

(2) Why is it important for cleaning and maintenance to be undertaken in a business?

(3) What types of support does the administration and IT department provide for software applications?

(4) True or false?

The administration and IT department provides services to the business's employees rather than to its customers.

(5) Give two examples of what might happen if a business did not have an administration and IT department.

Portfolio practice

Zepryl plc

Zepryl plc is a large company with factories all over the world. It produces compact discs which are used for storing computer data or music. The business has administration, maintenance, cleaning and security staff.

This week the business faces a number of challenges.

✪ The design team has been carrying out research into new production methods. Dust can ruin compact discs, so some of the research takes place in a dust free, uncontaminated area. This area has to be kept clean at all times and only researchers must be allowed in. And all other areas used for research must be kept clean, tidy and well organised.

✪ The company wants all parts of its business, throughout the world, to know about the research department's findings. So far, they have been written by hand and kept in a folder of about 300 pages.

✪ One of its factories has an 'education zone' as part of its marketing programme. This is an area that people can visit and find out about the company's production methods. A large school party is visiting on Thursday morning.

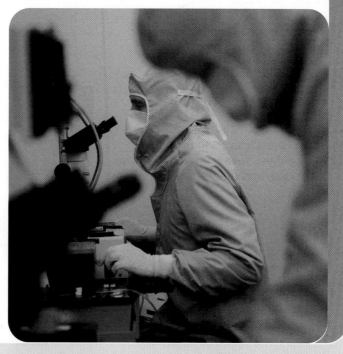

1. Identify the administration and IT staff at Zepryl plc. (2 marks)

2. Which type of staff would be most suited to help with each of the three challenges faced by the company? (6 marks)

3. Explain how each type of administration and IT staff might help the business to deal with the three challenges. (9 marks)

Getting started...

Businesses use INPUTS such as raw materials, components, buildings, machinery, tools, equipment and people to make products. The products are called OUTPUTS. The process of changing resources into goods and services is called PRODUCTION. A business has to make the best use of its resources. Look at the resources used by the businesses below.

Case 1 *Rexam plc*

Rexam is one of the leading packaging groups in the world. It makes a variety of packaging products for well known companies. These include plastic containers to hold butter for St.Ivel, envelopes for American Express, polythene covering for Hovis bread, plastic beauty packaging for Givenchy, Avon and Chanel, and glass jars and bottles for Uncle Ben's Chilli and Carlsberg Pilsner.

Source: adapted from Rexam plc, *Annual Report and Accounts*.

Case 2 *Northern Foods plc*

Northern Foods is a leading UK food manufacturer employing around 15,000 staff. Its products include meat and savoury products, speciality bread, cakes and puddings, biscuits, fresh chilled dairy products and frozen foods. The company supplies retailers from twenty factories all over the UK.

Source: adapted from Northern Foods plc, *Annual Report and Accounts*.

Case 3 *Thistle Hotels plc*

Thistle Hotels operates 56 hotels in England, Scotland and Wales. The company provides restaurants, bars, fitness centres, swimming pools, saunas, steam rooms and meeting rooms in most of its hotels.

Source: adapted from Thistle Hotels plc, *Annual Report and Accounts*.

Describe the resources being used and the products being produced by:
(a) Rexam
(b) Northern Foods
(c) Thistle Hotels.

What types of production are there in business?

What is production?

Figure 1 shows what happens when pizzas are produced. A food manufacturer uses inputs such as flour, salt, water, tomatoes, cheese and mushrooms. It then uses a number of PROCESSES such as dough making, moulding, base cutting, freezing, garnishing, baking and packing, to change the inputs into outputs. The outputs are the pizzas that are sold to retailers.

Figure 1 *Pizza production*

INPUTS
SALT   FLOUR
WATER   TOMATOES
CHEESE   MUSHROOMS

PROCESSES
DOUGH BAKING
MOULDING
BASE CUTTING
FREEZING
GARNISHING
BAKING
PACKING

OUTPUTS
MUSHROOM PIZZA

Labour and capital intensive production

Some industries are LABOUR INTENSIVE. This means that the most important resource being used in production is people. Service industries such as health care, financial services and leisure are labour intensive. A CAPITAL INTENSIVE industry is one that uses large amounts of plant, machinery and equipment in production. Car manufacturers, food processors and oil refiners are often capital intensive.

Job production

JOB PRODUCTION is where a business produces one product from start to finish before moving on to the next. Each item produced is likely to be different. Examples might include the building of a bridge or a road, or the design of an advertisement. The main advantage of this method is that quality and worker motivation is usually high. But it is slow and can be expensive.

The construction of a chemical factory is an example of job production

Batch production

BATCH PRODUCTION is where a number of the same product is made at the same time. Production takes place in stages. Each operation in the process is completed on all products in the batch before moving on to the next. Bread is often made in batches. A batch of dough is made, the loaves are shaped and then baked. Then another batch is made. Components such as nails and screws are also made in batches.

The advantages of this method are that workers can specialise and production is cheaper because more goods can be made. However, specialisation can mean that tasks are boring. Also, the machinery may have to be adjusted after each batch to do the next job.

Components produced in batches

Flow production

FLOW PRODUCTION is used when large numbers of goods are being produced continuously. For example, in car production, cars are produced on a production line which moves all the time. A car is assembled in stages as it moves along the line.

Flow production uses a huge amount of machinery and equipment which can be very expensive to buy. Flow production is often limited to the production of standardised products. It can be boring for workers and a breakdown might shut the whole line down. But generally, it is efficient and costs per unit are very low.

Process production is where a product flows continuously through a plant rather than on an assembly line. Different processes are carried out as it passes through. Examples include oil and chemical production.

Car production on an assembly line

key terms

Batch production – a method of production that involves completing one operation on all products in a batch before moving on to the next.
Capital intensive - production that uses large amounts of plant and machinery.
Flow production – a method of production that involves making a single product continuously.
Inputs – the raw materials used in production
Job production – a method of production that involves making a product from start to finish.
Labour intensive – production that uses large numbers of people.
Outputs – the goods or services resulting from production.
Processes – operations used to convert inputs into goods or services.
Production – the conversion of resources into goods or services.

Quick quiz

1 True or false?

(a) The Ford Motor Company uses job production to make cars.

(b) A construction company is likely to use job production.

(c) Workers are likely to get bored when using job production.

2 Which of these is not an input for a clothes manufacturer?

(a) Cotton. **(b)** Buttons.

(c) Sewing machine. **(d)** Fabric.

3 Which of these is not a process?

(a) Cutting.

(b) Welding.

(c) Packaging.

(d) Machinery.

4 State two advantages of batch production.

5 State two disadvantages of job production.

Portfolio practice

UX Oil

UX Oil is a large oil company in the UK and one of its main products is petrol. It converts crude oil, which has been extracted from the ground, into petrol, which can be used in cars.

UX Oil uses flow production in its large refineries. Crude oil is pumped into the refinery and a number of processes is then used to convert it into liquid. These processes largely rely on computers and do not need many people. The crude oil flows continuously through the refinery until it comes out as petrol.

1. State one input and one output for UX Oil. (2 marks)
2. Does UX Oil use labour or capital intensive methods of production? Explain your answer. (6 marks)
3. Explain the advantages and disadvantages of flow production to UX Oil. (8 marks)

11 Operations 2

Getting started...

When businesses produce goods or services, it is important to use resources efficiently. This helps to reduce costs and increase profits. A business can do a number of things to help use resources efficiently. Look at the things that these businesses do.

Case 1 Munton Engineering

Justine Devereux works for Munton Engineering. It is her job to buy all the resources that the company needs such as materials, components, tools, equipment and services. She has to buy the best quality resources available at the cheapest possible price. She often visits suppliers to see what they can offer. She is a good negotiator and can often drive suppliers' prices down.

Case 2 Cooper's Instruments

Cooper's Instruments makes surgical instruments for hospitals so it is important that the quality of their products is high. Staff are trained in quality control and are responsible for the quality of their own work. Cooper's products also have to meet high quality standards laid down by the British Standards Institution (BSI). Producing quality work means fewer faulty goods and more satisfied customers.

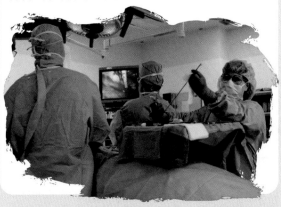

Case 3 Egg

Many businesses use new technology to make the most of their resources. Egg was one of the first banks to provide Internet banking. Customers can check their accounts and conduct transactions using the Internet from anywhere in the world. This helps to keep costs down and allows customers access to banking information 24 hours a day.

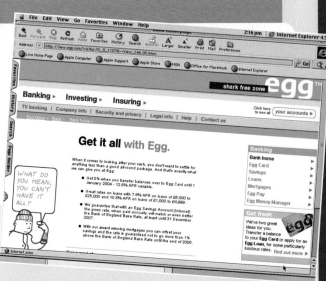

How do:
(a) Munton Engineering
(b) Cooper's Instruments
(c) Egg
make the best use of their resources?

How is production managed in a business?

Purchasing

Many businesses have a purchasing department. Specialist buyers are employed to buy all the business's resources. They have to buy or hire the best quality resources as cheaply as possible.

Getting resources cheaply means that costs will be reduced and profits will be higher.

Stock control

Some businesses keep stocks of raw materials, components and finished goods. Holding stocks incurs costs such as:
- storage;
- insurance;
- handling;
- opportunity cost - the money tied up in stock that could have been used to buy other things.

If too much stock is held, these costs will be high and profits will be lower. But if a business runs out of stock, production might have to stop or customers might have to wait for their orders.

Businesses must hold exactly the right amount of stock. Some businesses use JUST-IN-TIME (JIT) methods of production. This involves holding little, or no stocks. Stocks must arrive just before they are needed. JIT cuts costs, but businesses have to rely on suppliers to deliver stocks promptly and regularly.

Quality

If businesses produce high quality products, there will be less waste and they may also get more customers. Poor quality products have to be reworked or thrown away. Some businesses use TOTAL QUALITY MANAGEMENT (TQM) to focus their employees' attention on the need to deliver high quality products and services. This approach means that **all staff** must take responsibility for the quality of their own work. It requires training and commitment from everyone in the business.

Some businesses try to achieve quality standards.
- **Production standards, such as ISO 9000**. This is where a business sets out the quality it wants to achieve in its production processes. It must achieve this quality before it can show customers that it has the award. The award is given by the British Standards Institution (BSI) and other bodies. The business is inspected from time to time to show it has maintained quality.
- **Product standards, such as the BSI kitemark**. This is given to products such as children's toys or safety clothing which need to be safe for the customer to use.

Business can achieve quality standards in production processes and products

Technology

All industries are making more use of technology. Many manufacturers use robots and COMPUTER AIDED MANUFACTURING (CAM) to control the whole production process. COMPUTER AIDED DESIGN (CAD) may be used to help design new products. IT is used to improve communications and process information. Some of the advantages of new technology include:

- ✪ higher levels of output because machines are more efficient;
- ✪ lower labour costs because fewer staff are required;
- ✪ increased quality because machines and computers are more accurate;
- ✪ a safer, cleaner and quieter work environment for staff;
- ✪ better communications because electronic methods, such as e-mail, are faster;
- ✪ new methods of selling and promoting products.

Computer aided design can help to improve the design process

Improving efficiency

If businesses make better use of their resources, they become more efficient. This helps to reduce costs and raise profits. There are different ways in which a business might improve efficiency.

Changes to the workforce A business can make employees more efficient by improving incentives, providing better training, more specialisation, using teamwork and giving staff more responsibility.

Changes to the factory and office layout Machinery and workstations can be rearranged so that effort and costs are reduced.

Using technology Using automatic plant, machinery and computers will improve efficiency.

Using new production approaches LEAN PRODUCTION is a new approach developed in Japan. It involves using less of everything, including resources and time. Examples of methods used to achieve this include JIT, TQM, team working and KAIZEN. Kaizen is the Japanese word for continuous improvement. It means that staff are trained to avoid waste and look for ways of improving efficiency all of the time.

key terms

Computer aided design (CAD) – the use of computers to design products.
Computer aided manufacturing (CAM) – using computers to control production.
Just-in-time (JIT) – an approach to production that involves holding little or no stocks.
Kaizen – Japanese for continuous improvement.
Lean production – an approach to production that involves using less of everything.
Total quality management – an approach where everyone in the business takes responsibility for the quality of their own work.

key terms key terms key terms key terms key terms

Quick quiz

1 True or false?

(a) Just-in-time results in higher stock holding costs.

(b) The BSI awards kitemarks for products that achieve a certain quality.

(c) Efficiency is to do with making better use of resources.

2 Which of these is not a stock holding cost?

(a) Insurance.

(b) Storage.

(c) Opportunity cost.

(d) Advertising.

3 Which of these is not designed to improve the efficiency of the workforce?

(a) Team working.

(b) Just-in-time.

(c) Incentives.

(d) Better training.

4 State three methods that might be used in lean production.

Portfolio practice

Merton plc

Merton plc produces cotton garments such as shirts, blouses, dresses and skirts. The company wants to improve the quality of its products because they have not been up to standard. The company plans to invest to improve quality and has to choose between two options.

✪ Train the workforce to take responsibility for the quality of their own work and gain ISO 9000 accreditation.

✪ Invest in new technology. Some new machinery is available which reduces waste material and improves the accuracy of sewing and cutting. However, 200 staff will be laid off if this machinery is introduced.

1. State two ways in which better quality products will benefit Merton plc. (2 marks)

2. Explain how new technology will improve efficiency at Merton plc. (6 marks)

3. Which of the options should Merton plc choose to improve quality? Give reasons for your answer. (9 marks)

12 Marketing and market research

Getting started...

The marketing activities of businesses are concerned with meeting customers' needs. Before a business can satisfy its customers' needs, it has to find out what their needs are.

Case 1 *The Heyfield Water Company*

The Heyfield Water Company owns a mountain spring from which it collects sparkling spring water. It is thinking of selling a new product for business people who want a healthy drink at work. But it is worried that other businesses have already used this idea. It has just read a report on the market for spring water. It gives a list of all the producers and figures on sales of spring water. It also includes customers' opinions about the price of spring water and the type of people who are most likely to buy it.

The Spring Water Market
Report by TXC Market Research Agency

1. The main producers _____ Sales in 2003

Case 2 *Stellar*

Stellar is a coffee shop in Leeds. Esme and Chris, the owners, like to try out a new coffee with their customers every few months. Their latest favourite is a coffee from Central America. They are thinking of putting a small sample of the coffee and a list of questions in the shop, asking what people think of it. They also want to know if people in offices would pay to have coffee delivered.

Case 3 *Burnden Wines*

Burnden Wines imports a range of wines from Australia. It has noticed that some other wine import businesses are selling alcohol-free wines. It wants to know whether stocking these drinks would prove to be popular with its customers. Most of its customers buy the wine by mail order. They send in orders through the post or by email.

BUY NOW
Alcohol-free wines from Australia

Order by phone:
01234-56789
or email:
www.auswine.com

(a) How might each of these businesses find out about their customers' needs?
(b) What information might they find out?

What is marketing?

Marketing

MARKETING is concerned with meeting customer's needs. To do this a business must:

- **find out** what potential customers want;
- identify the type of **products** customers want;
- sell products in the right **place**;
- make sure products are **promoted**, so that customers know about them and want to buy them;
- sell products at the right **price**.

Businesses use marketing to help reduce the chance of making mistakes. A lot of new products come out each year, but many are unsuccessful. One of the main reasons for this is that they do not meet customers' needs.

Marketing is important in helping a business to meet its aims and objectives, such as making a profit or earning revenue. This can only be achieved if a business sells enough of its products. Marketing helps a business to do this.

Market research

MARKET RESEARCH is the way that businesses find out about their customers' needs. It can be carried out in a number of ways.

Using existing information A business might look at information that has already been collected and recorded. This is known as SECONDARY or DESK RESEARCH. For example, a business setting up a pizza take-away in a town centre might find out its competitors from a local directory of businesses. It might find out how many people live in the area from a local government publication. Examples of sources used for primary research are shown in Figure 1.

Primary research involves collecting information, often by asking customers questions

Collecting information from customers This is where a business collects information which was not available before the research began. It is known as PRIMARY or FIELD RESEARCH. It is done is by asking consumers questions face to face, on the telephone, in writing or by email. This allows businesses to ask detailed questions. For example, customers could be asked about the price they would pay for a product and where they would go to buy it.

One of the problems with market research is that it doesn't guarantee success. Just because market research suggests that a product will sell well, doesn't mean that it will. When Coca-Cola launched 'New Coke' it expected the product to be a success. But customers did not like the taste and it didn't sell well.

Figure 1 *Sources of secondary or desk research and the type of information*

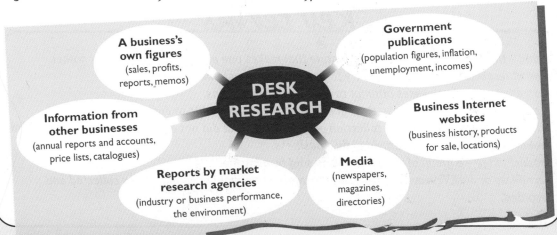

A business's own figures
(sales, profits, reports, memos)

Government publications
(population figures, inflation, unemployment, incomes)

Information from other businesses
(annual reports and accounts, price lists, catalogues)

DESK RESEARCH

Business Internet websites
(business history, products for sale, locations)

Reports by market research agencies
(industry or business performance, the environment)

Media
(newspapers, magazines, directories)

The product

A PRODUCT is a good or service provided by a business. A tin of pet food, a holiday in Majorca, a ride on a bus and a pair of shoes are all products. Larger businesses often have a PRODUCT RANGE. This is a group of similar products, sold by a business. Businesses often try to make their products different from others. How can they do this?

- ✪ Names. Most products have names that allow customers to distinguish them from others. Chocolate bars have different names such as Mars Bar, Lion Bar, Milky Way, Bounty and Twix.
- ✪ Design. Businesses make products with different designs to make them appeal to customers. Car manufacturers, for example, spend millions of pounds on the design of their cars.
- ✪ Packaging. Products often have unusual packaging to stand out from others on shelves. This allows consumers to recognise them more easily.
- ✪ Businesses often try to create a BRAND. This is a name, design, symbol or feature that makes one product different to another. Well known brands include Coca-Cola, Virgin and Microsoft. Businesses hope that customers will always buy a particular product because they recognise the brand.

The right place and the right time

It is important for businesses and their products to be available to consumers at the right PLACE and at the right time. A business selling petrol is likely to locate its petrol station on a busy road. A business selling products for people who are flying, such as socks to help circulation, will want to locate at an airport.

Products must also be available at the right time. For example, products such as Christmas puddings and Christmas trees are only wanted by customers in the run up to Christmas.

Well known brand names

key terms

Quick quiz

1 Complete the sentence.

One of the main reasons why many new products are unsuccessful is that they do not meet …… needs.

2 True or false?

To carry out secondary or desk research, a business might ask people questions about whether they will like a new product.

3 Which of the following are examples of market research?

(a) Designing new packaging for a product.

(b) Making sure that a product is available at the right time of year.

(c) Listening to customers' opinions about the quality of service that they are receiving.

(d) Finding out about the population of a village on a council website.

4 State two ways in which a business can distinguish its products from those of others.

5 Why is it important that products are available to consumers at the right place and at the right time?

Portfolio practice

Unilever

Unilever is one of the world's leading suppliers of consumer goods. The business has a number of widely known products in the areas of foods and personal care. In food, its most successful product range is called Knorr which consists of soups, sauces, noodles and complete meals. The Knorr range has sales of over £1.5 billion in over 100 countries. Other successful Unilever products and product ranges include Flora margarine, Bird's Eye frozen foods, Wall's ice cream and Brooke Bond tea. Unilever also sells personal care products under the name of Lux, Dove and Pond's.

Unilever believes that its success in selling huge quantities of these products lies in a number of areas. First, its ability to anticipate what consumers want and its policy of listening to customers. Second, the development of products to meet particular groups of consumers. Third, its willingness to introduce new and exciting products, such as the Magnum snack size and Cornetto miniatures for its ice cream market.

Source: adapted from www.unilever.com

1. Name two Unilever products. (2 marks)
2. Name three of Unilever's product ranges. (3 marks)
3. Is there any evidence of Unilever using market research? (4 marks)
4. Why might the names of Unilever's products be so important to the business? (4 marks)
5. Why do you think Unilever introduces new products onto the market? (6 marks)

13 Marketing – promotion, price and sales

Getting started...

The marketing activities of businesses are concerned with meeting customers' needs. A business might try different activities to market its products. It might change its price. It might advertise its products in many places. Think about the businesses below.

Case 1 Craytona Ltd

Craytona Ltd manufactures children's crayons. It decided to promote its product in shops that had play areas where parents left their children while they were shopping. The shops were given free samples of crayons for children to use.

Case 2 Abrett plc

Abrett plc has just opened up a range of shops selling lighting products. It is keen to attract customers in its first few months in business. So it has decided to set its prices as low as possible. Abrett is even prepared to make a loss on some products as long as it gets people into its shops.

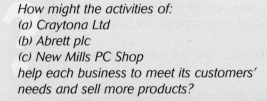

Case 3 New Mills PC Shop

New Mills PC Shop is popular with first time buyers of computers. It has just hired three new sales representatives. After a customer has bought a computer, a sales representative goes to the customer's house to demonstrate how it works. The sales representatives give individual support and attention to customers. They also tell customers about the range of extras that they can buy from New Mills PC Shop, such as digital cameras.

How might the activities of:
(a) Craytona Ltd
(b) Abrett plc
(c) New Mills PC Shop
help each business to meet its customers' needs and sell more products?

How does a business promote and sell its products, and how does it decide what price to charge?

Promotion

PROMOTION is the way that businesses make customers aware of their products. They do this in various ways, including:
- showing customers how the product will meet their needs;
- persuading customers to buy the product;
- letting customers know where the product is available and how much it will cost to buy;
- giving customers information about the product.

Advertising

ADVERTISING is a form of promotion which uses the MEDIA. It can be done in a number of ways.

Television, cinema and radio Advertising on TV and in the cinema can be effective, but it is very expensive. TV advertising is one of the best ways of reaching large numbers of people. For example, a TV advert at 7.00 pm on a Saturday can reach as many as 10 million people. Radio advertising is cheaper, but it reaches fewer people.

Newspapers and magazines TV advertising and advertisements in national newspapers reach millions of people. Local newspapers reach fewer people, but are likely to be cheaper. Advertising in magazines is a good way of reaching particular groups. For example, an advertisement for a guitar might be placed in a music magazine specialising in guitars.

Posters on taxis, buses and other forms of transport and on billboards This can be cheaper than other forms of advertising. It also enables eye-catching posters to be used which attract people's attention.

The Internet Some business use their own Internet websites to advertise their products. Some websites are designed to advertise certain things, such as jobs. Most businesses place their names on search engines to make it easier for customers to find them.

Many small businesses cannot afford to use some of these methods because they are too expensive. Such businesses often rely upon satisfied customers to tell others about their business. But large businesses use a variety of advertising methods.

Some businesses use an ADVERTISING AGENCY to help with their advertising. Advertising agencies help to produce advertisements. They also give advice on the most suitable media to use for an advertisement.

Advertising on television and billboards

Sales promotions

SALES PROMOTIONS are methods of achieving quick increases in sales. They include:

✪ competitions with prizes;
✪ free gifts;
✪ vouchers giving discounts off the next purchase;
✪ sponsorship;
✪ BOGOF promotions (buy one get one free)
✪ money off deals for buying two products.

Pricing

One of the ways in which businesses try to meet customer needs is by selling their products at the price which customers are prepared to pay. Businesses use a number of methods of pricing.

A price based upon the cost of producing the product A business might charge a price which covers its costs and then add an extra amount so that it makes a profit.

A price based upon the prices charged by other businesses A business might charge a similar price to those of other businesses. If it charged a higher price, it might lose sales to its competitors.

A price based upon what customers are willing to pay When a product is first sold, a business might charge a low price to encourage people to try it. But sometimes a business might charge a high price for a new product. This occurs mainly with new inventions and technologies. Customers might be prepared to pay a higher price because the product is new and only a few people have it. The business might lower the price later as sales increase.

Sales

Sales are the business activities concerned with selling products directly to consumers. This can take place in a number of ways.

Personal selling PERSONAL SELLING is where salespeople are involved in selling the product. This includes door to door sales, sales advisors in stores and other ways in which customers come into direct contact with someone trying to sell them a product. Personal selling is used widely to sell houses, insurance products and double glazing. It is also used by businesses selling products to other businesses. Those individuals involved in personal selling are often called SALES REPRESENTATIVES.

IT sales This area of personal selling has increased in recent years. It includes telephone sales, when salespeople call customers on the telephone. Text messages sent by mobile phone is a more recent personal selling method. More and more businesses are selling directly to customers through websites on the Internet or email.

Maintaining customer records Customer records provide information about customers. They might include data about where they live and work, their contact telephone number, when they were last contacted and their preferences. Developments in technology, such as the use of databases, allow businesses to keep extensive and up to date information on their customers.

key terms

Advertising – Promotion that is carried out through the media.
Advertising agency – organisations which produce advertisements and give advice on advertisements to other businesses.
Media – newspapers, magazines, TV and radio.
Personal selling – where salespeople are involved in selling the product.
Promotion – business activities which try to increase consumer awareness of products.
Sales promotions – promotions that try to cause a quick increase in sales.
Sales representatives – people involved in personal selling.

Quick quiz

1. Which of the following are examples of advertising?
   (a) A poster on a bus.
   (b) A free gift with each purchase.
   (c) A competition for a free holiday in Thailand.
   (d) A five minute commercial shown in cinemas.

2. Complete the sentence.
   To assist them with selling their products, many businesses employ an …… …… to contact customers personally.

3. True or false?
   Sales promotions are used to help businesses get quick increases in sales.

4. State three methods that businesses use to price their products.

5. State two ways in which IT developments have helped businesses in their sales activities.

Portfolio practice

The Latestop Weekend Holiday Shop

The Latestop Weekend Holiday Shop specialises in providing weekend package holidays for people who want to book a weekend break at the last minute. The weekend package includes the cost of flights and two or three nights' hotel accommodation.

The business is quite small and it uses a website which provides details of holidays and encourages customers to book online. But there is also a telephone booking service for those customers who don't want to book over the Internet. This service has a number of telephone salespeople who try to persuade customers to buy the business's products.

To get customers interested, The Latestop regularly holds competitions with prizes of free and discounted weekends away. The business also runs advertisements in national newspapers, usually on Sundays.

Prices for weekends away regularly change. The Managing Director, Keith Gordon, is directly involved in all pricing decisions. He spends a great deal of time checking the prices charged by rival businesses. He also keeps a close eye on changes in the costs of flights and hotel rooms, as he has to be careful to cover these costs.

1. State two examples of the methods of promotion that the Latestop Weekend Holiday Shop uses. (2 marks)
2. What pricing methods does the business use? (4 marks)
3. Using information from the case, explain any sales activities in which the Latestop Weekend Holiday Shop engages. (4 marks)
4. Recommend other suitable promotional methods that the Latestop Weekend Holiday Shop might use. (9 marks)

14 Customer service

Getting started...

All businesses need customers. It is important for businesses that they build good relationships with their customers.

Case 1 *Evercity plc*

Evercity plc supplies paint to aircraft manufacturers. It is important that these customers get their paint on time because delays can hold up production, which can be very costly. Evercity employs a team of customer service assistants. They work closely with the aircraft manufacturers to ensure that things run smoothly and that orders are delivered on time.

Deliveries always on time

Case 2 *Fawcetts*

Any problems? Repairs at no extra cost

Fawcetts is a roofing repair business. Nigel, the owner, always says the same thing to his customers if there are problems after he has repaired their roof. 'Ring me at once and I'll sort it out at no extra cost.' Because Nigel always keeps his word, he has built up a large number of loyal customers who always come to him for repairs. Also, they often recommend his services to others.

Explain how the services provided by:
(a) Evercity plc
(b) Fawcetts
(c) The Vishna Holiday Company
help them to build a good relationship with their customers.

Case 3 *The Vishna Holiday Company*

The Vishna Holiday Company offers a unique service to its customers. It organises family holidays to India and Nepal, but these can be costly if a few children are going with two parents. Some families find it hard to pay the cost of the holiday all at once. So Vishna allows families to spread the cost over one to three years, paying a little at a time.

Pay a little at a time

What customer services do businesses offer?

Customer services

CUSTOMER SERVICES is the part of a business that tries to make sure customers are satisfied with the good or service they are buying. Without customers, no business could survive. So the way businesses treat their customers is very important. Customer services can be:
- ✪ PRE-SALES SERVICES - services for customers before customers have made a purchase;
- ✪ AFTER-SALES SERVICES - services which are available to customers after they have made a purchase.

Staff working in customer services deal with matters such as making sure that products are delivered on time, providing help if the product breaks down and helping customers with small problems when they first take delivery.

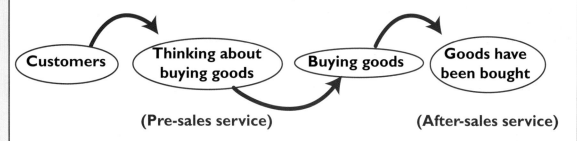

Figure 1 *Customer services*

Providing information and giving advice

This can be done before or after a sale.
- ✪ Before a sale, customer services can give valuable information about how a product might meet a customer's needs.
- ✪ After the sale, customer services help the customer to make the product work and explain some of its functions.

Technical products, such as computer equipment and specialised machinery, may need a lot of support before and after a sale has been made. Many businesses now use the Internet to provide advice and assistance. Their websites give information to support customers and include sections such as 'frequently asked questions'.

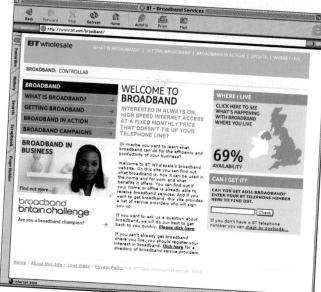

A website with customer information

The advice and information that customers need about some products is often complex. So it is important for customer services to work closely with others in the business, such as those involved in design, production and sales. This helps to ensure that the information and advice given to customers is accurate and helpful.

Credit facilities

A business might provide CREDIT FACILITIES. This allows customers to 'borrow' money to pay for goods and services. The money is then paid back a little at a time over a period. Some businesses allow customers to buy goods and pay it all later.

For goods or services costing more than £100, credit facilities are an essential part of customer service. Without credit facilities, many customers would not be able to buy the product. For example, businesses selling cars rely heavily upon credit facilities. Most cars are too expensive to buy with cash or credit cards.

Offering credit services

Delivering goods

This is an after sales service offered by businesses to customers. Some products can be bought and taken home straight away. But other products need to be delivered to customers. There are various reasons for this.

- ✪ The product may have to be made to fit the customer's requirements, for example, a new piece of machinery for a business.
- ✪ The product may be out of stock, so the customer has to wait for delivery.
- ✪ The product may be too big for the customer to carry away, such as a sofa.

Getting products when they need them is vital for customers. So customer services must agree with the customer when the product will be delivered. If delivery is late for any reason, the customer must be told. People dealing with deliveries must work closely with others in the business so the job is carried out effectively. For example, they need to work with transport personnel to make sure orders are delivered and with production staff to ensure goods are produced on time.

Handling customer complaints

Dissatisfied customers must be dealt with carefully by businesses. If they remain unhappy with their product, they might not buy a product from the business again. They are also likely to tell others about their complaint. This could harm the reputation of the business.

key terms

After-sales service – services available to customers after they have made a purchase.
Credit facilities – a service that allows customers to borrow money.
Customer services – the part of a business that seeks to ensure that customers are satisfied with the good or service they are purchasing or considering purchasing.
Pre-sales service – services for customers before they have made a purchase.

key terms key terms key terms

Quick quiz

1   Which of the following are examples of customer service?

(a) Dealing with a customer complaint.

(b) Arranging for a customer to borrow £10,000.

(c) Informing a customer that her order will arrive two days late.

(d) Giving a 20 per cent discount on repeat purchases.

2   What is the difference between pre and after sales services?

3   Which of the following are examples of after sales services?

(a) Explaining to a potential customer how a product will meet their needs.

(b) Arranging for a product to be sent to a customer within 48 hours.

(c) Arranging for a fault on a product to be fixed.

(d) Offering a refund.

4   Complete the sentence.

So that customers are able to purchase more expensive items ...... are often arranged to make them affordable.

5   State two reasons why customer services need to work closely with other areas of a business.

Portfolio practice

Roche Cottons Ltd

Roche Cottons Ltd manufactures shirts, jeans, jumpers and sports wear. All of its products are produced from pure cotton and the business has a good reputation for producing high quality goods. It supplies clothes to a number of major clothing shops.

The customer service department at Roche is a vital element in the success of the business. It works closely with the production department to make sure that clothes are delivered on time to customers. Jean Chadwick, the manager of the customer service department, keeps in close contact with customers, to check that any problems or complaints are dealt with quickly.

The customer service department takes orders from customers. It is also responsible for checking their precise requirements before the orders are made in the production department. Jean says: 'Without me and my team, we'd lose our customers in no time. I'm forever apologising about orders turning up late or sending the wrong clothes, and generally smoothing over problems'.

1. Identify one pre-sales and one after-sales customer service offered by Roche Cottons Ltd. Use information from the case to answer this question. (2 marks)
2. Explain three ways in which the customer service department at Roche Cottons Ltd benefits the customers. Use information from the case to answer this question. (6 marks)
3. Examine the reasons why the customer service department at Roche Cottons Ltd should be so vital to the business. (6 marks)

Research and development

Getting started...

If businesses want to carry on being successful, they must constantly develop new products. To do this, they carry out research to find out what customers want. They then use this information to help them to develop and produce new products.

Case 1 *The Beatty Partnership*

The Beatty Partnership is a travel agent. It books holidays with large travel companies but is finding it hard to compete with other travel agents. It has just seen a book with a list of small travel companies that offer specialist holidays, such as golfing or hiking weeks. The Beatty Partnership is wondering whether to offer these holidays, but it is not sure how its customers will react. So it has decided to ask people who visit the shop to answer a set of questions. It has also put these questions on its website.

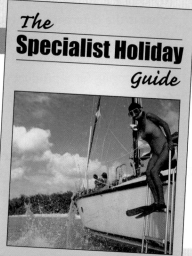

The **Specialist Holiday** *Guide*

Case 2 *Courtways*

Courtways makes soft drinks. Most of its sales are of small bottles of cola, orange and lemonade. It has noticed that other manufacturers have been selling a wider variety of flavours so it has been experimenting with new formulae for drinks. It is testing two new products in its laboratory.

✿ A lemonade which is yellow, rather than clear, and tastes more strongly of lemons.

✿ An orange and cranberry juice drink.

It has asked some of its existing customers to taste the drinks and give their opinions.

Case 3 *EFG Ltd*

SURVEY

Name: _____
Age: _____

Gender: Male ☐   Female ☐

Income: Less than £30,000 ☐
          £30,000 – £60,000 ☐
          £60,000 – £100,000 ☐
          Over £100,000 ☐

EFG Ltd makes luxury sports cars. The cars cost around £50,000, so generally the customers are middle-aged people on high incomes. The company thinks that it could sell more cars if its designs appealed to younger customers. It has sent out a list of questions in a car magazine asking people for information about their age, earnings and what they like about the cars they currently own. EFG has just seen some research showing how cars can be made from lighter materials and it wants to try this in its new designs.

How can each of these businesses find out about:
(a) the type of products that they might develop
(b) the type of products that their customers want?

How does a business research and develop new products?

Research and development

RESEARCH AND DEVELOPMENT is concerned with researching markets and products and then using the information to help in developing existing products or creating new ones. Businesses conduct research to find out:

- what customers think about products;
- what products it is possible to produce.

Businesses need to develop new and existing products so their customers will continue to buy their products rather than those of rivals. They also need to find out about new products that are coming onto the market and new technologies that will help them develop their products.

Customer research

Finding out what customers want from products involves carrying out market research. This gives businesses information about the markets in which they operate. It might mean finding out:

- how a business can sell its products to different age groups;
- what consumers think about rival products;
- how customers would like a business to improve its products.

The information can then be used to develop products. For example, customers in hair salons might be asked to try out a new shampoo. If most of them like everything about the shampoo except its smell, the manufacturer might change this before the shampoo is sold.

Collecting market research information

One of the main ways in which businesses collect market research information is through the use of SURVEYS. A survey involves asking people questions about themselves, their habits and their views. Surveys can be carried out in a number of different ways.

- Questions being asked over the telephone.
- Face to face interviews between two people.
- Postal surveys, where customers answer questions in writing and then send their replies by post.
- Internet or email surveys, where customers answer questions on a business website or send replies by email.

Businesses use various methods to persuade consumers to respond to market research questions. These include such things as entries into prize draws to win foreign holidays and cars.

Businesses might also obtain customer information from:

- customer panels, where businesses ask customers for their views about products over a period of time;

Face to face interviews

- tasting panels, where customers are invited to try out food products that a business is developing;
- observing customers shopping and, for example, recording how they move around a supermarket or what products they buy.

Businesses can also use information that already exists. For example, a business that wants to set up in a town centre might be able to find out:

- how many people live there from government records;
- what other businesses there are in the area from a local business directory.

ICT and market research

Information and communication technology (ICT) is becoming more and more important to businesses that carry out market research. ICT can be used to collect and store information.

Storing information Computer databases allow businesses to store huge amounts of information about consumers and their preferences. Businesses can also use databases to identify potential consumers. For example, a wine seller might be interested in people who subscribe to a wine magazine.

Collecting information ICT allows businesses to collect information about consumer habits and preferences. For example, electronic scanners at supermarket checkouts can monitor changes in sales patterns. The business can then use this information to decide whether it needs to buy in more or less quantities of the products it sells to its customers.

Product research

Businesses also need to carry out research into the type of products they can manufacture or sell. They might obtain this information by:

✪ finding out about innovations or new technologies that will enable them to develop new products or make changes to existing ones;

✪ testing new product ideas or inventions to see what is possible;

✪ comparing existing products or new products with similar ones being sold by other businesses.

Businesses that produce medicines often test their products in laboratories

Product development

PRODUCT DEVELOPMENT is about ways of improving products. As a result of market and product research, businesses sometimes find that they need to improve their existing products. This might lead to new ingredients such as 'New Formula Persil' or a special one-off product like 'Limited Edition Magnum' ice cream. Businesses hope that by doing this, their customers will continue to buy their products and will be less likely to buy similar products from their competitors.

New product development is about the development of new products. There is a number of stages to the process of developing a new product.

✪ Coming up with the idea for a new product. This also involves deciding which ideas are likely to succeed and those that are not.

✪ Creating the new product. This may involve designing the product and developing the technology needed to make the product. Or it might mean changing and improving a rival's product to produce a completely new product. This is called innovation.

✪ Testing out the new product to make sure that it works in the way it is meant to.

✪ Judging customers' reactions to the product.

✪ Introducing the new product to the market and selling it to customers.

key terms

Product development – the process of improving products for customers.
Research and development – researching markets and products and using this information to develop existing products and produce new ones.
Surveys – a method of collecting market research information. Surveys involve asking people questions about themselves, their habits and their views.

Quick quiz

1. Which of the following are examples of market research?
   (a) Developing a new vacuum cleaner.
   (b) Observing the reactions of consumers to a new ice cream.
   (c) Asking customers how they would like their house cleaning service to be improved.
   (d) Negotiating a discount on a new van for a customer.

2. State two ways in which a survey can be carried out.

3. Which of the following are examples of the use of ICT in market research?
   (a) Creating a database with details of existing customers.
   (b) Using email to find out the views of customers about a new product.
   (c) Doing a postal survey to gain further information on customer tastes and attitudes.
   (d) Purchasing a new item of software to help a business keep its accounts in order.

4. Complete the sentence.
   To remain competitive, many businesses are constantly engaged in …… so that their products continue to improve.

5. State the five main stages of a new product's development.

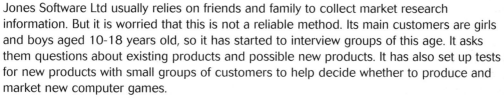

Portfolio practice

Jones Software Ltd

Jones Software Ltd develops computer games for customers to use on their personal computers. It is a small business in a market dominated by large companies such as Sony and Nintendo. But the company thinks its small size is important in a fast changing market. It has healthy sales and profits to prove it.

Jones Software Ltd usually relies on friends and family to collect market research information. But it is worried that this is not a reliable method. Its main customers are girls and boys aged 10-18 years old, so it has started to interview groups of this age. It asks them questions about existing products and possible new products. It has also set up tests for new products with small groups of customers to help decide whether to produce and market new computer games.

The approach to new product development is straightforward. New games are developed in teams made up of three employees. Each employee is responsible for a different part of the development.
- One develops the software in the company's workshop.
- One arranges for it to be tested with the customer test groups.
- One introduces it to the market.

The teams often visit technology and games exhibitions to find out what tomorrow's games might be. The initial ideas for new products often come from conversations during break times and nights out together.

1. Describe how Jones Software Ltd gathers market research information and product research information. (4 marks)
2. Identify the different stages in the development of a new item of the company's computer software. (4 marks)
3. Evaluate the likely effectiveness of the company's market research activities. Use information from the text to support your arguments. (9 marks)

16 The use of IT in business

Getting started...

Information technology (IT) is the recording and use of information by electronic means. Businesses use IT to help them run more effectively and efficiently. IT can be used to cut costs and improve goods, services, communications and productivity.

Case 1 *Checking over the Internet*

A customer has ordered something on the Internet from Amazon UK. It has not yet arrived. He is checking the progress of the order on his computer.

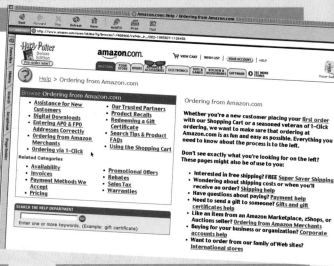

Case 2 *Checking a bank balance*

A customer wants to check her bank balance by phone. The telephone assistant replies: 'Certainly. But first of all, can you give me the first and third letters of your password and your place of birth?' The details are then shown on the customer's records on the bank's computer.

Case 3 *Sending money abroad*

A sales manager wants to buy from a French supplier. She does not want to send a cheque or money in case they get lost. She has contacted her bank to ask if the money can be transferred directly from the company's bank account into the French company's account in Calais.

(a) What particular business problem is illustrated in each of the above cases?
(b) How does IT help each business to deal with its problem?

How can IT support and improve business?

External communications

IT can help businesses communicate with various people and organisations outside the business. For example, many businesses now have a website on the INTERNET that provides information about their business. The Internet is available to everyone who has a computer and a modem. Businesses have websites that show information, take orders for goods and receive payments. For example, airlines such as Easyjet allow people to book directly through their website. Many of the large supermarkets, such as Tesco, offer Internet shopping. Customers can also email businesses to ask for details about their products.

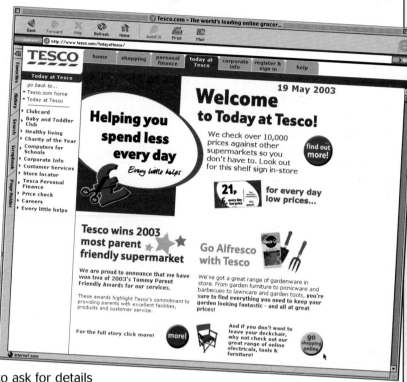

Electronic communications between departments

In the future, new technologies such as email and the INTRANET may replace the telephone and internal mail as the main methods of business communication between departments. They are a much cheaper way of sending long and complicated messages. They also make sure that most messages get through to the right person quickly.

Email allows people to send messages and an attachment to someone else's email address in a different department. That person can then pick up the message when it is needed. The intranet is similar to the Internet but it is only available to those within a business who access it by using a password. Information on the intranet is confidential, whereas information on the Internet is available to the public.

Facilities to share common data

IT can help businesses share and update data that is common to all employees, quickly, efficiently and with potentially large cost savings. The intranet is a good way of enabling people to access files such as stored records, certain types of financial data and orders. One of the biggest savings with the intranet comes from the sending of standard information throughout the business. For example, information such as internal phone numbers, diaries and timetables quickly goes out of date. But in electronic format, it can be revised as soon as a change occurs. These changes can then be made available to all staff through a 'browser'.

Security systems

When large amounts of information are stored on computers, businesses must ensure that the information is safe and that only the right people can access it. There are certain ways to protect information on computer systems.

Anti-virus software Businesses can have problems with viruses that have been created by 'hackers' who want to change or destroy the information on their systems. A simple way of introducing a virus onto a company's system is by email. Emails, with viruses attached to them, are sent

to individuals in the business. Once the email attachment is opened, the virus attacks that computer and can then spread very quickly to all the company's computer systems. Businesses can buy ANTI-VIRUS SOFTWARE to protect their computers against viruses. The software can detect and remove viruses before they enter the system. The software needs to be regularly updated because new viruses are being created all the time.

System back ups If a computer's hard disk crashes, becomes corrupted by a virus or is destroyed through fire or flood, the company will need to have a back up. A back up is a copy of all the files and programs that are kept on a computer system.

Confidentiality and passwords Although a lot of business information is shared, some of it is confidential and has to be restricted, such as staff records or sensitive financial information. In such circumstances, the files will be password protected. That means that a password needs to be typed in before anyone can gain access to the information.

On-line support for customers

Companies can now provide customers with on-line support via the Internet. Customers can check progress on their orders, search out new products, buy goods and send enquiries to a business. For example, many people now use on-line banking. This means that they can check their accounts and examine all their transactions.

Electronic transfers

Businesses are making increasing use of the electronic transfer of information. Most shops now use bar code systems at till checkouts. This allows a business to record all sales transactions and cash receipts. It also provides immediate receipts and invoices to customers. As the business can also see what stock has been sold and what stock remains, the information is also used for stock control. Through the use of electronic transaction services, such as Switch and Solo, customers can pay for things immediately because the funds are transferred from their bank account to the business's at the point of purchase.

key terms

Anti-virus software – computer software that allows a computer to be checked for viruses and removes them before they do any damage.
Internet – a worldwide method of communication that is available to everyone with access to a computer and a modem.
Intranet – similar to the Internet but messages can only be received by members of a business who use a password.

Quick quiz

1. How is the intranet different from the Internet?
2. Name three ways of making computer data safe and secure.
3. Name a company that does business on-line.
4. Switch and Solo are examples of what?
5. Name four services that customers could access on a business's on-line service.

Portfolio practice

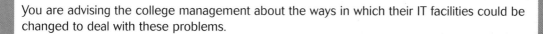

Capel College

Capel College has decided to upgrade its IT system for a number of reasons.

- The computer network keeps getting new viruses that are destroying staff and students' work.
- It's a large college and staff often need to access student files. At the moment they can't do this easily because they have to go over to the central office.
- The college is only advertised in the college brochure. The brochure is often out of date.
- There is no easy way for staff to get messages to each other.
- Students would like to be able to access their course worksheets, notes and exercises from home.

You are advising the college management about the ways in which their IT facilities could be changed to deal with these problems.

1. Explain two ways in which the college could prevent viruses from affecting the computer system. (4 marks)
2. What IT improvements could the college make that would help:
   (a) the staff; (6 marks)
   (b) the students; (6 marks)
   to carry out their work?

Getting started...

People COMMUNICATE with each other every day in business. The operator of a machine asks another worker for help with a problem. A customer tells a taxi driver where she wants to go. A printing business orders stocks of paper from a supplier. Think about the people communicating with each other below.

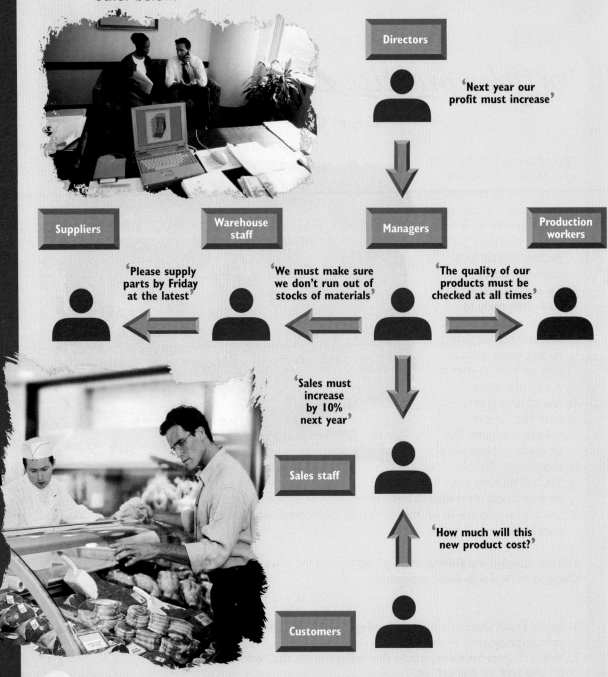

Directors

'Next year our profit must increase'

Suppliers

Warehouse staff

Managers

Production workers

'Please supply parts by Friday at the latest'

'We must make sure we don't run out of stocks of materials'

'The quality of our products must be checked at all times'

'Sales must increase by 10% next year'

Sales staff

'How much will this new product cost?'

Customers

(a) Identify the communications that are taking place above. In each case, say who is communicating and what they are communicating.

What is communication and who communicates in a business?

Communication

Communication is when information is passed between people. This can be in words, sounds, images and numbers.

Communication has two sides to it. There is a sender and a receiver. For example, a customer might telephone a salesperson to ask about the price of a product. The customer is the sender and the salesperson is the receiver. When the salesperson tells the customer the price, the salesperson is the sender and the customer is the receiver.

In some cases, there may be a number of senders or receivers. For example, a sales manager might hold a team meeting with her ten sales representatives to give them information on a new product they will be selling.

SENDER ⟶ **RECEIVER**

Information passed from sender to receiver

Figure 1 *Communication*

Communication within a functional area

The functional areas of a business include marketing, production, human resources and finance. People within these areas communicate with each other in many ways.

Marketing A sales manager might discuss some market research results with the staff that have carried out the surveys. Or two employees might discuss the best way to promote a new product.

Production Two members of a quality control team might discuss why a piece of machinery is not operating as well as it should be. Or a production worker might discuss flexitime arrangements with his manager.

Human resources Two staff might discuss organising a training course for some new employees. Or a manager might ask an employee to look up the latest information on redundancy law.

Finance An employee might ask a colleague how to use the computer's accounts program. Or an accountant might ask finance staff for figures to produce the company's annual accounts.

Communication within the production department - two workers discussing a problem in the factory

key terms

Communicate – to pass information from a sender to a receiver.

key terms key terms key terms key terms key terms key terms

Communication outside a functional area

People often have to communicate with those in other functional areas of the business. They may do this in the workplace by holding meetings with colleagues from other departments or by sending emails. Or they may do this informally, outside work, for example when they meet for lunch or have a night out. There are various reasons why they need to communicate.

- **Discussing problems.** Managers from different departments might meet to discuss how they can work together to improve the business's efficiency.
- **Passing on instructions.** The board of directors might tell its managers about changes that it wants in the following year. Or an employee from the sales department might pass information to the finance department about current sales.
- **Providing training.** An employee from the human resources department might hold a training course to give health and safety information to employees from other departments.
- **Passing on information.** Some companies produce newsletters or business magazines to tell all their employees what is happening in the business. This may also be done on the business's intranet or website.
- **Supporting other departments.** Administrative staff who carry out support duties, such as filing and photocopying, would ask departments about their needs.

Some companies produce magazines or newsletters to give employees information about the business

Communication outside the business as a whole

Businesses communicate with people outside the organisation.

- **Suppliers.** Businesses need to communicate with suppliers to order materials, parts or ingredients. Suppliers will tell the business the price and when the order can be delivered.
- **Customers.** Customers might ask about the price of goods, where they are sold and how they work. Businesses give customers a great deal of information about their products.
- **Government.** Businesses need to communicate with government departments, for example to pay their taxes or to apply for grants.
- **Outside interests.** The shareholders of the business need to be told how the business is performing. They get this information from the company's Annual General Meeting and the Annual Report and Accounts.
- **The local community.** A business might give information to a local newspaper about a new factory it is building, for example.

Communication problems

Not all communications are effective. There are many reasons why communications may break down.

- The sender of a communication may not explain himself or herself very well.
- The sender might use complicated language or jargon that the receiver does not understand.
- The receiver may not have being paying attention.
- The receiver might not see or hear the information.
- The message may have been passed to other people first who have interpreted it differently.
- The information might not be received on time.
- The technology used to send the information might be faulty.

Quick quiz

1 What is meant by communication?

2 True or false?

(a) Asking suppliers to deliver goods on time is an example of communication within a functional area of the business.

(b) An example of a communication difficulty is when an employee does not know how to operate a database even though he has been given training.

3 Match the communications (a)-(c) to the people sending and receiving them (i)-(iii).

Communication	**Sender and receiver**
(a) Outside the business.	**(i)** The production manager tells her machine operators that they have not met that month's production targets.
(b) Within a functional area.	**(ii)** A customer telephones a ticket agency to ask when tickets for a concert will be on sale.
(c) To another functional area.	**(iii)** A researcher explains some market research information to the research and development team in the production department so that they can make changes to a new product they are working on.

4 List five barriers to communication.

Portfolio practice

Handlecare

Handlecare manufactures children's toys that it sells to toyshops. Caleb is the manager of the marketing department. He is going to hold a team meeting to discuss ideas for a new advertising campaign that will try to attract new customers.

Caleb also wants to get ideas from other functional managers in the business as he thinks that their ideas might help to improve the campaign. He does this by sending an email with the advertising campaign attached. Unfortunately, the finance manager is out of the office for the next few days and the human resources manager's computer is not working properly.

At the meeting, Caleb explains that the business should try to increase its sales to the large, national toy chains. He gives the team a huge file containing detailed information about sales in different shops. He asks for their opinions, but there is a lot to understand in such a short time.

1. From the text, identify examples of communication that takes place:
   (a) within a department;
   (b) between functional areas of the business;
   (c) outside the business. (3 marks)
2. Explain the communication problems that Caleb has experienced and why they might cause difficulties. (7 marks)
3. What changes could Caleb make to improve communications? (6 marks)

18 Business communication methods

Getting started...

People in business use a variety of methods to communicate with others. They might talk to people in the same office or send a note to colleagues about a meeting. They might telephone or email someone in another office or send an invoice to another business asking for payment. They might tell customers about a forthcoming sale in an advertisement.

Case 1 *Human resources manager*

Case 2 *Receptionist*

Case 3 *Sales manager*

(a) What methods of communication might be used in each of the above cases?

What are the different ways of communicating information?

Oral communication

This is when people talk to each other. There are many methods of oral communication.

Verbal messages This is often the quickest way to communicate. It is where the sender talks to the receiver of a message. It allows the message to be explained and discussed. But because the message is not written down, the receiver may forget it.

Telephones, mobile phones and answer machines Telephones are still one of the main ways of communicating with someone who is not close by. They are relatively cheap and easy to use, but they can be engaged or the person being called may be out. Answering machines or voicemail solve these problems as they can receive and store messages. But some people find these machines impersonal and they will not leave a message. People can carry mobile phones around and they can be used to send text messages and pictures. But they can be expensive to use and some areas of the country have poor reception.

Telephone conferencing This is where people are linked together via telephone lines. Each person can talk to others as if they were in the same room. The advantage is that people can have discussions without having to be in the same place. This can save on time and travelling costs.

Meetings Sometimes it is important that everyone meets face to face to discuss business issues. Usually, an assistant writes down what was discussed and agreed. These are called the minutes and everyone gets a copy. One problem of meetings is that they take time and have to be planned in advance to make sure that everyone can be there.

Video communications

More and more people are able to communicate by video link. VIDEO CONFERENCING is a method of communication that allows individuals in different locations to communicate as if they were in the same room. With the use of a camera, individuals can see each other on monitors and talk to each other via telephone lines. The advantage of this type of communication is that people can talk to and see other people from anywhere in the world. As this saves on the time and cost of travelling to meetings, many businesses find it cost effective. But it is not quite the same as meeting people face-to-face and video conferencing is expensive to set up because of the equipment costs.

This technology is now available over the Internet. Also, video phones that allow people to see and talk to each other are becoming more common. In time, both of these should reduce the cost of video communications.

Graphical communication

These include drawings, graphs and images. They can help to communicate ideas and messages in a way that is clearer than words or text. For example, if sales have risen faster in one month than another, this can be shown clearly on a bar chart. Graphs are often followed by text, video and oral information to give a fuller explanation.

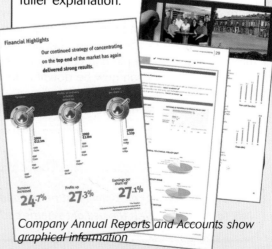

Company Annual Reports and Accounts show graphical information

Written communications

Written communications are often used when information has to be passed on formally or when a permanent record is needed. Written communications come in many forms.

Letters Letters contain information written on paper or typed and printed. The advantage of a letter is that it is a cheap and easy way to communicate in writing. But it does take time to word process, check and print, and then send it out in the post.

Memos Memos are short, informal written messages that are used for internal communications in a business. They are usually sent by the internal mail system or by email. As the message is brief, it is unlikely to be forgotten. But many business people say that these days so many memos are sent that some of them are ignored.

Financial documents and forms Petty cash books, sales ledgers, cash flow statements, balance sheets and other financial documents are written methods of communicating a business's performance. But they can be difficult to understand if a person has not had accountancy or financial training. Businesses also use various forms such as expenses forms, timesheets, and stock request forms to give information. They can be filled in quickly and easily, are simple to file and the information can be retrieved and confirmed quickly.

Advertisements Advertisements in magazines, newspapers and the Internet are all examples of written communication. Information about a product can be communicated to customers in a persuasive way and it can be updated and changed regularly. But as customers see so many adverts, they do not all make an impact and some adverts work better than others. Customers often want to see how a product works, so radio advertising is not suitable for certain products.

Email Email allows people to communicate immediately with others by word processed text or images on a computer. The communication takes place immediately and it will stay in the computer until the receiver picks it up. Another benefit is that large documents can be sent as attachments. But emails can only be sent to people who have a computer. Also, if people get a lot of emails, they might not bother to read all of them.

Fax Faxes are similar to email but the information is sent by a fax machine. Both the sender and receiver must have a fax. The fax machine sends messages instantly and the receiver does not have to be there to receive the message. Sometimes the quality of the received fax is poor and it can take a long time to send a lengthy item.

Notices and electronic notice boards Notices are a quick way of sending a message. They are often found in places where a lot of people pass through such as the entrance to business premises. Electronic notice boards send messages by monitors or screens and can be quickly updated. A problem with notice boards is that not everyone looks at them. Also, the information does not always apply to everyone who reads it.

Multimedia, the Internet and the future

More and more businesses communicate by multimedia and the Internet. Mobile phones and websites can now send messages with images, text and graphics. Memos can be sent by email as a video rather than text. Letters can be sent as email attachments with links to Internet websites. People can communicate with each other via live chat rooms. Forms and various documents can now be downloaded from the Internet. New websites are set up every day that provide information about all types of activities. In the near future, all homes are likely to have computers linked to the Internet and all businesses will have computer networks.

key terms

Video conferencing - a communication method that allows people in different places to see and talk to each other with the use of cameras and telephones.

Quick quiz

1 Complete the table below, showing at least one advantage and one disadvantage for each method of communication.

Method of communication	Advantages	Disadvantages
Fax		
Mobile phone		
Verbal		
Letter		
Email		

Portfolio practice

Clayson Design and Builders Ltd

Clayson Design and Builders Ltd is a construction and design company working in the London area. Young families and single people find it difficult to afford the expensive housing in the area, so they are looking for cheaper and smaller 'starter homes'.

Clayson has just started to build 20 new houses. Erica Clayson, one of the designers, has produced detailed housing plans for the team of builders. She has had a meeting with them to discuss the need to follow the designs carefully and to meet deadlines. She faxed a memo to the business's managers outlining the main points of the meeting and what was said.

The business is facing a number of problems.
- It buys some of its materials from abroad and the materials haven't arrived on the date when they are needed. The business must find out where these materials are and have them delivered as soon as possible.
- In the meantime, workers must switch jobs so that they do not lose time. This must be organised quickly.
- Clayson has built a 'show home'. Customers can visit it and see what the houses will look like when they are finished. The company must attract customers to come and look at the show home before the houses are completed.

1. Identify three these methods help communication in the business. (3 marks)
2. Explain how these methods help communication in the business. (7 marks)
3. Evaluate the most suitable methods of communication that could be used by the business in solving its problems. (9 marks)

19 Business competitors – making products competitive

Getting started...

Businesses must find ways to make their products competitive against those of their rivals. This will allow them to win and retain customers. Think about the following businesses.

Case 1 *Stanley Park Foods*

Stanley Park Foods is a small delicatessen shop in Liverpool. Its main competitors are the large supermarket chains that offer similar products. Because of this competition, the business tries to stock a larger range of specialist foods, such as local and foreign cheeses. It also uses local suppliers who do not sell their products to the supermarkets.

STANLEY PARK FOODS
'Local cheeses a speciality'

Case 2 *Salop Meat Supplies*

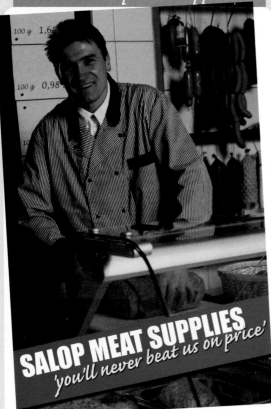

SALOP MEAT SUPPLIES
'you'll never beat us on price'

Salop Meat Supplies has a motto; 'You'll never beat us on price'. It sells to butchers and supermarkets. It buys its meat from a number of European countries and is always looking for the cheapest price.

Case 3 *Bon Mot*

Bon Mot imports Belgian chocolates and sells them to a small number of specialist hotels. The hotels give chocolates free to customers in their most expensive rooms. Bon Mot is careful to check the taste and appearance of the chocolates it imports. It is important that their customers think they are being offered a product that is special and of the finest quality.

Explain how:
(a) Stanley Park Foods
(b) Salop Meat Supplies
(c) Bon Mot
are trying to make their products competitive against those of other businesses.

How can a business make its products competitive?

Competition

Nearly all businesses face competition from other businesses. COMPETITION is where rival businesses aim their products at the same customers and try to win and keep their custom.

Take chocolate bars as an example. There is a huge range of products available. Because of competition, companies such as Nestlé, Mars and Cadbury Schweppes must find ways to make sure that customers buy their chocolate bars rather than those of their rivals. And once customers have bought their goods, businesses must make sure that they come back and buy them again. So businesses must also retain customers.

Quality and status

Sometimes, the price of a product gives a signal about the quality or status of the product. In these markets, businesses may charge what they think the customers expect to pay. For example, a business selling designer clothes will want to charge a price that suggests high quality. Other examples of goods which customers might expect to pay a high price for are Rolls Royce cars and Rolex watches.

Availability

Businesses may try to win customers by making sure that their products are available where they want them. For example, a car driver in a rural area might want to buy petrol. There might be a number of petrol stations selling quality fuel at a low price. But if they are all 20 miles away, he may choose to use a local petrol station even though it is charging a slightly higher price.

Being available when customers want products is also important. More and more shops are staying open later in the evening or on Sundays. Some supermarkets are now open for 24 hours.

Price

Sometimes, customers just want to buy the cheapest service or product available, for example, when buying basic products and services such as electricity, gas or a bag of potatoes. In markets where businesses have close rivals, they must make sure that their prices are similar to those of their competitors. If they are not, the business could lose customers. If they can charge a slightly lower price, they might win customers from other businesses.

Motor car businesses and mobile phone companies compete with rivals using prices

Identifying competitors

A business needs to be able to identify the other businesses it is competing with. One way is to look at businesses with similar **products**. For example, a train company would identify other train companies as its competitors.

Another way is to think about other businesses that offer similar **benefits** to customers. So, for example, a cinema might identify businesses offering leisure and entertainment as its competitors. These might be bowling alleys and adventure games such as 'laser quest'.

Today, businesses face competition from all over the world, not just their local area. There are three main types of business competitors.

✪ Local – these are businesses based in the same part of the same country.
✪ National – businesses based in the same country.
✪ International – businesses based abroad.

Competition and technology

Developments in technology have made markets more open to competition from a range of businesses. For example, the growth in air transport has created an international market for fruit and vegetables because they can now be transported all over the world by air.

One of the main technological developments affecting business competition is the growth in information and communication technology (ICT). One example of this is the sale of products via websites on the Internet. This means that a business operating from one country can compete all over the world without needing to have a factory or office in other countries.

key terms

Competition – *where a number of businesses try to sell their products to the same group of people, attempting to win their custom at the expense of rivals.*

key terms key terms key terms

Quick quiz

1. In one sentence explain why businesses need to compete.
2. Identify three ways in which businesses compete for customers.
3. Complete the sentence.

   Businesses are able to identify their competitors by examining those businesses offering the same ...... and the same ...... to customers.
4. Give two examples of technology increasing competition for businesses.
5. Explain the difference between local and international competitors.

Portfolio practice

Roma Pizzas

Hatherbake is a small town in the Peak District with a population of just under 12,000. It is in a rural area and the nearest other town is seven miles away.

In 1992, Luigi Fererra moved to Hatherbake and opened Roma Pizzas, the town's first pizza take-away. When he first started, there was only one other take-away business in the town. This was a well established fish and chip shop called the Hatherbake Chippy.

To make his business successful, Luigi worked long hours and stayed open as long as possible. He has been happy with the sales from his business and he has made a good living. Although Luigi's pizzas are more expensive than a portion of fish and chips, he has been careful never to cut corners. He is proud of his pizzas. They are cooked in a special pizza oven and he uses only the finest fresh ingredients.

But Luigi wonders whether the good times are coming to an end. An Indian restaurant has just opened and a new supermarket with a café has been built just outside the town centre.

1. How does Roma Pizzas compete with other businesses? (4 marks)
2. Explain why it is important for Roma Pizzas to compete with other businesses. (4 marks)
3. Evaluate the extent to which Roma Pizzas faces competition for its customers. (9 marks)

20 Business competitors - targeting customers

Getting started...

Different groups of customers have different needs. Businesses that are in competition with each other need to TARGET these groups in the right way.

Case 1 *Harrods*

Harrods, the London Department Store, offers a wide range of high quality goods and services and has a reputation for stocking the best products. Although its customers include a wide variety of individuals, it is geared up to meet the needs of high-income earners from both the UK and abroad. A part of Harrods' business is with tourists and other visitors to London.

Case 2 *Boots No 7 range*

Boots No 7 is a range of competitively priced make-up including lipstick, eye shadow and nail varnish. Boots has been marketing No 7 to women and teenage girls for over twenty years and it has been one of the company's most successful product lines.

Case 3 *Saris*

Saris are the traditional dress for Asian women. Manufacturers in the UK sell to British Asian women. There is also a growing trade in selling saris to non-Asian women.

(a) At what groups of customers is each of these businesses aiming its products?

How does a business target its customers?

Market segments

Some products are aimed at nearly all consumers, for example staple food items such as sliced bread and potatoes. Businesses selling these products do not always carefully plan who will buy their products.

But most products are aimed at particular groups of consumers. This does not mean that other consumers will not buy them. But it does mean that the majority of purchases will be made by people in the TARGET GROUP.

Targeting products at particular groups of consumers allows businesses to better meet their needs. By doing this, businesses hope that they will increase their sales and gain more loyal customers. Think about the market for shoes. If businesses did not target their customers, they would probably sell a fairly limited range of shoes that only varied according to their size. Young and old, rich and poor, and men and women would end up wearing the same style of shoes. Clearly identified groups of consumers are called MARKET SEGMENTS by businesses.

Identifying customers

Businesses need to identify the groups of customers at which they want to aim their products. Consumers can be grouped in various ways. These are shown in Figure 1.

Figure 1 *Market segments*

Grouping by age

Infants, teenagers and the over 80s all have very different needs. For this reason, businesses often target consumers according to their age. Clothes are usually designed with the needs of certain age groups in mind. Some products are designed for particular age groups, for example baby milk, meals for young children or mobility aids for the elderly.

Grouping by location

Customers in some parts of the country have different tastes to those in other parts. For example, those living in the countryside might be more likely to buy Wellington boots than those living in cities. Some foods are bought mainly in certain parts of the country, for example, haggis in Scotland and Kendal Mint Cake in Cumbria.

Grouping by income

Businesses target certain income groups with particular products. Luxury sports cars and exotic holidays are expensive so they are aimed at those with high incomes.

But budget shops are targeted mainly at those on lower incomes.

Grouping by lifestyle

This refers to the way in which people live their lives. For example, some house building companies try to sell their properties to young people in their 20s and 30s who live in cities, enjoy eating out at restaurants and socialising in bars. Some holiday companies advertise to older people who regularly take holidays abroad. Some products are aimed at vegetarians.

Grouping by gender

Grouping by gender is done according to whether the customer is male or female. Many products, including clothes, drinks, and cars are aimed at a particular gender. Magazines are often produced mainly for males or females, such as *Men's Health* or *Mizz*.

key terms

- **Market segments** – *clearly identified groups of consumers who share something in common.*
- **Targeting** – *aiming products at an identified group of consumers.*
- **Target group** – *a group of customers or market segment with similar tastes at which businesses are aiming their products.*

key terms key terms key terms key terms key terms key terms

Quick quiz

1. Complete the sentence.
   Businesses aim their products at clearly identified groups of consumers known as
   ....
2. Give one reason why businesses target their products at a particular group of consumers.
3. Which of the following ways of classifying groups of consumers might be used by a business selling soft drinks?
   (a) Lifestyle.   **(c)** Hair colour.
   (b) Age.   **(d)** Method of travelling to work.
4. Why might a business be interested in people's lifestyle?

Portfolio practice

Next

Next is a clothes retailer that has successfully targeted particular groups of consumers. Its stores have sections for men, women, and children. The company's Head Office is in Leicester and it has over 300 shops on the High Streets of most towns and cities in the UK. In 2001 it had a turnover of £1.9 billion and was the third in the market behind Marks and Spencer and Arcadia, which owns shops like Top Shop. One of Next's main market segments is fashion conscious men and women in their thirties, and their children.

During the 1990s, Next tried to capture a new group of customers - younger people in their late teens and twenties. This venture did not succeed. Next was left with too few business suits and too many micro-minis on its shelves.

Source: adapted from ICSG.org and The *Guardian*, 27.3.1998.

1. Using evidence from the text, identify two methods of targeting consumers used by Next. (2 marks)
2. Explain how targeting particular groups of customers has helped Next to become a successful business. (4 marks)
3. Explain two alternative methods of targeting consumers that Next might use. (6 marks)
4. Evaluate the success of the Next consumer targeting strategy. (6 marks)

Getting started...

Businesses are affected by many factors. Some of these factors are influenced by the state of the country's economy. For example, if banks increase their interest rates, businesses have to pay more for the money they borrow. Businesses cannot control these ECONOMIC CONDITIONS. Think about the economic conditions that have affected these businesses.

Case 1 The Newquay Surf Shack

Joel Zanick is the owner of The Newquay Surf Shack.

'When I started my surf shop, I had to buy the surfboards to sell to my customers. To do this, I borrowed money from the bank. The bank charges me interest on the loan. I worry about paying this interest. But if I had started the business two years ago, it would have cost me even more because interest rates were higher then.'

Case 2 MGP Warehouses

MGP Warehouses is a UK business that holds stocks of paper. It keeps many different sizes and styles which it sells to printers. Most of its paper is bought from mills abroad which make the paper. Last year, the price that the mills sold the paper for fell. But MGP Warehouses has just received an email from a paper mill in Sweden saying that paper prices are going to increase by 5 per cent next month.

Case 3 The Shoe Company

Elaine McGovern buys shoes for The Shoe Company.

EVERY YEAR I GO TO A FACTORY IN SPAIN AND BUY THOUSANDS OF PAIRS OF SHOES TO SELL IN OUR SHOE SHOPS IN BIRMINGHAM. THE SPANISH CURRENCY IS THE EURO, SO I HAVE TO PAY THE FACTORY OWNER IN EUROS. I GET THESE FROM MY BANK.
LAST YEAR I GOT 1.5 EUROS FOR EACH POUND BUT THIS YEAR I GOT LESS.

Identify the factors that have affected:
(a) The Newquay Surf Shack
(b) MGP Warehouses
(c) The Shoe Company.

What are the main economic factors affecting businesses?

Interest rates

Most businesses need to borrow money. This could be when they first start up or when they want to expand. INTEREST RATES affect how much it costs a business to borrow money. When interest rates rise, a business has to pay more. But when they fall, this helps the business because it has to pay less. The problem businesses face is that they cannot control interest rates and they do not know when rates are going to change.

Interest rates and business

What if a business needs to borrow £5,000 from its bank? The interest rate is 12%. Table 1 shows that this will cost the business £600 a year. Table 1 also shows how a change in the interest rate to 18% or 6% will affect the business.

✪ An increase to 18% will cost £900 a year. This is £300 a year more.

✪ A reduction to 6% means that the business will pay £300 a year. This is £300 a year less.

Table 1

Amount borrowed	Annual interest rate	Annual interest paid
£5,000	**12%**	**£5,000 x 12% = £600**
£5,000	18%	£5,000 x 18% = £900
£5,000	6%	£5,000 x 6% = £300

Prices

A business will set prices for the goods and services it sells to customers. Prices can go up or down. When there is a general rise in all prices in the economy, this is known as INFLATION. When there is a general fall in prices, this is called DEFLATION.

Exchange rates

When UK businesses buy or sell goods outside the UK, they are affected by exchange rates. The EXCHANGE RATE is the price or rate at which one CURRENCY can be exchanged for another. Currency is the money that is used in a country. In the UK it is the pound, in the USA the dollar and in many European countries it is the euro.

✪ A business that wants to buy products from another country will need the currency of that country to buy its products.

✪ A business selling to another country will be paid in that country's currency.

So, for example, a UK business buying products from the USA will have to exchange pounds for dollars to buy the USA products. A UK business selling to the USA will be paid in dollars and will need to change the dollars back to pounds.

Prices and business

Changes in prices can affect a business.

Rises in price If prices rise, a business will pay more for the things it buys, such as its packaging. This will increase its costs. If costs rise, the business might have to put up the price it charges its customers. It will earn more money from each good it sells. But if it raises its price too much, customers might buy fewer goods.

Falls in price. If prices fall, a business will pay less for the things it buys. This will reduce its costs. If costs fall, the business could cut the prices it charges its customers. But it could also leave its prices the same and make more profit.

Exchange rates and business

Changes in exchange rates affect businesses in two main ways.
- They affect the cost of buying goods and services from abroad.
- They affect the price at which goods and services are sold abroad.

Exchange rates can either go down or up.

A fall in the exchange rate What if the exchange rate of the pound for the US dollar goes down, from £1 = $2 to £1 = $1? How will this affect a UK toy business? This is shown in Figure 1.
- The business could reduce the price charged abroad. A £1 toy will only cost $1 instead of $2. The UK business might be able to sell more toys at a lower price.
- The cost of buying goods and services

from abroad should go up. A $2 part that used to cost £1 would now cost £2. Fewer products might be bought from abroad.

A rise in the exchange rate What if the exchange rate of the pound for the US dollar goes up, from £1 = $1 to £1 = $2? How will this affect a UK toy business?
- The business could raise the price charged abroad. A £1 toy now costs $2 instead of $1. The UK business might sell fewer toys at the higher price.
- The cost of buying goods and services from abroad should go down. A $2 part that used to cost £2 would now only cost £1. More products might be bought from abroad.

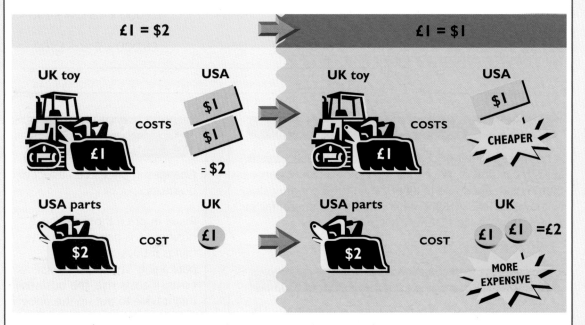

Figure 1 *How a fall in the value of the pound from £1 = $2 to £1 = $1 affects a UK toy business*

key terms

Currency – *the type of notes and coins used in a country.*
Deflation – *a general fall in prices.*
Economic conditions – *situations that result from the operation of the economy, such as changes in prices or exchange rates.*
Exchange rate – *the price, or rate, at which one currency can be exchanged for another.*
Inflation – *a general rise in prices.*
Interest rates – *the percentage charge made by banks and other lenders for borrowing money.*

key terms key terms key terms key terms key terms key terms

Quick quiz

1 True or false?

Businesses want interest rates to increase so that they can borrow money more cheaply.

2 How much interest will a business pay each year on a loan of £5,000 with an annual interest rate of 8%?

(a) £400. **(b)** £200. **(c)** £100. **(d)** £480.

3 Fill in the missing words.

Price   Currency   Rate   Price

The exchange ...... of the pound is the ...... of the pound in relation to the ...... of another ....

4 True or false?

A fall in the exchange rate of the pound, from £1 = $2 to £1 = $1, will help a British business buying cotton from the USA.

5 Complete the sentences.

A general rise in prices is called .... A general fall in prices is called ....

Portfolio practice

The Trans-Pennine Mountain Bike Company

The Trans-Pennine Mountain Bike Company has recently seen an increase in the demand for its mountain bikes. They are assembled and sold from a small factory and shop in Hebden Bridge which the company rents.

The business wants to expand, but it does not have enough room to assemble more bikes. So instead, it has decided to buy some mountain bikes from a business in California. The bikes will cost $6,000 and the exchange rate is £1 = $2. The owners of Trans-Pennine are concerned. They think that they might need to borrow £10,000 from their bank next year. But inflation is quite low at around 2 per cent a year.

1. How much in UK pounds will it cost The Trans-Pennine Mountain Bike Company to buy the bikes from the Californian company? (2 marks)
2. What would be the effect on The Trans-Pennine Mountain Bike Company of an increase in annual interest rates from 12 per cent to 18 per cent? (5 marks)
3. Explain how inflation might affect The Trans-Pennine Mountain Bike Company and evaluate how much it might be affected.(10 marks)

22 Economic conditions - government, businesses and the economy

Getting started...

The government is involved in a range of activities that affect businesses. It tries to create an environment in which businesses can be successful.

Case 1 *Dunscar Ltd*

The government has recently reduced the tax that small businesses have to pay on their profits. Dunscar Ltd is a manufacturer of sports quipment. On last year's profits, it paid tax of £175,000. But this year it only expects to pay £150,000.

Tax cut for small business

Case 2 *Evans Winslow*

The Chancellor of the Exchequer is the person in the government who makes decisions about the economy. He has decided to spend more money on the NHS and this means that some new hospitals are going to be built. Evans Winslow, a construction company, hopes to win a contract to build one or more new hospitals.

Government spending to increase

Tax on diesel to rise by 1%

Case 3 *Wright Robinson Ltd*

Some of the most heavily taxed goods in the UK are petrol and diesel. The government is responsible for setting the rate of tax. Wright Robinson Ltd is a haulage company that transports goods all over the UK in its fleet of 120 lorries. The government has increased the tax on diesel by 1 per cent, so the business expects its fuel costs to rise by £15,000 a year.

(a) Describe how each of the above businesses has been affected by the government's decisions.

How do the government's activities affect businesses?

Governments and the economy

Governments see one of their most important roles as helping to create an environment in which:

○ businesses can plan to meet consumers' needs;
○ consumers are willing to spend their money on products.

Consumer spending is vital for businesses. The more that people spend, the more likely businesses are to be successful. Successful businesses that work hard to meet consumers' needs are also important. They supply the products that consumers want to buy.

Governments try to prevent uncertainty. If businesses and consumers are worried about what might happen in future, they are less likely to spend or invest their money. In more stable conditions businesses and consumers can plan for the future with confidence.

Managing the economy

To achieve its aims for consumers and businesses, the government has to manage the ECONOMY. The economy is a system that decides what is produced, how it is produced and who receives the products. All businesses operate in at least one economy. It could be local, national or international. Many large businesses operate in several different economies.

The government tries to manage the economy by:

○ spending money;
○ taxing businesses and consumers;
○ changing interest rates;
○ encouraging competition.

One of the main aims of government is for the economy to grow. If the economy is growing, consumers are likely to have more money to spend and businesses will have more opportunities to sell their products. But the government also wants stable conditions. So it would not want high levels of growth in one year, followed by no growth next year.

Government spending

GOVERNMENT SPENDING is the money that the government spends on a wide range of areas including schools, hospitals and roads. When the government increases or decreases its spending, this affects businesses. For example, a road building business would benefit if the government decided to build a new motorway. On the other hand, if the government cancelled a new road building scheme, this would reduce the work for a road building business.

Education

Health

Road building

Public services, such as parks, street lighting and refuse collection

Defence

Housing

Figure 1 *Examples of government spending*

Taxes

The government taxes businesses and consumers. TAX is money which the government takes from businesses and consumers to pay for its spending.

Three of the main taxes are:
- ✪ income tax – paid by most people on their income;
- ✪ corporation tax – paid by limited companies on their business profit;
- ✪ VAT – paid by consumers when they spend money on certain products and services.

Increases and decreases in taxes affect businesses and consumers.

Increasing taxes If the government increases the income tax that consumers pay on their earnings, this would have several possible effects. Consumers would have less money to spend on products and services, so a business's sales might fall. But the government would have more to spend. This could benefit both consumers and businesses.

Decreasing taxes When taxes are reduced, consumers have more money to spend on business products. But the government may have to cut its own spending and this can affect such things as education and health care.

Interest rates

The UK's interest rates are controlled for the government by the Bank of England.

Changes in interest rates can affect businesses and consumers. An increase in interest rates will lead to an increase in the cost of borrowing money and this generally means that consumers and businesses have less to spend.

A decrease in interest rates is likely to have the opposite effect. It is likely to lead to lower costs of borrowing and more spending by consumers and businesses.

Competition policy

COMPETITION POLICIES are government policies that try to make businesses more competitive. If businesses do not face much competition, they might exploit consumers, by charging high prices and sell poor quality products. For this reason, the government has a range of policies to encourage competition between businesses.

For example, the government has set up the Competition Commission. This organisation prevents businesses from taking over its competitors. It also tries to make sure that businesses don't charge high prices to make large profits at the expense of customers.

key terms

○ **Competition policies** – *policies devised by the government to try to make businesses more competitive.*
○ **Economy** – *the system that determines what gets produced, how it is produced and who gets the products.*
○ **Government spending** – *money spent by the government on areas such as schools and hospitals.*
○ **Tax** – *money paid by consumers and businesses to the government, which partly helps to pay for government spending.*

key terms key terms key terms key terms key terms

Quick quiz

1 Complete the sentence.

If consumers are worried about the future they may be less likely to ....

2 State four ways in which governments try to manage the economy.

3 Give two examples of government spending.

4 Give two examples of taxes.

5 A decrease in income tax will normally lead consumers to:

(a) spend more;

(b) spend less;

(c) spend the same amount;

(d) stop spending completely.

6 In one sentence, explain why governments have competition policies.

Portfolio practice

Beatty Taylor

Beatty Taylor is a large construction business involved in major building projects such as office complexes, public buildings and hospitals. It borrows money from banks and other institutions to pay for its building work.

The business's biggest customer is the government and the various agencies, such as local education authorities, National Health trusts and government departments, which are responsible for spending government money.

The directors of Beatty Taylor always pay close attention to any possible changes in the economy and to government policies. At their end of year financial meeting in 2003, the business's economic advisors outlined the following possible changes over the coming two years.

✪ An additional £1 billion will be spent by the government on new school and university buildings.

✪ Corporation tax will be increased by 1 per cent.

✪ Interest rates will go down by 1 per cent.

✪ Consumer spending in the high street will decline.

The directors weren't sure how to react to the above.

1. How might a £1 billion increase in spending on new school and university buildings affect Beatty Taylor? (4 marks)

2. Beatty Taylor borrows large amounts of money to finance its building work. How will the 1 per cent fall in interest rates affect the business? (4 marks)

3. Explain the advantages and disadvantages to Beatty Taylor of the changes that may take place. (9 marks)

23 Environmental constraints

Getting started...

The environment is the surroundings that people live in. Business activities can have a damaging effect upon the environment. This might be noise, waste materials, congestion or destruction.

Case 1 *A power station*

Case 2 *Building a road*

Case 3 *An outdoor concert*

(a) Describe the types of environmental problem that might be caused by the business activities in each of the above cases.

How can businesses damage the environment and what can be done about it?

What damage can be caused?

As a result of their activities, businesses can have a damaging effect upon the environment. This is called POLLUTION.

Air pollution Air pollution is caused by businesses emitting waste or gases into the air. Amongst the main causes are fumes from vehicles run on petrol and diesel, and emissions from power stations and factories.

Water pollution Water pollution is mainly caused by businesses dumping waste products into rivers, streams and the sea. Examples include chemicals being leaked into rivers and untreated sewage being dumped into river estuaries and near beaches.

Noise pollution This is an increasingly common form of pollution. Examples include noise from factories disturbing local residents and noise from the customers of businesses, such as nightclubs, or large events, such as an outdoor concert or a sports event.

Other types of damage to the environment include the following.

Traffic congestion Business activities might cause traffic congestion in a local area which can result in delays and accidents.

Wasted use of resources This is the unnecessary use of scarce resources, for example, the use of disposable carrier bags. Because of this, some retail businesses such as supermarkets encourage their customers to reuse their carrier bags. It also includes packaging of products and customer litter.

Destruction of the environment and wildlife Sometimes, when building work takes place, the surrounding area can be ruined. Also, some building work destroys areas of natural beauty and wildlife habitats.

Traffic congestion can harm the environment

Why do business activities affect the environment?

There are various reasons why some business activities might cause damage to the environment.

The type of business activity Some businesses are more likely to damage the environment than others because of the products they are making or the services they are providing. For example, a business in the chemical industry might be more likely to damage the environment than an advertising agency. A haulage business whose lorries use diesel is likely to cause more air pollution than a bicycle courier business.

The cost of processing waste and preventing pollution Unless they face a fine or some other form of punishment, it may be easier and cheaper for a chemical business to dump waste into a river than to

pay for it to be processed and disposed of safely. Similarly, it may be cheaper for a sewage disposal business to dump untreated sewage into the sea. This is because the cost of dealing with pollution caused by dumping untreated materials is not paid for by the business.

The attitudes of people in business The environmental attitude of businesses can vary considerably. Some businesses know that their activities are harmful to the environment, but choose to ignore the damage that they cause. Other businesses try to prevent environmental damage and many of them now have environmental or 'green' policies. So, for example, some businesses offer incentives to their employees not to travel to work by car so that they cause less air pollution and traffic congestion.

Preventing damage to the environment

How can environmental damage caused by business activities be prevented?

Self-regulation This is when businesses regulate themselves. SELF-REGULATION works well if everyone running the business agrees that their activities should not damage the environment. But this is not always the case.

A business that tries to prevent damage to the environment might face additional costs, such as the cost of disposing of dangerous chemicals properly. This can be expensive so the business might not be able to compete with other similar businesses whose costs are less because they ignore environmental issues. This suggests that self-regulation on its own might not be enough to prevent environmental damage.

Some businesses now recycle their waste products. This prevents waste and produces resources which can be used to make other products, such as glass or paper.

Government regulation GOVERNMENT REGULATION uses laws to make environmental damage illegal or to place charges and restrictions on pollution. It includes the following.

- ✪ The Clean Air Act and the Environmental Protection Act. These set limits on the emissions that businesses can make into the air. Businesses which exceed these limits can be fined.
- ✪ The LANDFILL TAX. Landfill is a way of disposing of waste by burying it in the ground. The landfill tax aims to encourage businesses to produce less waste, for example through recycling. It also tries to encourage businesses to use more environmentally friendly methods of waste disposal rather than simply dumping it.
- ✪ Road pricing. One of the main ways in which businesses contribute to air pollution is through the use of business vehicles. Road prices and charges try to encourage businesses to use less environmentally damaging ways of transporting their goods.
- ✪ Permits. These allow a certain amount of pollution in areas where the government thinks that it is safe.
- ✪ Planning permission. This is where the government allows building to take place in areas where damage to the environment will not be too great. A business will also need to meet certain conditions, such as repairing damage to the landscape.
- ✪ Taxes on diesel and petrol. Taxes on fuel encourage businesses to try to find energy saving ways of transporting goods. The taxes also aim to reduce the number of journeys made by customers.

key terms

Government regulation – *the laws, taxes and charges which governments use to control the behaviour of businesses.*
Landfill tax – *a tax charged on businesses that dispose of their waste products on land based sites.*
Pollution – *damage or contamination caused to the environment. It can be in various forms including water, air and noise.*
Self-regulation – *the process by which businesses control and monitor their own activities.*

key terms key terms key terms key terms key terms key terms

Quick quiz

1 State five ways in which businesses can damage the environment.

2 Which two of the following businesses are most likely to directly damage the environment?

(a) A firm of accountants specialising in small business accounts.

(b) A road haulage business that uses diesel powered lorries.

(c) An open cast mining business extracting coal and lead.

(d) A paper recycling business.

3 Complete the sentence.

Many businesses cause damage to the environment because of the ...... of processing waste materials.

4 Give one reason why self-regulation may not be a very effective way of protecting the environment from pollution.

5 Which of the following are examples of government regulation of business activity?

(a) Taxing businesses that dump waste.

(b) Making it illegal for businesses to emit noises higher than a certain level.

(c) Persuading business leaders about the need to protect the environment.

(d) Holding demonstrations outside factories that cause pollution.

Portfolio practice

The Admiral Bar and AZI Chemicals

The Admiral Bar

The Admiral Bar is notorious amongst local residents for its Saturday night disco. Many of them complain that they can't get to sleep or hear their TVs. People hang around the street drinking and leave their bottles lying around. Some local residents find if difficult to park next to their own houses on a Saturday night. Even during the week there are problems because vans delivering goods block the road and the residents can't get in and out of their houses.

AZI Chemicals

The AZI chemical works was found to be responsible for leaking acid into a local river ten years ago. Even now, fish in the river have not completely recovered despite the efforts of local nature conservationists to clean the water and put new fish back in. The business also finds that it has a lot of packaging to dispose of because some of the chemicals that it buys are delivered in drums. Most of this packaging is disposed of in a local landfill site.

1. Describe two types of pollution being caused by each of the business activities above. (4 marks)
2. Explain possible reasons why each of the businesses is engaged in polluting activities. (6 marks)
3. For each business, what are the best methods of regulating the businesses' activities? Explain your answer. (9 marks)

24 Stakeholders

Getting started...

All businesses have STAKEHOLDERS. Stakeholders are the individuals and groups of people who have an interest in how the business is run. They are said to have a 'stake' in the business. Their interests and expectations, what they expect to get from the business, are often different. They will agree on some things, but disagree on others. For example, employees might want high wages. But owners of a business might want to keep wage costs down so that they make more profit. Think about a business, such as The Carphone Warehouse, that sells mobile phones.

Case 1 *Buying and selling mobile phones at The Carphone Warehouse*

Case 2 *Setting up a new Carphone Warehouse shop*

Case 3 *Making mobile phones to be sold in Carphone Warehouse shops*

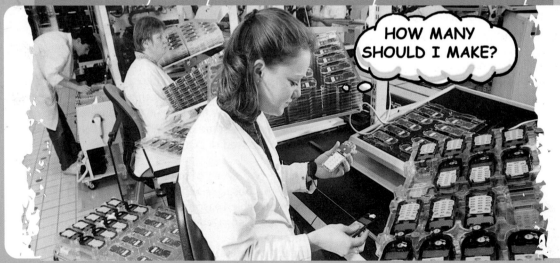

(a) Who are the stakeholders in each of the cases above?
(b) What interests and expectations might each of these stakeholders have in The Carphone Warehouse?

Who are the stakeholders in a business?

Customers

People who buy goods or services from the business. They want quality, value for money and good service. If they don't get these things, they are likely to spend their money somewhere else.

Employees

People who work for the business. They want good pay, job satisfaction, a secure job and a chance of promotion. Employees who feel that they are treated unfairly may not work as well. This could affect the owner's profits.

Pressure groups

Groups of people that try to influence the way a business operates. PRESSURE GROUPS are interested in such things as pollution, the safety of products and the welfare of the local community.

Suppliers

Businesses that sell their goods and services to other businesses. When a business is doing well, its SUPPLIERS hope to get more orders. If it does badly, their orders will be reduced. This will affect the suppliers' own profits.

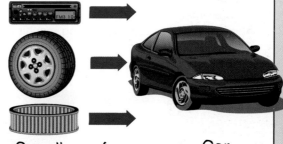

Suppliers of parts

Car producer

Local community

People and organisations in the local area. If a business is doing well, it creates jobs for local people. They will then spend their wages in other local businesses. If it is doing badly, employees might have to take a pay cut or even lose their jobs. They then have less money to spend.

Financiers

Organisations, such as banks, who lend money to businesses. FINANCIERS want the loan and interest charged to be repaid on time. If a business doesn't repay its loan, the bank may sell the business's assets to get its money back.

Managers

People employed by the owner to run the business. They want the same things as other employees. If the business is doing well, they may also expect to be paid bonuses. They are responsible for the day to day running of the business. So they have a big influence on the business's activities.

Owners

In smaller firms these are people who put money in to start the business. They want the greatest profits so that they earn more from the business. So they want high sales and low costs. In companies, the owners are called shareholders. The money they put in buys shares, which makes them part owners of the business.

Government

A body of elected Members of Parliament who run the country. When a business is doing well, the government receives more in taxes from businesses' profits and from employees' wages. If a business fails and employees lose their jobs, no taxes are paid. Also the government has to pay out unemployment benefits. In areas where there is high unemployment, the government helps local businesses. It might give money to help with such things as building factories, buying machinery and hiring workers.

MONEY IN

MONEY OUT

Tax paid by people

Tax paid by businesses

Benefits to people

Help for businesses

Services such as Health and Defence

key terms

Financiers - *organisations that lend money to businesses.*
Pressure groups - *groups of people that try to influence how businesses operate.*
Stakeholders - *individuals, groups and organisations that have an interest in how a business is run.*
Suppliers - *businesses that sell their goods and services to other businesses.*

key terms key terms key terms key terms key terms key terms

Quick quiz

1 Match each stakeholder in the table with one of the descriptions below.

(a) This organisation wants its loan repaying on time.

(b) This person wants good wages.

(c) This person wants the maximum profits from the business.

(d) This person wants quality and value for money when he or she buys goods.

(e) This group wants the business to stop polluting the local river.

(f) This person wants high bonuses.

(g) These people want the business to provide more jobs in the area.

(h) This business wants to supply more of its goods to other businesses.

(i) This body receives taxes from the profits that businesses make.

Stakeholder	Description
Customer	
Employee	
Manager	
Owner	
Local community	
Government	
Pressure group	
Supplier	
Financier	

Portfolio practice

Manchester Airport

Manchester Airport has built a second runway and this has created more jobs. 700 builders were employed to build the runway, a new fire station, public viewing area and electricity sub-stations. New staff were also taken on to cope with the extra passengers. These included baggage handlers and check-in, security and catering staff.

Manchester City Council was enthusiastic about the building of the second runway. For them, it meant more wealth for the city through increased tourism. The government was pleased with all the new jobs because they added to the country's wealth.

But not everyone was happy. Some nearby villages said that their quiet lives would be affected by traffic and noise. Pressure groups tried to stop the runway from being built. They argued that fields and hedgerows where wildlife lived would be lost when the runway was built. But they were not successful.

Source: rylibweb.man.ac.uk/data2/spcoll/runway/airport.html

1. Identify four stakeholders in Manchester Airport. (4 marks)
2. Explain the interests of two of these stakeholders in the building of the runway. (4 marks)
3. Do you think that Manchester Airport should have been allowed to build the second runway? Give reasons for your answer. (9 marks)

25 Investigating job roles 1

Getting started...

All employees who work in a business have different roles to play. These are the things that they are expected to do in the business. Different employees within a business will have different job roles. Think about the following employees in businesses in the motor industry.

Case 1 *Production*

Case 2 *Designing*

Case 3 *Selling*

Case 4 *A directors' meeting*

(a) What type of job is each person likely to be doing?
(b) What is likely to be their main job role?

What are the main job roles in a business?

Job roles

For a business to be successful, everyone must know what they should be doing. They also need to know what other people in the business should be doing. These are their JOB ROLES. This is particularly important when there are large numbers of people in a business. Employees are more likely to do their job successfully if they know exactly what their job role is.

Job descriptions

Employees who start a job need to know such things as their main tasks and conditions of work.

Figure 1 *What is in a job description?*

All these are included in a JOB DESCRIPTION, as shown in Figure 1. For example, a McDonald's sales assistant will take a customer's order, tell kitchen staff the order, put the order together, handle cash, carry out some clearing duties and be responsible to the sales supervisor.

Organisation charts

The job roles that people have can be shown in an ORGANISATION CHART. The chart shows how the job an employee's job fits in with other jobs in a business.

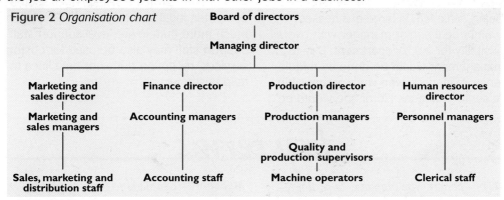

The chart has a number of **layers**. The board of directors and managing director are shown at the top. Employees, such as shop floor workers, are shown at the bottom. This is called a HIERARCHY. Below the managing director are specialist directors in charge of the FUNCTIONS of a business. In this business:

✪ the marketing and sales director is responsible for the marketing department. Job roles in this department might include advertising products and market research;

✪ the accounting director is responsible for the

work and the employees in the accounting department. Job roles in this department might include invoicing, bookkeeping and preparing the annual accounts;

✪ the production director is responsible for production. Job roles in this department might include manufacturing products and checking quality;

✪ the human resources director is responsible for the personnel department. Job roles in this department Invent might include recruiting and training staff.

Level of job within a business

The organisation chart in Figure 2 shows the different job roles in a business. The further up the hierarchy people are, the more responsibility and control they have.

Directors Large companies have thousands of shareholders who own the business. They can't all be involved in its running. So they elect DIRECTORS to represent them. There might be a managing director in charge of the business and directors for each department, such as finance and marketing. A **board of directors** will be responsible for overall planning and co-ordination of the business. Directors must be experts in a field, such as marketing. They need leadership, planning and communication skills. They also need to respond to shareholder's concerns and to understand the business's overall strategy. Directors may have shares in the business, so they have an interest in its success.

Managers Directors make plans and think ahead. But MANAGERS take everyday decisions and make sure that things get done. Communication and leadership are also parts of the manager's role. They must be able to monitor progress and report to directors. For example, a finance manager would be expected to know what the business's profit target was and whether it was being achieved. In large businesses there might be a senior manager with overall responsibility for each department. Day-to-day management would be done by middle and junior managers, who were responsible to the senior manager. He or she would be their LINE MANAGER.

Supervisors A SUPERVISOR'S role is to make sure that employees carry out work to the standard that managers and directors want. Today some companies organise their workers in **teams** and no longer need supervisors to oversee their work. Instead, teams plan and organise their own work and report directly to senior managers. Many car plants have production teams that are responsible for meeting targets and quality control.

Operatives In a factory OPERATIVES are shop floor workers who operate machines or production equipment. In service businesses, such as a bank or a shop, operatives are people that have direct contact with members of the public they are serving. Operatives do the work that managers and directors plan.

Support staff SUPPORT STAFF provide services to help the day-to-day work of the business. A business may have an administration support team that provides word processing, cleaning or security for all departments. In large businesses each department might have its own support staff. Some businesses have senior support staff who provide professional services such as computer, legal and tax advice. They earn much more than lower level support staff. Support staff may also be used for customer services, reception duties or help lines to help customers.

key terms

Directors – people who plan and co-ordinate business activity.
Function – a division of a business according to the type of activity it undertakes, such as marketing or production.
Hierarchy – the levels of authority in a business, from top to bottom.
Job description – a description of an employee's job role.
Job role – the tasks an employee undertakes and the responsibilities he or she has.
Line manager – an employee who is responsible for the work of others below them in the hierarchy

Managers – people who from day-to-day carry out the plans of directors and organise the work of people in their own department.
Operatives – shop floor workers who operate machines or have direct contact with members of the public.
Organisation chart – a diagram that shows the different job roles in a business and how they relate to each other.
Supervisor – a person who oversees the work of others to check it is satisfactory
Support staff – staff who provide services to others in the business or to those outside the business, such as customers.

Quick quiz

1 True or false? A job role is the tasks and responsibilities that an employee has.

2 Complete the sentence. A diagram that shows the relationship and levels in an organisation is called an ....?

3 What is a hierarchy?

4 Match the statements (a)-(e) to the jobs (i)-(v).

Statement	Job
(a) Someone who has overall responsibility for a particular function or department in a large organisation.	**(i)** Operative.
(b) Someone who does the jobs that managers and directors have planned.	**(ii)** Managers.
(c) Employees who provide a service to other employees in the business.	**(iii)** Director.
(d) People who take day-to-day decisions and organise employees' work.	**(iv)** Supervisors.
(e) People who check on the work of operatives.	**(v)** Support staff.

Portfolio practice

ComCare

You are the personnel manager of a computer business called ComCare. The directors have asked you to produce a booklet for the business to show how it is organised. This should include a description of the different levels within the business. You have the following information.

A There is a managing director and a board of directors.

B There are the following departments in the business.
  • Computer production.
  • Sales and marketing.
  • Finance.
  • Distribution.
  • Human resources/personnel.
  • Customer services.
  There is a director for each department.

C The production department and the sales and marketing department have 2 managers. All other departments have one manager.

D There are also the following jobs.
  • 2 secretaries in the human resources/personnel department.
  • 2 account clerks.
  • 2 customer services support staff.
  • 10 telesales staff.
  • 30 shop floor operatives.
  • 2 production supervisors.
  • 5 distribution staff.

E There is also a separate computer maintenance department that has:
  • a senior technical and computer manager;
  • a computer support technician.

1. Describe the different levels of job at ComCare. (10 marks)
2. Complete Table 1 to show the category that each job fits into. (5 marks)
3. Produce an organisation chart for ComCare. (10 marks)

Table 1 *Jobs at ComCare*

Directors	Managers	Supervisors	Operatives	Support Staff

26 Investigating job roles 2

Getting started...

People do different tasks in different jobs. They have different responsibilities. And they need different skills. Think about the following.

Case 1 *Machine operator*

'I must make sure that I meet my production target for this week.'

Case 2 *Receptionist*

'Please hold for a moment. I will put you through to someone who'll be able to help you.'

Case 3 *Quality controller*

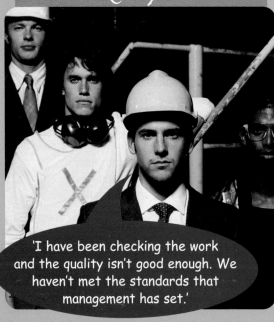

'I have been checking the work and the quality isn't good enough. We haven't met the standards that management has set.'

Case 4 *Sales manager*

'We need to increase sales by 10 per cent by improving our marketing. I will be holding a meeting with the whole marketing team soon to explain how we might do this.'

? *(a) What tasks will each person have to carry out in the situations above?*

What tasks, responsibilities, skills and qualities are needed for a job?

Job analysis

JOB ANALYSIS is investigating and breaking down what a job involves. It will include the tasks and activities, responsibilities, skills, qualifications and personal qualities, and job security, pay and benefits of the job.

Job tasks and activities

There are many different tasks and activities that make up a job. For example, a person responsible for computer support in a business might carry out the tasks shown in Figure 1.

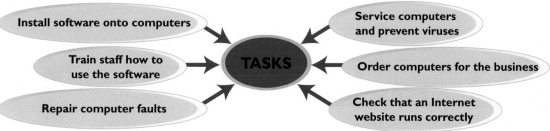

- Install software onto computers
- Train staff how to use the software
- Repair computer faults
- **TASKS**
- Service computers and prevent viruses
- Order computers for the business
- Check that an Internet website runs correctly

Figure 1 *The main tasks of a person responsible for computer support*

Tasks will vary depending on the level of job in a business.

Planning and decision-making Directors and managers are responsible for overall planning and decision-making. They plan how a business will make or sell its products. They make decisions so the business achieves its objectives. For example, McDonald's sells products at certain times of the year, like a Cadbury Egg McFlurry at Easter. Marketing directors must decide what the products will be, their price, when they will be sold and how to promote them.

Organising and co-ordinating These involve making sure that people are doing things at the right time and in the right way. For example, personnel managers organise training. Marketing managers co-ordinate promotion, such as radio advertising and sending leaflets to customers.

Setting and achieving targets Directors may set targets for departmental managers. Managers may set targets for employees to achieve. Examples might be:
- ✪ call centre employees given targets for the number of calls answered per hour or per day;
- ✪ sales representatives given targets for the amount of sales they make in a year;
- ✪ machine operatives given targets for the number of components they make in a week.

Supervisors will check that the targets are being achieved by comparing the results with targets.

Problem solving Problem solving is deciding how to cope with business problems when they take place. Solving problems might not be part of a worker's job role. But they may be expected to respond to situations when they arise. For example, a BT engineer may be called out to fix a customer's telephone line, but find that the problem is the telephone. The engineer might solve this problem by ordering a new telephone.

Delegating DELEGATING means giving responsibility and authority to someone else to complete a task. Managers might give others the responsibility to plan, organise, make decisions, solve problems, co-ordinate and complete a task. For example, a production manager in a car plant may give responsibility to her supervisor and operatives to plan how to check the quality of cars being produced.

Responsibilities

These are the main aspects of a job for which an employee can be held accountable. They also include who the employee might be in charge of and who is in charge of the employee. Examples in an insurance company are shown in Table 1.

Table 1 *Responsibilities of jobs in an insurance company*

	Job title	Responsibilities	Responsible for	Responsible to
Manager	Marketing manager	Setting targets and organising work	Marketing department employees	Directors
Supervisor	Sales	Ensuring targets are met and reporting to the manager	Salespeople	Manager
Operative	Salesperson	Selling insurance to clients	No-one	Supervisor/ manager
Support staff	Clerical assistant	Filing, photocopying etc.	No-one	Manager

Skills, qualifications and personal qualities

Different skills, qualifications and personal qualities are needed for different jobs.
- Finance directors and managers are often qualified accountants with experience. They need skills in planning, organising, co-ordinating, problem solving and managing. They also need drive and ambition.
- Supervisors need the ability to work with people. They also need to be able to judge whether targets have been met.
- Operatives need the training and qualifications to work a machine or carry out a task. They also need to be accurate and reliable.
- The qualifications and skills of support workers depend on their job role. A clerical assistant is likely to need maths and literacy skills. A technician may need a high level of skill and experience in repair work.

Pay and benefits

Some jobs in a business have a higher salary or wage than others.
- Directors are the most well paid. They may be given bonuses if a business does well. They may also be paid dividends if they own shares. Managers in large businesses are also well paid. They may be given a bonus if a department meets its target. They may also get benefits such as company cars or private health care.
- Supervisors are often paid more than operatives. The pay of operatives may be a set amount each month or week. But they may also be given a bonus or overtime. The business may also contribute to their pension scheme.
- The pay of support staff depends on their job. Low level support assistants are often paid least. Technicians and higher level support staff may be paid more than operatives.

Job security

If a business is doing well, the jobs of all employees should be secure. If a business is doing badly, shareholders may vote out directors and managers, and operatives and support staff may be made redundant. Managers often have permanent jobs. The jobs of support staff or operatives might be permanent jobs or temporary jobs, for a limited period of time.

key terms

Delegating – passing down the responsibility and authority for a task to someone further down in the hierarchy of the business, with a lower level job role.
Job analysis – investigating and breaking down the different aspects of a job.

key terms key terms key terms

Quick quiz

1. True or false? Job analysis means advertising for a job in a newspaper.
2. What three things would be included in the responsibilities of a job?
3. Match the activities (a)-(e) to the type of tasks that would be involved in a person's job role (i)-(v).

Activities

(a) Thinking about developing a new camcorder and deciding what to call it, how to advertise it and what price to charge for it.

(b) Organising a car show.

(c) A production manager giving someone in his department the responsibility of devising new production methods.

(d) A marketing manager of a perfume company setting new sales targets and checking they have been achieved for the latest men's aftershave.

(e) A customer service representative successfully dealing with a customer's problem.

Tasks

(i) Problem-solving.
(ii) Delegating.
(iii) Planning and decision making.
(iv) Organising and co-ordinating.
(v) Setting and achieving targets.

Portfolio practice

Jake Purcell, Personal Assistant

Jake Purcell works for a medium sized advertising company in Glasgow. He is the personal assistant for Jon Williams, the design director at the company. His main tasks are to schedule meetings for his boss and arrange trips for Jon to visit clients. This includes Jake writing a timetable for Jon, buying train tickets, booking hotel rooms and generally making sure that Jon knows what is going on. He also takes calls for his boss and attempts to solve any problems that he can without having to bother him. He oversees a clerical assistant who works in the business.

Jon thinks that Jake works well and has potential. He is keen to delegate some of his management jobs to Jake to help him develop his career. He is giving Jake the responsibility of organising a new design brief for a small client that the company is dealing with. Jake has a salary of £22,000 a year and receives a bonus at Christmas of £2,000. He also receives free membership of the local gym.

Jake has a permanent job and his prospects look good. The company is growing and has been recruiting and promoting staff rather than making any employees redundant. The company is successful and it is likely that this will continue.

1. What are Jake's main responsibilities? (3 marks)
2. List the tasks and activities that make up Jake's job. (3 marks)
3. What is Jake's pay and what other benefits does he receive? (3 marks)
4. Are all of Jake's tasks routine? (3 marks)
5. Do you think that Jake's job is secure? (6 marks)
6. To what extent does Jake need to plan, make decisions, organise, delegate and solve problems? (8 marks)

Getting started...

When employees start working for a business, they agree to their work arrangements with the employer. These arrangements set out details about their work. Will they work full-time or part-time? How many hours will they work? Where will they work and how much will they be paid? Look at the following case studies.

Case 1 *Manager talking to an employee*

TONIGHT YOU NEED TO WORK AN EXTRA FOUR HOURS SO THAT WE CAN COMPLETE THE ORDER ON TIME.

I HAVE A LETTER SAYING THAT MY WORKING HOURS ARE 9.00AM TO 5.30PM. IT ALSO SAYS THAT I WILL BE GUARANTEED OVERTIME IF I WORK OUTSIDE THOSE HOURS.

?

(a) What work arrangements have been changed in each of the case studies?

(b) How will the changes affect both the employee and the employer in each of the case studies?

Case 2 *Letter to an employee*

FASTECH LTD

Benyon Street
Glasgow

Dear Employee

Due to a rise in profits in the last year, all employees have been given a 6 per cent pay rise. Your salary will increase from £25,000 to £26,500, starting next month.

Case 3 *Sales representative*

The company has increased our yearly holidays from 20 to 25 days a year. They also want all the sales team to spend more time visiting clients and less time in the office.

What are the main work arrangements of employees?

Employment contracts

By law, employees are entitled to have a CONTRACT OF EMPLOYMENT when they start work. This is a formal agreement between the employer and employee. The contract will show the TERMS AND CONDITIONS of employment, as in Figure 1.

The type of employment and whether it is full-time or part-time

The number of hours the employee is expected to work by the employer

TERMS AND CONDITIONS

The place the employee will work

The pay and benefits provided to the employee by the employer

Figure 1 *Terms and conditions shown in an employment contract*

Employers and employees have to obey these terms and conditions. It is unlawful to break them unless they both agree.

Place of work

The contract of employment also states where an employee will work. Sometime this will be in an office, shop or factory that belongs to the business. But some people work from home. They include farmers, shop owners and hotel owners. Employees working at home might also be tele-workers. They use a computer or phone to do their work. Mobile workers are workers that don't have a fixed place of work. They are expected to move from one site to another on a regular basis.

Types of employment

Permanent employment This is where there is no limit on the length of time a worker is employed. Employees work for a business until they leave. They could leave for a number of reasons.
- They might move to another job.
- They may have been forced to leave because they have broken their contract of employment.
- They might be made redundant. This is where there is no longer a job for them to do in the business.
- They might retire.

Temporary employment This is when employees are employed for a limited period. There are various reasons why businesses have temporary jobs.
- Employees might be hired at busy times. For example, shops hire extra staff at Christmas. Farms employ seasonal workers during the harvesting period.
- To cover for staff that are absent. For example, a business might employ someone to cover for an employee's maternity leave.
- To carry out a 'one-off' task, such as installing new machines in a business.

Full-time employment Full-time employees work the full working week of a business. The European Union Working Time Directive suggests that full-time work should not be more than 48 hours per week for most workers.

Part-time employment Part-time employees only work a proportion of the full working week of a business, eg less than 30 hours. Part-time workers are helpful to a business because they give it flexibility. For instance, they might be employed to work just at the busiest times, such as weekends in a pub. Or they might be hired to allow supermarkets to stay open late in the evening. Part-time work can also benefit employees. Lone parents, who may have difficulty working full-time, are able to work.

Hours of work

Part-time workers work fewer hours than full-time workers. But there are other things that can affect the number of hours employees work and when they work during the week.

Shift work Some employees are expected to do SHIFT WORK. Shift work is often found in businesses that operate machinery for 24 hours. For example, the first shift might work from 8am to 4pm. The next might work from 4pm to 12pm and the last from 12pm to 8am. Shift work might also be used in businesses that provide a 24 hour service, such as telephone banking.

Flexitime Employees might be allowed to work FLEXITIME in their contract of employment. This means that they can work at different times during the week or month. But they must work the total number of hours agreed in the contract for that week or month. For example, an employee might work 8am to 7pm on Monday, Tuesday and Wednesday, and then 9am to 4pm on Thursday. This would allow the worker to take Friday off, rather than working from 9am to 5pm each day.

Flexitime can benefit a business. An advertising company might need to present its ideas to a client within a very tight deadline. The designers might work longer hours one day to get the presentation ready on time. It can also benefit employees. They may need to be home at a particular time to pick up children from school or to allow workmen to carry out jobs. But some businesses and employees prefer set hours of work. Flexitime might be a problem if a lot of employees want to be off at the same time.

Overtime Some employees are expected to work OVERTIME. This is when businesses want employees to work more hours than their usual agreed hours. Businesses often pay higher rates for overtime.

Breaks By law, employees are entitled to breaks during their work. This might be a break in the number of days worked each week or in the number of hours every day or night.

Pay and benefits

Pay A contract of employment states the rate of pay for the job and whether the employee is paid a wage or salary. A wage is paid weekly and the rate of pay is shown by the hour, eg £5.00 per hour. A salary is paid monthly and the rate is shown as an annual salary figure, for example £20,000 per year.

The contract of employment may also say that a **bonus** or **commission** will be paid in addition to the wage or salary. A bonus is an amount paid to employees if a target is reached, eg an insurance telesalesperson may be paid a bonus for selling a certain number of policies. Commission is an amount paid to employees for each item that they sell. For example, a car salesperson may receive commission on every car sold.

Benefits The benefits that the employer is offering the employee are also included in the employment contract. This includes the number of days paid holiday per year. Other benefits could include the employer providing the employee with private health insurance or a company car.

key terms

Contracts of employment – *a formal agreement between the employer and employee that describes the rights and responsibilities of employers and employees in work.*

Flexitime – *where employees can work at different times during the week or month as long as they work the total number of hours in their contracts of employment and do not exceed them.*

Overtime – *when businesses want employees to work more than their usual agreed hours, usually at higher rates of pay.*

Shift work – *when different employees work different times over a set period of time.*

Terms and conditions – *the rights and responsibilities of the employer and employee. These usually include the type of employment, the hours of work expected from the employee, the place of work and the pay and benefits provided to the employee.*

key terms key terms key terms

Quick quiz

1 What are the four main terms and conditions usually contained in a contract of employment?

2 Give three reasons why an employee in permanent employment might leave the business.

3 Complete the sentences.

   (a) The term used when employees are employed for a limited period is called …… employment.

   (b) By law, employees are entitled to …… in the number of hours or days they work.

4 True or false? Full time employment is when an employee usually works fewer hours than the usual working week of the business.

5 What term is used to describe employees who work from 9am to 5pm one week and from 2pm to 10pm the next week?

Portfolio practice

The Tandoori Club

Farzana Ahmed runs a restaurant in Manchester. She employs various people at the restaurant. Her chefs are full-time, permanent employees. They are paid £15 per hour and work 40 hours per week. They are also expected to work shifts. They have 20 days holiday a year and one of the benefits of the job is that they are can help themselves to the food they cook without having to pay for it.

Farzana also employs permanent full-time and part-time staff to serve customers. At busy times, such as Christmas or Eid, she also employs temporary staff. She expects her staff to be flexible, so permanent employees have flexi-time contracts. They are not allowed to take time off when the restaurant is busy. If they want time off, they have to agree it with Farzana a week in advance.

1. State four of the terms and conditions of the chefs' contracts of employment at the Tandoori club.
(4 marks)
2. Describe how the Tandoori Club might use shift workers. (3 marks)
3. Why does the business employ both full-time and part-time staff? (4 marks)
4. Why does the business also employ temporary staff at certain times of the year? (3 marks)
5. Do you think that flexitime is in the interests of both Farzana and her employees? (6 marks)

28 Working arrangements – flexibility and change

Getting started...

Businesses sometimes need to change their employees' working arrangements. This might mean a change in the hours that they work, when they work, where they work, who they work with, how they work and what equipment they use. Working arrangements often change so that businesses can improve the way in which they operate. Think about the following businesses.

Case 1 *A call centre*

'Our performance last month was poor. The main problem is that operators are not dealing with enough calls per minute. They are not productive enough. From now on we will be checking more carefully that everyone is meeting their targets. We may even give bonuses for employees that can answer more calls and deal with problems quickly and correctly.'

Case 2 *A producer of machine parts*

'More and more of our engine parts are being made by machines. We've just bought a new computer-guided cutting machine. It can produce 30 products an hour instead of the usual 5. This means that some of our employees won't be needed any more. But we might need to take on a few new employees who can work the machine. They can help to train other workers.'

Case 3 *A local veterinary surgery*

'There's been lots of talk about a new veterinary practice opening up in the area. We've been the only vets in the town for many years. But we will have to change if we want to compete with this modern, larger surgery. I think that we should stay open longer in the evening. Some of our staff will have to work longer hours. And we may need to ask some people to work at different times.'

(a) Why do you think these businesses in the case studies have made changes in their employees' working arrangements?

(b) How are these changes likely to affect the employees?

Why do businesses change their working arrangements?

To increase productivity

A business might change working arrangements so that PRODUCTIVITY improves. This is the amount that can be produced with a certain number of workers and equipment.

Most businesses want to know about their labour productivity. This is the amount produced by each worker. For example, a business might ask its workers to work longer hours, so more is produced. Or it might want a worker to learn to operate two different machines instead of just one. Some workers might be asked to work in the afternoon and others in the evening so that the business can stay open longer. If workers are FLEXIBLE like this, productivity is likely to improve.

To improve the quality of their products

A business might change its working arrangements to improve the quality of its products.
- A business might have a quality controller to check the quality of finished goods. But quality might be improved if all workers were responsible for checking quality during production. Faults might be spotted before products are made, which then have to be thrown away.
- A business might want to produce more innovative products. Employing more full-time staff in the Research and Development (R&D) department might help it to do this.
- The quality of services might be improved by changes in work practices. A business that sells to another country might send its sales staff to work abroad.
- A business might want its workers to visit clients more, rather than stay in the office.

To be more competitive

A business might change its working practices so that it can compete better with other businesses.
- Businesses sometimes ask workers to work longer or at different times. Supermarkets now stay open late in the evening or even 24 hours to compete with other shops, for example.
- A business might set up an office abroad and ask workers to move there if it is competing with a foreign company.
- Workers might be asked to work flexitime so that the business can produce urgent orders. A business that is not able to meet deadlines might lose custom to a rival.

To introduce new technology

Working arrangements might change because a business wants to introduce new technology. New equipment might be introduced in a number of ways.
- Faster, more efficient, computer operated machines that require fewer workers might be used in producing goods.
- A new computer system that deals with orders might be introduced into the administration department. Workers' job roles might change as a result.
- Communication technology might make it easier to work from home and send information to the business via email. Businesses might use part-time home workers rather than hire full-time workers who work in the office.
- Business might find it easier to communicate with customers via email and the Internet. Workers may be hired to run a business's website.

key terms

Flexibility – being able to change in response to different situations.
Multi-skilled – being able to do more than one type of job.
Productivity – the amount that can be produced with a certain number of workers and equipment.

To introduce team-working and multi-skill practices

Working arrangements might change when a business introduces new methods of work. A business might make goods on a production line, where each worker has his or her own job and works

Working arrangements might have to change if workers work in teams

alone. But the business might decide that productivity would increase if workers worked in teams. Employees would then need to learn to work together. They might receive pay based on the team's performance.

A business might also want its workers to be MULTI-SKILLED. This means that they would do a number of jobs, rather than just one. If workers have many skills, it makes them more flexible. They can cover for staff who are off ill, for instance.

Effects of changes on employers

Changes in working practices can affect employers.

Reorganisation of the business Changes in working practices might affect the organisation of the business. For example, if workers are made more responsible for their own jobs, fewer managers might be needed to look after them. Team working might mean that certain jobs are no longer needed. A business might also need to be reorganised if part of its operation moves abroad.

Increased costs Changes in working practices might increase business costs. Workers need to be trained. They might be paid bonuses. Extra highly skilled workers might be needed. But some costs can be cut, if a business uses part-time workers, for example.

Management The introduction of new technology and the introduction of teamwork can disturb how a business works. Employers must make sure that there is as little disruption as possible. Employers must also check that home workers are doing their job when they are not working at the business. And they must decide which workers are to lose their jobs or which new workers will be hired.

Motivation Employers must motivate workers to cope with the changes. For example, they must decide what pay and other benefits will be used to motivate employees to be more productive.

Effects of changes on employees

Changes in working practices can affect employees in a number of ways.

Longer hours Employees may be asked to work longer hours if, for example, a business wants to produce more goods or provide more services.

Different hours or patterns of work Workers may be asked to work shifts or flexitime to meet deadlines. This will allow a business to compete better with its rivals and be more productive.

Training Employees will need to learn new skills if new machinery is being introduced or if they are expected to be multi-skilled. Training might also be needed if team working is introduced.

Earnings Workers' earnings might change when working practices change. Some workers will be paid more in overtime bonuses. A business might also pay workers to motivate them to be more productive.

Job security The introduction of new machinery often means that some workers lose their jobs. A business trying to compete with rivals might take on part-time or temporary workers to reduce its costs. But workers with skills may have to be hired when new machines are used or if the business is trying to improve the quality of its products.

Different job tasks or job roles The introduction of new technology, such as computers, can change workers' job roles. Before clerical workers might have been responsible for simple tasks like typing. The new technology might mean that they are responsible for emails and other forms of communication.

Quick quiz

1 Fill in the missing words.

**Trained   Sacked   Internet
New technology   Representatives**

The introduction of .... can lead a business to change its working arrangements. For example, a business might decide to sell its products over the ...... rather than using its sales .... These workers might then be ...... to do other jobs or ....

2 True or false?

(a) Workers who are multi-skilled are only ever likely to do one job.

(b) A business that wants to improve its productivity will not be helped if its workers are more flexible.

(c) A shop that wants to compete better with other businesses might ask its workers to work on Sunday so that it can stay open longer.

3 Which of the following statements (i)-(v) are about the (a) employee and (b) the employer?

(i) Might be asked to work overtime to meet deadlines.

(ii) Might have to reorganise work if new technology is introduced.

(iii) Might have to be trained to be more productive.

(iv) Might have to ensure that people working from home are doing their job.

(v) Might need to cut costs so the business is more competitive.

Portfolio practice

Baccino kit cars

Tony Baccino runs a business which makes reproduction sports cars in 'kit form'. Customers buy the kits and make up the cars. Tony employs 2 designers, 7 engineers, 3 body builders and 15 welders and mechanics who work in the garage. He also has 2 administrators in the office. One deals with customers. The other deals with finance. Over the last 10 years there has been growing demand from customers for cheap, high quality kits. Competition has grown to meet this demand. Tony has seen sales fall and costs rise as a result. He has decided that he will have to make some changes to the way he runs the business.

At the moment everything is done by hand. So work is slow and the business can not produce as many kits as it would like. Each worker specialises in their own job. Tony noticed that when the car bodies are being built the welders and mechanics don't do anything. He also realises that there are now machines that will body press panels instead of them all being hand produced.

Tony's designers design everything by hand. Office workers sometimes still use a typewriter in the office and some documents and letters are still written by hand. When customers ring up, the finance employee can not answer questions about orders. Tony's staff work a 38 hour week. Some are motivated and will work longer when an order is urgent. But others will not.

1. Describe the present working arrangements in Tony's business. (3 marks)
2. Suggest one reason why the production workers (2 marks) and one reason why the office workers (2 marks) are not very flexible.
3. Explain the factors that might change the working arrangements of the business in future. (6 marks)
4. Discuss:
   (a) how the business might change its work arrangements in future; (8 marks)
   (b) how these changes might affect Tony's employees. (6 marks)

29 Rights of employers and employees

Getting started...

Employers expect certain things from employees in a business. And employees expect certain things from their employers. These are the 'rights' of employers and employees. Employers and employees need to be clear about what is expected of them if they are to work together and the business is to be successful. Look at the following case studies.

Case 1 A factory

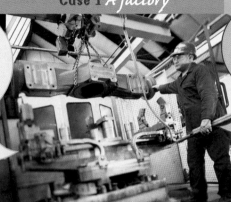

Employer
'We need people to work overtime this week to make sure this new order is produced on time. You all signed an agreement to do this when you joined the company.'

Employee
'I don't remember agreeing to that. I will need to check my contract. I haven't even been shown how to use the new machinery.'

Case 2 A sales team

Employer
'We expect everyone to work hard to sell our new product.'

Employee
'But the salesperson in the office next door is being paid more than me for doing exactly the same job. That doesn't seem right.

Case 3 A building site

Employee
'I don't think I should be climbing this ladder. We should be using scaffolding.'

Employer
'Workers must always wear protective gloves and a hard hat on the building site'.

? In each case:
(a) what does the employer expect from the employee?
(b) what does the employee expect from the employer?

What do employers and employees expect at work?

Employers

Employers provide employees with contracts of employment. These state what is expected from the employee. The contract will show what the employee's job is and the number of hours to be worked each week, for example. Employers expect their employees to meet the terms of their contracts of employment. For example, they expect employees to work the number of agreed hours a week.

Employers also expect employees to work together with managers and other employees to help a business meet its objectives, develop and grow. Employers often want employees to be flexible to meet the changing needs of a business. For example, a business might introduce new technology to help it expand. Employers need employees to be trained to use this new technology.

Employers expect employees to follow health and safety regulations. This is to make sure that no one is injured or harmed at work when they are carrying out their jobs. Injuries can result in employees being off work, which may affect the profitability of the business.

Employees

Employees expect to be paid according to their contracts of employment. They also will want to work in a safe environment. Employees might be injured if they work in dangerous conditions. This may affect their ability to work or enjoy life.

Employees also expect to be trained so that they can carry out their jobs. Without proper training, employees can become DEMOTIVATED because they do not know how to carry out a task.

Employees expect employers to allow them to join a trade union or staff association. Trade unions or staff associations protect their members. They negotiate pay and other terms and conditions of employment, such as working hours, benefits and working conditions.

Businesses often keep records about their employees. The records could be about their wages or the number of days they have been absent. They may be written records or files kept on computer. Employees expect this personal information to be accurate and to be able to check whether the information is correct.

Employees must not be discriminated against by gender, race or disability

Laws that protect employers and employees

Employees expect their employers to deal with them fairly and to follow the law.

Equal pay

Employees doing the same or similar work as those of the opposite sex are entitled to equal rates of pay and conditions. This is covered by the **Equal Pay Act 1970**.

Discrimination

Employees are protected against DISCRIMINATION over gender, race and disability.

- **The Sex Discrimination Act 1975** states that it is unlawful for a person to be discriminated against because of their gender. So advertisements for most jobs cannot say that they prefer a man or woman. Job titles must be 'genderless', as in salesperson rather than salesman. Interviews should not be biased towards one gender. Men or women should be promoted on ability rather than gender.
- **The Race Relations Act 1976** makes it unlawful to discriminate on the basis of race. So a business that didn't promote a suitably qualified employee who was Indian, Chinese or African-Caribbean would be discriminating.
- Disabled people should not be discriminated against without 'substantial' reason, according to the **Disability Discrimination Act 1995**. For example, a person in a wheelchair might be the best person for a job. Not giving that person the job because they are in a wheelchair is illegal. But a substantial reason for not employing the person may be if the company had to move premises to meet their needs.

Health and safety

Making the work environment safe might involve providing safety equipment and clothing on a building site. Or it could be making sure there are washing areas in a food manufacturing company. A business must protect its workforce to prevent accidents, injuries and illness. These could lead to absences and lost production. Businesses must also protect people outside the business, such as those living near a chemical plant. Employees are also responsible for health and safety in a business. **The Health and Safety at Work Act 1974** is the main law that covers health and safety issues.

Access to information

The Data Protection Act 1998 allows employees to look at their records to check that there are no mistakes.

Employment rights and working hours

When employees take a job the employer must provide them with a written statement and contract within a certain time. This sets out the terms and conditions of employment, such as job title, working hours, main responsibilities, benefits and holidays.

- At work, adult workers must be paid a minimum wage in the UK according to the **Minimum Wage Act 1998**.
- **The Employment Act 2002** gives employees the right to maternity and paternity leave for mothers and fathers when children are born. They can also ask to work flexible hours.
- Employees must be given pay during periods of illness.
- Employers must explain their rules of conduct at work to employees. Employees must also be told what happens if these rules are broken.
- **The Employment Relations Act 1999** states that employees have the right to join a trade union.
- **The European Working Time Directive 1998** restricts the number of hours employees can work. It also allows employees to take breaks during the day and to take holidays.

A person can be made redundant by a business if the job 'no longer exists'. They are then entitled to **redundancy pay**. An employee who is unable to do a job or is involved in misconduct can be **dismissed**. The employer must follow procedures to do this, including warnings. If they do not, the employee can take the business to a tribunal. It will decide whether the employee has been unfairly dismissed.

key terms

Demotivated – *employees who may not be willing to work hard at their job because they are unhappy with it.*
Discrimination – *favouring one person rather than another. In the UK it is illegal to discriminate in most jobs on the grounds of race, gender or disability.*

Quick quiz

1. Give the correct answer a, b or c.
   An employee will expect workers to work to the terms and conditions stated in their: **(a)** wage slip **(b)** contract of employment **(c)** training manual.

2. True or false? Employees expect to be given training and to work in safe conditions. This will benefit the employee, but not the employer.

3. Complete the sentence. Employees doing the same or broadly similar work to other employees are entitled to …… pay.

4. Name three different groups that are protected by discrimination laws.

5. Match the following situations to the laws they apply to.

Situation	Law
(a) A worker's computer has a faulty lead that is not repaired.	**(i)** The Race Relations Act.
(b) A man is paid more than a woman for overtime.	**(ii)** Minimum Wage Act.
(c) A baker is not hired because she was not born in England.	**(iii)** The Health and Safety at Work Act.
(d) A man aged 21 in the UK is not paid the minimum wage.	**(iv)** Equal Pay Act.

Portfolio practice

The Halifax

In 2001 the Halifax bank asked people from the Chinese community in Manchester to consider working for the bank in the area. 30 people applied in two weeks and six people were offered jobs. They were attracted by recruitment posters written in English and Chinese. The employees can speak the language used by many customers in the area, such as Mandarin or Cantonese. Mortgages have increased by 30-40 per cent amongst the Chinese community as a result.

The business also has employees from other ethnic minority groups. The Halifax allows some employees to change their working hours because their religion means they cannot eat at certain times of the day.

The Halifax is flexible in other areas. This allows the business to attract extra staff and stay open for longer. Some employees can work part-time or share jobs. One employee worked 4.5 days a week so he was able to pick up his son from school on Mondays. But the business still expected him to work a 37 hour week.

Discrimination is not only prevented in the case of ethnic minorities. All employees receive training based on the company's 'Fair's Fair' policy. This includes women, older workers and people with disabilities. 3.3 per cent of employees who work at the business are disabled. The business would like this to be closer to the national average of 9 per cent. Any worker using racist or inappropriate language gets a warning from a manager. The business also encourages workers to learn sign language.

Source: adapted from People Management, 8.11.2001.

1. (a) Give two examples of what the Halifax expects of its employees. (2 marks)
   (b) Give two examples of what Halifax employees might expect of the company. (2 marks)
2. Explain how the business ensures fair practice. (5 marks)
3. Do you think that the business is meeting the needs of its employees and employers? (8 marks)

30 Resolving disagreements

Getting started...

Sometimes disagreements take place about the way employees are treated at work. The disagreements might be about their pay or work conditions. They might be over discrimination when applying for a job or being made redundant. Employers and employees must find ways to resolve these disputes. Think about the following examples.

Case 1 Ford

In 2003 Ford, the motor car company, agreed a pay settlement with the T&G trade union. 22,000 manual workers were given pay rises. They were 4 per cent in the first year, and 3 per cent or the rate of inflation plus 0.5 per cent in the second year. The deal also increased maternity leave for mothers taking time off to have children from 40 to 52 weeks.

Source: adapted from Labour Research, January 2003.

Case 2 Threedles UK Ltd

Threedles UK Ltd is an engineering business. It has recently lost a number of orders and needed to reduce its costs. It decided to cut its working week from 6 days to 5 days. This meant that workers would get less pay. The employees took their case to The Employment Appeal Tribunal. The Tribunal ruled that putting workers on shorter time and pay without agreement was not lawful.

Source: adapted from Labour Research, January 2003.

Case 3 The Post Office

In 2002 The Post Office was in dispute with its workers. Workers wanted a 5 per cent rise in pay and a minimum wage of £300 a week. The Post Office offered less than half this amount. Workers belonged to the CWU communications union. They agreed to delay taking any action for 28 days while discussions took place with the ACAS conciliation service, which would help them try to find a solution to the disagreement.

Source: adapted from Labour Research, March 2002.

(a) What disagreements were taking place at:
  (i) Ford
  (ii) Threedles UK Ltd
  (iii) The Post Office?
(b) How were the disputes resolved at Ford and Threedles?
(c) What steps were taken to try to settle the dispute at the Post Office?

How can disagreements be resolved between employers and employees?

Grievance procedures

A grievance is where employees have a complaint against other staff or against their treatment at work. They can use a business's GRIEVANCE PROCEDURE to resolve the complaint. It provides a fair way for employees to raise problems. Businesses do not need a formal grievance procedure by law. But they must give employees the name of the person who they can approach with a complaint.

Most grievance procedures explain:
- how, and to whom, an employee should make a complaint;
- who an employee should go to next if they are still not satisfied;
- the time it should take for a complaint to be dealt with;
- that employees can be represented by someone else, such as a member of their trade union.

European Court of Justice

Employees could take their complaints to the European Court of Justice. It is a court that decides whether countries that belong to the European Union (EU) conform to EU law. For example, a business in the UK, which is part of the EU, might discriminate against a female employee. The employee might win her case under the EU Equal Treatment Directive.

Negotiations with trade unions or other representative organisations

Employees might think that a business has not really dealt with their grievance. Or they might feel that the grievance will affect other employees in the business. In such cases, employees might contact their TRADE UNION or another organisation to represent them.

A trade union is an organisation of workers who join together to further their own interests at work. Trade unions negotiate and bargain with employers on behalf of their members over pay, conditions of work, job security and grievances, for example.

Unions might take industrial action to further their members' interests. For example, they might call a strike. Employers sometimes consult unions before making changes to pay or working arrangements. This can help to prevent disagreements right at the start.

Unions might take industrial action to further their members' interests

Arbitration services

Sometimes employers and employees cannot agree on a solution. In these situations the Advisory, Conciliation and Arbitration Service (ACAS) can help. ACAS provides a wide range of services to employers and employees.

Industrial disputes Employers or unions can ask ACAS to become involved in a dispute. It will try to encourage a settlement between employers and unions that they both can agree upon.

Arbitration and mediation ARBITRATION is where employers and employees explain their case to ACAS. ACAS then judges which is strongest and makes a final decision that employers and employees have to agree on. MEDIATION is where ACAS makes a decision, but leaves it to the employers and employees to discuss a settlement.

Advisory work ACAS can advise employers and unions. It may help to answer questions on issues such as contracts of employment, employment laws, and recruitment and selection.

Individual cases ACAS investigates unfair discrimination or unfair dismissal, for example whether an employee has been unfairly sacked.

Employment tribunals

Where employers and employees cannot resolve a dispute, even with the help of ACAS, the case may go before an Employment Tribunal. They are like a court, with legal decision making powers, but less formal.

Tribunals are made up of three people. A lawyer chairs the Tribunal and there are two other people, often with industrial experience. Both employers and employees, often with a union representative, present their case for the Tribunal to rule on. Tribunals hear complaints about unfair dismissal, redundancy and discrimination.

Employees that win their case may be given their old job back (REINSTATED), offered a new job by the business or paid compensation for losing their job.

key terms

Arbitration - where employers and employees in a dispute put forward their case to ACAS.
Grievance procedure - the steps that an employee should follow when making a complaint about other staff or their treatment at work, and how the business will deal with that complaint.
Mediation - where ACAS makes a decision but then leaves it to the employers and employees to find a settlement.
Re-instated - when employees are given their old job back after winning an industrial tribunal decision.
Trade union - an organisation of workers who join together to further their interests at work

Quick quiz

1 Complete the sentences.

To help solve disputes a business might have a ...... procedure. It might tell an employee who to talk to if they have a .... Employees are able to be ...... by others if they are in dispute at work.

2 State four different services offered by ACAS.

3 Match the activities (a)-(c) to the institution (i)-(iii).

Activity	**Institution**
(a) Negotiates on behalf of its members with employers.	**(i)** European Court of Justice.
(b) Makes decision based on EU directives and laws	**(ii)** Trade unions.
(c) Has the power to make legal decisions over unfair practice but is less formal than a court.	**(iii)** Employment tribunals.

4 What three decisions might be made in favour of an employee who has won her case in an employment tribunal?

Portfolio practice

The firefighters dispute of 2002/03

In October 2002, firefighters voted nine to one in favour of industrial action in support of their pay claim. The Fire Brigades Union (FBU) represents firefighters. It wanted a 40 per cent increase in wages so that qualified staff would be on £30,000 a year.

The employer rejected this claim and offered 11 per cent over two years. The offer was linked to big changes in working practices which would mean increased working hours. This was in line with the independent Bain report that investigated firefighters' pay and working conditions. The unions rejected the employer's offer and tried to negotiate a higher increase, but the talks broke down.

In December 2002, FBU called a number of four day strikes to try to persuade the employer to increase the offer. The employer did not give in. The union then organised more strikes, but postponed these when ACAS were asked to try to find a way to resolve this dispute.

ACAS talked to both sides. ACAS said that the dispute would not be resolved quickly because of the difficult issues involved. But it was confident that, by talking to each side separately and trying to find common ground, an agreement would eventually be reached.

Source: adapted from BBC website.

1. (a) What is the firefighter's grievance? (1 mark)
   (b) What do the firefighters want to resolve their grievance? (1 mark)
2. Why do you think the employer and firefighters are in dispute? (4 marks)
3. Why has ACAS been called in to help? (4 marks)
4. To what extent do you think that ACAS will be successful? (7 marks)

31 Recruitment and selection

Getting started...

For a business to be successful, it has to take on people with the right skills for the job. A business will want to attract the best people to apply for a job. This is called recruitment. Then the most suitable person must be chosen from the people who have applied. This is called SELECTION.

Case 1 *Hesling Ltd*

Jeff Gooding is the transport manager at Hesling Ltd, a delivery company. 'We are based near Newcastle and deliver goods in the North of England. We are desperate to take on some extra, permanent drivers as our orders are piling up. I have placed this advert in the local newspaper each night next week. If I don't get the right people, I'll have to ask the Gateshead Drivers' Agency for some temporary local drivers from its list'.

---

helsing ltd

Heavy goods vehicle drivers required
We have work waiting in the Newcastle and surrounding area for HGV Class 1 and 2 drivers with experience.

We will pay a basic wage of £6.50 per hour. Overtime is paid at time and a half. Additional payments for weekends are negotiable. You will be expected to work a minimum of 40 hours a week.

Please apply in writing to:
Mr J Gooding, Hesling Ltd, Acre Park, Gateshead.

Case 2 *Gofast*

Gofast is a film production company. It makes programmes that it sells to television companies. One of its best film producers has just left. The managing director said: 'It's a pity to lose her. She was very good at meeting deadlines. Also, she could organise everyone on the film crew, such as the camera people and sound recorders, so that programmes were produced on time. She knew exactly what programmes would work best on TV. But I think we may have other people in the company who can do the job. I'll put the details of the job on our website and a notice in the office.'

(a) How have these businesses tried to recruit workers?
(b) What skills will applicants need to be selected for these jobs?

What are the steps involved in recruiting and selecting a new employee?

Identifying the vacancy

A business will need to recruit a new employee if a VACANCY exists. This is where there is a job to be done, but no one to do it. A business might have a vacancy because:

○ a worker has left a job, retired, been promoted or been dismissed;
○ a new job has been created because there is more work to do.

Drawing up a job description and person specification

A job description states the title of the job and outlines the tasks and responsibilities of the employee. A business also needs to decide what skills, experience, attitudes, qualifications an employee needs. These are shown in a PERSON SPECIFICATION. The things a candidate must have are often classed as essential. The things that it would be useful for a candidate to have are classed as desirable. Figure 1 shows a job description and person specification for a senior hair stylist.

Figure 1 *A job description and a person specification*

Job description for a senior hair stylist
Job title Senior Hair Stylist responsible to the owner of the salon.
Day-to-day tasks Styling, blow drying, colouring, building up new client portfolios.
Responsibility Responsible for two junior trainee stylists.

Person specification for a senior hair stylist
Essential
Qualifications NVQ Level 4 Hairdressing.
Experience 5 years experience working in top grade salon.
Skills A broad portfolio of hair-cutting styles.
Training and development Ability to train and develop junior staff.

Desirable
Attainments Prizes at hair shows.
Contacts A large client portfolio.

Advertising the vacancy

Businesses must decide whether to advertise internally or externally.

Internally This is where a business advertises the job to people who already work in the business. Internal recruitment has certain advantages.

○ People who already work there will know how the business works and other employees. They should settle into a new job more quickly.
○ It shows other employees that they can progress in a business. This can help to motivate staff.
○ It is fairly cheap because vacancies can be advertised on a notice board, on the company intranet or newspaper, or by word of mouth.

Externally A business could recruit people who do not work for the business at the moment. People who are new to the business might have fresh ideas and be very motivated. External advertising gives a wider choice of people for the business to select. It could do this in a number of ways.

○ **Employment and recruitment agencies**. Employment agencies have lists of people looking for work. They match these people up with vacancies in businesses. Many agencies specialise in clerical, nursing, computing or teaching staff to fill part-time or temporary jobs. Recruitment agencies help business to recruit and select employees and might also suggest the best ways to advertise vacancies.
○ **Job centres**. These are government run offices that help the unemployed find jobs and local firms to fill vacancies. Vacancies tend to be for lower paid jobs.
○ **The media**. Vacancies can be advertised in the local and national press, in technical journals, on television and through the Internet.

Short-listing

People applying for jobs send a letter of application and a CURRICULUM VITAE (CV) or fill in an application form. These contain personal details (name, address, age, nationality), qualifications, experience, hobbies and reasons why they are suitable for the job. They also include names and addresses of referees. These are people who can confirm the employee's details or give more information about them.

A business cannot usually interview all the applicants, so it will just choose a small number. This is known as SHORT LISTING. It is usually done by matching the application to the person specification.

Selecting and appointing

Sometimes interviews are not the best way to choose an employee. Interviewers might be biased. They might not like how a candidate looks, for example. So a business might use other methods to select the most suitable candidate.
- ✪ Tests. These might be aptitude tests, to measure how well a candidate copes with a business problem. They might be attainment tests, such as a word processing test. Or there could be a test to see if the candidate has a suitable personality.
- ✪ Selection exercises. These include role play exercises, group presentations and simulations. They allow candidates to show whether they have the skills for a job.

After interviews and tests, a business will select and appoint the most suitable candidate. If the wrong person is chosen, this could be a problem. They might not do the job well. They might find the job boring or hard and leave. It would then be costly for the business to replace them. Businesses that choose the best candidates are likely to be able to compete better with other businesses.

Interviewing

Applicants who short-listed are usually asked to come to an interview. Here the interviewers can find out more about candidates by asking questions. Candidates can also expand on their CVs and letters of application. The information is used to help businesses decide which candidates are suitable for the job. Interviews also allow candidates to find out more about the job.

Legal and ethical rules that affect recruitment

Businesses must follow the law when recruiting and selecting employees. They cannot discriminate against employees based on sex, race or disability. This might affect a business in a number of ways.
- ✪ It cannot advertise vacancies to one particular sex apart from where this could be essential to the job.
- ✪ It cannot say that people of an ethnic minority must not apply for a job.
- ✪ Interviewers are not allowed to ask questions which might lead them to discriminate against a candidate. For example, it would be illegal to ask female candidates about childcare arrangements if the same question was not asked to men.
- ✪ It cannot refuse to appoint a disabled person simply because they use a wheelchair.

key terms

✪ Curriculum vitae – a list of the main details about a person applying for a job. .
✪ Person specification – shows the skills, experience, attitudes, qualifications that are required from a candidate to carry out the job detailed in the job description..
✪ Selection – where a business attempts to choose the most suitable person for the job from candidates.
✪ Short-listing – reducing the number of candidates down to those that will be interviewed.
✪ Vacancy – where a job exists but the business has no one appointed to do it.

key terms key terms key terms

Quick quiz

1 Give four reasons why a vacancy may arise in a business.

2 True or false? A job description lists the skills, experience, attitudes, qualifications that a person needs to do the job.

3 Complete the sentence. The term used for reducing the number of applicants to those being interviewed is ....

4 Match the following descriptions (a)-(d) to the terms (i)-(iv).

Descriptions	Terms
(a) A test to show a business how well an applicant could cope with a business problem.	**(i)** An advertisement on a company notice board.
(b) A government run office that helps the unemployed find jobs and businesses to find employees.	**(ii)** An aptitude test.
(c) A fairly cheap way to recruit workers for a new post from existing employees.	**(iii)** An interview.
(d) A method of selecting candidates which allows questions to be asked and expanded upon.	**(iv)** A job centre.

5 What is the main problem of just using interviews in the selection of candidates?

Portfolio practice

A tale of two businesses

4T Graphics and Bellemonde are two design and graphics businesses that offer services such as producing company logos and advertising brochures. Each company is successful and needs to attract new staff. The two businesses select and recruit in different ways.

4T Graphics

When a vacancy arises at 4T Graphics, the business produces a job description and person specification. Then it asks a recruitment agency to advertise the post and short-list the candidates. The short-listing is based on candidates filling in detailed job applications that show their experience and why they want to work for the company. Once candidates have been short-listed, the business selects the best candidate using tests and an interview. 4T Graphics employs a greater proportion of women and ethnic minorities in high positions than the national average. But this attention to detail in recruitment and selection is expensive.

Bellemonde

Bellemonde's approach is informal. If a senior job needs to be filled, the business appoints from within. When other vacancies arise, staff are asked to contact friends or relatives who might have the right skills and who might be interested in the job. If the business doesn't find anyone this way, it advertises in the local paper. Candidates are asked to apply by letter. A manager looks at these letters and selects some people for interview that he thinks might fit in with the business. This is often based on the school they attended and whether they have good A level results in history, Latin and economics. Candidates are chosen on how they look and whether they have the right social skills.

1. 4T Graphics produces job descriptions for each vacancy. What is usually included in a job description? (2 marks)
2. 4T Graphics also produces person specifications for each vacancy. What is the difference between a job description and a person specification? (4 marks)
3. What are the differences in the way that 4T Graphics and Bellemonde recruit and select? (6 marks)
4. Do you think 4T Graphics or Bellemonde is best at recruiting and selecting? (8 marks)

32 Job applications

Getting started...

When people apply for a job they need to present a good record of their achievements. They also need to prepare well for an interview or any other tests and selection exercises. Good preparation and practice are essential for anyone who wants to get a job.

Case 1 *A letter of application*

Rob Settler
      Runway Road
      Islington
      London

To the persson in chag

I'd like to apply for the job your advertised in the local Islington paper.
Could you please send me an application from as soon as possible.

Rob Settler

Case 2 *At an interview*

WHERE WOULD YOU LIKE TO BE IN THE BUSINESS IN A FEW YEARS TIME?

I HAVE NO IDEA. I HAVEN'T EVEN THOUGHT ABOUT IT.

Case 3 *Preparing for an interview*

I MUST MAKE SURE THAT I SEARCH THE INTERNET FOR INFORMATION ABOUT THE COMPANY AND ITS PRODUCTS BEFORE I GO TO THE INTERVIEW.

Look at the situations. What (a) poor practices and (b) good practices when applying for a job are shown?

What is involved in applying for a job?

Application forms

Application forms are designed by businesses to find out about people that want a job. The same form is sent to all applicants. Most forms start with personal details, such as name, address, age and gender. Then they might ask about education, experience, interests and hobbies. There might also be a section where people can say why they are applying for the job.

Application forms might ask for the names and addresses of referees. These are people who have experience of working with or educating the applicant, such as a manager or lecturer. They can confirm the applicant's details. They can also give further information about them, such as their skills, whether they are hard working and if they are always on time.

The advantage of an application form is that applicants all answer the same questions. And the answers are all in the same style. This makes it easier for the business to compare them.

A curriculum vitae

Instead of an application form, some businesses ask candidates to send a curriculum vitae (CV) and a letter of application instead. A CV is a factual record of the applicant's details. It usually has a series of headings.

- A list of personal details - name address, age and nationality.
- Educational qualifications, with the most recent first.
- Paid and unpaid work experience, starting with the most recent. Next to each job will be its title, a short description of the tasks and responsibilities, the dates worked and the employer's name.
- Hobbies and interests. This gives an idea of the applicants' wider interests. It might also show that they can work in a team and have good social skills.
- Names and addresses of referees.

Preparing for interviews and tests

People preparing for an interview should think about what the business will want from a successful applicant.
- How well they can do the job. Applicants should be clear about what tasks are involved in the job and how they can show their abilities at doing the job in the interview.
- How well they will fit in at the business. Finding something out about the business and the way it operates can make a good impression.
- Having good social skills. Preparing answers and questions to ask the interviewers will help. Giving confident answers in the interview is also a good idea.
- Good presentation. Smiling at the interview, wearing smart clothes, making suitable gestures, and showing enthusiasm help to make a good impression.

How can you prepare for a test?
- People must be honest in personality tests. They can be caught out if they try to give the answer which they think an interviewer wants.
- It is useful to practice the skills that are being tested before a test takes place.
- In teamwork exercises, people should think about how they can be involved in group activity. But they must not try to dominate too much.

Good presentation and preparation are important at interviews

Writing a letter of application

A letter of application will go into more detail about what applicants have done, why they are applying and why they would be good at the job. The letter is a chance for applicants to 'sell' themselves honestly, so they stand out from others. There are important things to remember when writing a letter of application. These are shown in Figure 1.

❶ Take into account what the person specification wants. There is no point writing about experience of childminding if a job wants relevant experience of management.

❷ Be honest, otherwise a business might find out in the interview. Or it might find out later and the employee might lose his or her job.

❸ Make sure that the letter is well written and there are no spelling and grammatical errors. This could give the impression that the application is rushed. Typing the letter will make it easier to read.

❹ Show confidence in your ability and be enthusiastic for the job.

❺ Be precise and concise. Make points clearly. Don't write much more than two sides of A4 paper.

Dear sir / madam

I am writing with reegard to your new leisure centre in Crosby, which is due to open in the near future. I hope to demonstrate through my experiences that I would be ideally suited to work as a General Manager.

I have always had an interest in leisure and sports services. I took a degree in Leisure Studies with Business, where I specialised in sport and business theory. During that time I studied sports development, events management and leisure management, as well as the theory of business strategy, the business environment and the organisation of human resources. My course provided me with an opportunity to experience a variety of posts in sports leisure, such as youth coaching and supporting and implementing sports in the community initiatives at a Premier League Football Club Academy. These experiences enabled me to carry on working at the Academy during the summer months of my degree, working full-time as scout and youth coach. Throughout this period I was able to put into practice some of the ideas and concepts learned during my university course. I also developed skills in coaching, training and the management of a sporting organisation and sporting events.

Since graduating I have not been able to find suitable full-time employment. However, I have taken unpaid posts in a couple of leisure centres where I have developed further skills. In addition, I have been keenly involved with sports in the community through my coaching of Crosby Stewarts Under-12 football team which I have coached for 5 years. I have also continued with scouting activities.

I see the new leisure complex as an ideal opportunity. It has arrived at the right time for me to be able to pursue more fully my primary interest in leisure management and, at the same time, continue with my sports in the community activities. Sport and recreation has always been my passion. Throughout my years studying in this area and working in voluntary positions I have shown commitment, dedication, enthusiasm and a willingness to work as part of the team. I have also realised the importance of sport for individual fulfilment and development. A combination of my personal qualities and skills and my varied work experiences would make me ideally suited to work for Parkfield Leisure in Crosby.

Yours faithfully

A purpose-built modern leisure centre has recently been completed in the Crosby area and is about to open in the near future. Parkfield Leisure is currently recruiting for three new posts.

Swimming instructor
Aerobics instructor
General Manager

Each post attracts a well paid salary linked to 5 weeks' holiday and other benefits. If you would like more details please contact Jackie Henshaw on 0151 100 6785.

Figure 1 *An example of a job advert and a letter supporting an application*

Quick quiz

1. What does CV stand for?
2. What headings would you include in a CV?
3. Who are referees?
4. (What type of people might be asked to be referees?
5. True or false?

   (a) It's sometimes makes sense to be dishonest in your application, particularly if you have something to hide about your experience.

   (b) Businesses are concerned about how you will fit in and whether you can do the job.

   (c) A person preparing for a teamwork exercise will try to work out how to control others in the team. A dominant person is likely to get the job, even if they don't work well with others.

Portfolio practice

Advert
Part-time sales assistant required in a shoe shop. £5.50 per hour, up to 15 hours per week. For further details contact Joanne Moore in Personnel. Apply with CV and letter of application.

Job description
Job title – sales assistant.
Tasks – customer advice on range of shoes, fitting shoes for customers, using a cash till, stock taking.
Responsibility - responsible to shop manager.

Person specification
Qualifications - GCSE in Maths and English, good social skills, enthusiastic and hardworking, experience as a sales assistant

---

Applicant 1 – Holly Jeffs – CV

Name: Holly Jeffs.
Address: 13 Seymour Grove, Blackpool
Tel : ?
Age : 17
Qualifications:
GCSE Maths   Grade B
GCSE English   Grade B
GCSE PE   Grade A
GCSE History   Grade D
GCSE Geography   Grade B
Education: Bilton School, Blackpool.
St Paul VI Farm College – stuing AVCE Leisure and Tourism.
Work experience: Baby sitting for a friend.
Interests: Watching TV and going out.

Applicant 2 – Paul Simmons - part of an interview

Interviewer – Why have you applied for the job?
Paul Simmons – My mum thought it might be a good idea. It would get me out the house and I could also pay her some keep.

Interviewer – What do you know about being a sales assistant in a shoe shop?
Paul Simmons – You sell shoes to customers. That's it, isn't it?

Interviewer – Why do you want the job?
Paul Simmons – I need extra money to help my mum and dad with all the expenses of running the home. Plus I like to go out with my mates quite a few nights a week and this costs money.

---

1. Look at the job description. What are the main tasks required to do the job? (2 marks)
2. Look at the person specification. What are the main things that the shoe shop wants from the person doing the job? (2 marks)
3. How would you improve Holly Jeffs' CV? (4 marks)
4. Would you employ Paul Simmons if you were the interviewer? (4 marks)
5. Draw up a list of five questions that you would ask applicants if you were interviewing for this job. In each case explain why you would ask that question. (10 marks)

33 Staff development and training

Getting started...

If a business wants to be successful and compete with other businesses its employees must be well trained. A business that does not develop and train its employees could have problems.

Case 1

WHEN HE STARTED THIS JOB HE WASN'T GIVEN ANY TRAINING ON HOW TO USE THE MACHINE PROPERLY AND WHO TO SEE IF HE WAS INJURED.

Case 2

WE'VE ONLY HAD THESE NEW MACHINES A WEEK, AND I DON'T UNDERSTAND HOW THEY WORK.
I'M ALWAYS MAKING MISTAKES. LOOK AT ALL THESE FAULTY PRODUCTS.

REJECTS

Case 3

THE SALES DEPARTMENT IS REALLY BUSY TODAY. COULD YOU HELP THEM OUT FOR A WHILE?

BUT I'VE NEVER WORKED THERE BEFORE. I DON'T KNOW IF I CAN DEAL WITH CUSTOMERS.

SALES

(a) What problems do the employees and the businesses have in the above examples?
(b) What type of training could the businesses give the employees to prevent those problems?

Why and how do businesses train and develop their employees?

Reasons for training

Why do businesses train employees?

- **Legislation.** Changes in the law may mean that employees need training. For example, new laws could mean that a health and safety officer in a business has to learn about new practices.
- **Technology.** Employees need training to work with new or improved software or machinery. This should make them work better. It should also prevent accidents. For example, British Gas engineers now use new electronic recording probes to check home boilers.
- **Improving skills.** Employees must have the necessary skills to do their jobs. Many businesses today need a multi-skilled workforce. If workers have many skills they are more likely to be flexible and to be able to do more than one job.
- **New jobs or work situations.** Workers may need to be trained to cope with new situations. For example, a worker may change jobs in a business and will need to be trained to do the new job.
- **Motivation.** Training can help to motivate employees by giving them the skills to do more interesting work.
- **Promotion.** Gaining new skills through training may help employees to get promotion.

Induction training

When employees first start a job they are often given INDUCTION TRAINING. Figure 1 below shows what it might involve.

A tour of the workplace to help new employees find their way around.

Health and safety training and what the business's rules are.

INDUCTION TRAINING

Something about the history of the business and how it is organised.

Introductions to the people they will be working with.

The business's main policies, such as quality and customer service.

Figure 1 *Induction training*

On-the-job training

ON-THE-JOB TRAINING takes place while the job is being done. There are various ways in which this may happen.

Watching another worker A new employee could watch a more experienced employee doing the job and copy them. The trainee might work next to a machine operator or travel with a salesperson. This can be a cheap and easy method of training. Employees are taught to do the job in the way that the company expects. But not everyone is good at showing others how to do a job.

Coaching An expert could work with an employee for a short time to show them the best way of doing something. For example, a computer technician could train an operator to use new software.

Mentoring A trainee could be paired with a more experienced employee for a period of time. The trainee does the job, but can discuss problems and how to solve them with the mentor from time to time.

Job rotation An employee could work in different departments for short periods, picking up skills from each. This is sometimes used for employees that a business expects to promote quickly. They get a better overall view of the business.

Off-the-job training

OFF-THE-JOB TRAINING is carried out away from the workplace. It can be a college course, a specialist course provided by a training company or a course at a business's training centre. These courses tend to cover the theory of the job, while the practical skills are learnt on-the-job. Businesses often allow employees to take a day off each week to follow a course. Off-the-job training tends to be expensive because the business has to pay for the course and because employees are not producing anything when they are being trained.

Training initiatives and National Awards

To help improve skills levels, employers and the government are keen for people to gain training qualifications. They also want to develop training initiatives and national awards that will be recognised by all employers. How is this done?

- ✪ **Learning and Skills Councils** (LSCs) identify, encourage and deliver training needs in the local areas in which they operate. They manage government funds, making payments to businesses that are training employees.
- ✪ **National Vocational Qualifications** (NVQs) are qualifications gained in the workplace. They include qualifications in catering, hairdressing, engineering and plumbing.
- ✪ **Modern Apprenticeships** aim to increase the number of young people going into work with training. Modern Apprentices work for a business, earn a wage and are trained in technical, craft or junior management skills up to NVQ level 3.
- ✪ **The New Deal** is where the government provides money to businesses to employ and train 18-24 year olds who are unemployed.
- ✪ **National Traineeships** give young people NVQ level 2 qualifications. After they have finished, trainees move onto Modern Apprenticeships or another form of training.
- ✪ To achieve **Investors in People (IiP)** status, employers must agree to train and develop all their staff. They must also plan their training and regularly review how successful it has been. Businesses that gain the IiP status can display a plaque.

Appraisal

After a period of time, such as a year, a business may review how well an employee has done the job. This is called APPRAISAL It often involves a supervisor drawing up a performance review and discussing with employees how well they have met their targets. When the appraisal takes place, the supervisor might decide that the employee has STAFF DEVELOPMENT needs. For example, an employee might not have met a production target because they had not been trained to use a new machine that works quicker.

Re-training

Many of the UK's 'traditional' industries have almost disappeared. So skills in shipbuilding, coal mining, textiles, or steel making are no longer needed. The government has helped people with these skills to be retrained, often in new technology.

Changes within a business might mean that employees need to be re-trained. For example, banks are providing more of their services by telephone, so many local branches have been closed down. Rather than make employees redundant, banks have retrained them to deal with customers over the telephone.

The success of training

Businesses want to make sure that the costs of training are worthwhile. They want training to lead to better performance from employees and to greater profits. If employees' performance improves after training, this suggests that it has been successful. For example, after taking a word processing course, an employee might be able to key in more words per minute accurately on a computer than before.

Quick quiz

1 Match the statements (i)-(vi) to the training methods (a)-(f).

2 **Statements**

(i) Training given to employees when they first start a job with a business.

(ii) Training that takes place while doing a job.

(iii) Training by watching an experienced worker doing the job.

(iv) Training that involves working in different departments for short periods.

(v) Training that is done away from the workplace.

(vi) Pairing a trainee with a more experienced employee to discuss problems and get advice.

Training methods

(a) Job rotation.

(b) On-the-job training.

(c) Off-the job training.

(d) Mentoring.

(e) Working next to another employee.

(f) Induction training.

key terms

Appraisal – where a business reviews an employees' performance.
Induction training – training given to employees when they first start a job.
Off-the-job training – training that takes place away from the job.
On-the-job training – training that takes place while doing the job.
Staff development – the improvement of employees' skills through training.

Portfolio practice

Emporium Charalambous

Andreas Charalambous started Charalambous Hairdressing in 1995. He now owns three salons in Leicester and hopes to open a fourth next year. Andreas wants to improve standards in the hairdressing industry and sees training as vital to doing this.

The company aims to provide the highest quality customer service using the best hairdressing techniques and products. It sells mainly to 25-35 year olds who have high fashion expectations.

Andreas says: 'When we're recruiting hairdressers we look for people with enthusiasm and good social skills. But, often we have to recruit unskilled people because there are not enough ready-trained hairdressers around.'

One of the salons Andreas owns has The Charalambous Training School on the floor above. The school provides training for NVQ levels 2 and 3 and Modern Apprenticeships. Andreas uses both on-the-job and off-the-job training.

Andreas says: 'During quiet periods our trainee hairdressers work with experienced stylists. They can watch and learn new styles of cutting and drying. When it's busy, it's difficult for stylists to have trainees around them. Trainees need to be given time to develop their basic skills in the school and to achieve their NVQs.'

Andreas realises that even his senior stylists need training to be aware of new hairdressing techniques. He appraises his stylists once a year. Each stylist is then given a plan for the next twelve months, showing what training they will be given.

Andreas says: 'Joan has been hairdressing in one of my salons for quite a while, but she only has NVQ level 2. She is very capable, but she needs to develop her advanced cutting skills. When I do her appraisal next week I'm going to suggest that she attends a specialist training college one day a week for three months to gain these skills. It's a cost to us. But I know it will more than pay for itself with the extra customers another fully trained stylist will bring in.'

1. What could Andreas include in an induction programme? (4 marks)
2. Explain two reasons which the business needs to train its staff. (4 marks)
3. What two types of training are given to trainees? (2 marks)
4. Using your answer to question 3, compare the advantages and disadvantages of each type of training for the business and its employees. (8 marks)
5. How would Andreas evaluate whether the training received by his employees was effective and why would he need to do this? (7 marks)

Getting started...

Customers are extremely important to businesses. To attract and keep customers, businesses must use a variety of techniques. They must also try to satisfy their customers' expectations.

Case 1 *Vodafone*

Vodafone is constantly looking for ways of offering new services to its customers. Customers want to use their mobile phones for a wide range of activities including email, playing games, shopping, chatting on-line with friends and sending still and moving images.

Case 2 *Hightown Pie Shop*

Customers of the Hightown Pie Shop in Wigan have clear needs. They want to be able to buy a wide range of freshly baked pies at sensible prices. And they don't want to queue for more than ten minutes at lunchtime.

Case 3 *Gates Cleaning Ltd*

Gates Cleaning Ltd offers a cleaning service for office buildings and hotels in Brighton. Its customers need their offices to be cleaned outside office hours, at a competitive price and with particular care over the cleanliness of such areas as kitchens, toilets and hotel rooms.

Case 4 *Catch plc*

Catch plc provides specialist holidays in Southern Europe for young people. They want action packed holidays in locations with beaches and plenty of clubs.

For each business:
(a) Who are the customers?
(b) What expectations do they have?

Why are customers important to a business?

The importance of customers

No business could survive without customers. Without customers, businesses would not be able to sell any of their products and they would not get any revenue. CUSTOMER SERVICES is the part of a business that tries to ensure that customers are satisfied with the goods or services they are purchasing or thinking about purchasing.

The benefits of good customer services

How can good customer services benefit a business?

⚙ Keeping customers. Businesses need to work hard to ensure that their existing customers stay with them.

⚙ Gaining new customers. Most businesses need to keep finding new customers because there is no guarantee that they will be able to keep all their existing ones. This is because existing customers will naturally want to try other businesses' products.

⚙ Keeping customers happy with their products. This is especially important because it helps to maintain the business's IMAGE AND REPUTATION. A business's image and reputation determines how consumers view it.

⚙ Offering customers information about the products that are available.

⚙ Providing customers with good service, or better service than competitors, helps businesses to increase their sales revenue and their profits.

Internal and external customers

Customers must be offered good quality customer services if a business is to win their custom and keep it. Customer services are important for both internal and external customers.

INTERNAL CUSTOMERS are customers within the same business. Internal customers are most commonly found in large businesses. For example, if the production department requires health and safety training for some new employees, this will be provided by the training department. In this situation, the production department is an internal customer because it is using the services of the training department.

EXTERNAL CUSTOMERS are customers outside the business. They might be individual consumers or other businesses purchasing products.

Figure 1 *Internal and external customers*

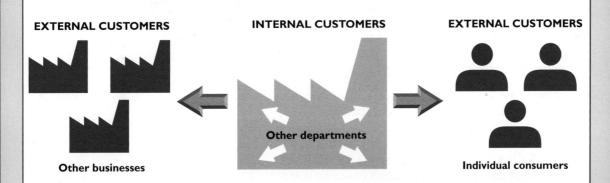

EXTERNAL CUSTOMERS

Other businesses

INTERNAL CUSTOMERS

Other departments

EXTERNAL CUSTOMERS

Individual consumers

Customer expectations

CUSTOMER EXPECTATIONS are about what people buying goods and services expect from a business. If businesses are going to offer a good quality of customer service, they must meet all reasonable expectations of their customers. These include the following.

- Providing a good after-sales service. This might be replacing faulty goods immediately or repairing them. Good after sales service might make customers feel more confident about buying a product.
- Providing competitively priced products so that customers feel they are getting value for money.
- Offering help when customers are buying a product by providing product information. This might be help from a sales assistant who can explain the variety of products available or information in a brochure on how a product works.
- Responding to enquiries from customers within a reasonable time. This might make customers feel that their custom is valued and that a business cares about them.

Sometimes, customers may have expectations that a business cannot reasonably meet, so it is important for businesses to set realistic expectations for their customers. For example, a car manufacturer may offer to provide full breakdown cover for three years on all new cars. But it would not claim that a new car will never break down in its first three years. Customer services play a vital role in establishing and meeting the reasonable expectations of customers.

A sales assistant can help customers when buying goods

key terms

Customer services – the part of a business that attempts to ensure that customers are satisfied with the goods or service they are purchasing.
Customers' expectations – what consumers expect from a business.
External customers – customers outside the business.
Image and reputation – how consumers view a business.
Internal customers – customers within the same business.

key terms key terms key terms key terms key terms

Quick quiz

1 Complete the sentence.
Customer service helps to ensure that customers are ...... with a product.

2 State three benefits of good customer service.

3 What is the difference between internal and external customers?

4 True or false? A business with high quality customer service will never lose any customers.

5 Which of the following might be examples of realistic customer expectations in a fast food outlet that specialises in selling burgers and soft drinks?

(a) Customers to get their burgers within 10 seconds of entering the store.

(b) No question refunds to be offered on poorly presented and badly cooked burgers.

(c) Customers to be given a free meal with every purchase.

(d) The restaurant to provide a clean and safe environment for consuming the burgers.

Portfolio practice

Raffles Ltd

Raffles Ltd is a shoe shop in Norwich town centre. The business owns one shoe shop and has to compete with other well-known high street stores. A new shoe shop has recently opened in the town centre. It has a reputation for excellent customer service. Raffles knows that it must improve its customer service to compete with this new shop.

Raffles has had some complaints in the last few months.

☺ Over one third of the business's weekly takings are on Saturday between 10.00 a.m. and 3.00 p.m. This is the shop's busiest time and customers have complained about delays in getting served.

☺ Customers want to know about the available stocks, sizes and styles of shoes before they visit the store. Customers have complained that when they ring up, the telephone is not answered quickly enough.

The managers and the staff have had a meeting. They have agreed to set a number of targets for customer services.

☺ The telephone at the customer help desk will be answered before it rings six times.

☺ On Saturday, customers must not wait for more than ten minutes before being served.

☺ A numbered ticket system will be used to manage queues of customers at busy times.

1. Describe three benefits of good customer service for Raffles Ltd. (3 marks)

2. Are the new service levels meant to benefit internal or external customers? Explain your answer. (4 marks)

3. What is likely to be the effect of the new customer service levels on the number of shoes sold each week by Raffles Ltd? (9 marks)

Getting started...

Businesses need to investigate aspects of their customer service. One of the most important things is to find out how satisfied customers are with what they have bought.

Case 1 *Bling Ltd*

Bling Ltd supplies software for computer games. It is a new business and has three games designers and a website where customers can buy games on the Internet. The website also has a special section where customers who have bought games are asked for their views on the company's products generally and on particular features of the games.

Case 2 *SETCON*

SETCON leases and maintains office equipment, such as photocopiers. All its customers are asked to respond to a range of written questions about the quality of its service.

Case 3 *Perth Opticians*

Perth Opticians likes to find out its customers' views on the service that it provides. Its main method of doing this is by speaking to customers when they come into the shop. Jackie McDonald, the owner, regards this as one of her most important duties.

? *(a) How does each of the above businesses find out how satisfied their customers are?*

How do businesses find out how satisfied their customers are with their service?

Customer satisfaction

Satisfied customers are important to businesses. If a business can keep its customers satisfied, it is more likely to be successful. It is not always easy for businesses to judge how satisfied their customers really are. So they use a range of techniques to measure customer satisfaction.

Measuring customer satisfaction

As well as asking customers for their views about products, businesses have other ways of measuring customer satisfaction.

Analysing sales performance The SALES PEFORMANCE of a business is concerned with the number and type of sales that a business has achieved. This is measured by looking at the number of actual sales recorded, the number of customers making purchases and how often customers have made purchases. Some businesses give loyalty cards to their customers to encourage regular purchases, for example the Nectar card offered by Sainsbury's. Loyalty card records are a good means of providing sales information because customers' purchases can be analysed.

Comparing sales performance with competitors It is vital for businesses to compare their sales performance with that of other businesses. Businesses are often more concerned with how they are doing in relation to their competitors than they are with their own sales.

Recording the number of complaints By recording the number of complaints, returned goods and the reason for their return, businesses can get a good indication of their customers' satisfaction. Businesses who react to their customers' views in a positive way will hope to get fewer complaints and fewer returned goods over time.

Collecting information on customer satisfaction

Businesses use a number of different methods to collect information on customer satisfaction.

Questionnaires Customers can be asked a series of carefully prepared questions known as a QUESTIONNAIRE. Questionnaires can be carried out by asking customers to give written replies to questions.

Interviews Customers may be asked questions in an INTERVIEW over the telephone or face to face. This gives the person answering the questions a chance to discuss the questions with the interviewer.

Customer panels A CUSTOMER PANEL is a group of customers who have been selected because of their experience of a business's products. They are asked to answer questions on products over a period of time. They might be asked what they like or dislike, and to suggest improvements.

Observation Businesses can observe customers as they use a product or at the point that they buy it. For example, a restaurant owner might want to observe customers' reactions to the meals they are eating as a way of judging their satisfaction.

On the spot questions This is where customers are asked what they think about a business's products at the time when they are buying them. Many employees are now trained to regularly ask on the spot questions about customer satisfaction with a product.

Websites and emails Many businesses use their websites to invite comments on customer satisfaction. Customers are asked to respond to questions and send their views by email.

Investigating customer service

Different businesses often have very different types of customer service. Customer service can vary greatly between small and large businesses, for instance.

What features of customer service can be different?

- ✪ The quality of customer service offered by staff. This could be the accuracy and quality of information that provide, the way they treat customers face to face, on the telephone or by email, and the effectiveness with which they communicate information.
- ✪ The product. A number of features of a product which are important to customers are how it is packaged, the information provided with it, how easy it is to assemble and use, its safety, and whether it performs as the advertising says it should.
- ✪ After-sales care. This includes how complaints are handled, whether repairs are undertaken and how quickly, and whether exchanges or refunds are given on unwanted or broken products.
- ✪ Delivery. Sometimes customers have to order goods and wait for them to be delivered. Customer service would be concerned with whether the goods are available for delivery, how quickly they are delivered and whether they are delivered when promised.

- ✪ Premises where the purchase is made. Features of customer service would include the customer facilities such as toilets, adequate signposting, facilities for the disabled and cleanliness.
- ✪ The use of Information and Communications Technology (ICT). Many businesses now use ICT to improve and develop their customer services so it is important for them to have USER FRIENDLY business websites. These are websites which are easy for customers to use.

A feature of customer service might be information given by staff

key terms

✪ **Customer panel** – *a group of customers who have been selected to answer questions.*
✪ **Interview** – *asking questions either face to face or by telephone.*
✪ **Questionnaire** – *a series of questions prepared in advance.*
✪ **Sales performance** – *the number and type of sales that a business has achieved.*
✪ **User friendly** – *the ease with which customers can use something, for example a business website.*

key terms key terms key terms key terms key terms key terms

Quick quiz

1 Complete the sentence.

In order to collect information on their customer services, a business can devise a series of questions to be included in a …… conducted through a face to face …… .

2 State two methods that a business can use to measure customer satisfaction.

3 What is a customer panel?

4 True or false? A business which provides customers with opportunities to give their views, and has very low levels of complaint, is likely to have satisfied customers.

5 Which of the following would be effective in investigating a supermarket's customer service?

(a) The communication skills of check out staff.

(b) The number of employees under the age of 30.

(c) The cleanliness of the food displays.

(d) The price of a can of baked beans.

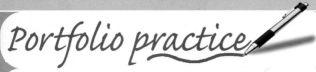

Portfolio practice

Sort-it plc

Sort-it plc sells cheap, self-assembly furniture in large stores with small numbers of sales staff. The business asked a group of customer service experts to investigate its customer service. Figure 1 shows some of the information collected by the group.

Figure 1

Sort-It plc Customer Service Report

- Customers said that many of the staff working in the stores were unhelpful and unwilling to offer advice. This information was given in customer panels that the business used to obtain views.
- In a questionnaire, customers said that the products offered by the business were extremely good value.
- Customer complaints were increasing. For the last three years they had been higher than those of rival home furnishing businesses.
- Many customers complained about the poor after-sales service. And they also said that their telephone calls to the stores were not answered.
- A frequent complaint was about the instructions for self-assembly furniture. Even after hours of trying, some customers had not been able to assemble the furniture they had bought. Some even got rid of it at the local tip. Many of these complaints had been registered on the business website, www.sort-it.com
- There had been large increases in sales levels over the previous year.

1. Using the information in the case, describe how the customer service experts investigated customer service at Sort-it plc. (3 marks)
2. Identify and explain three ways that the team of experts investigating Sort-it plc has collected information on customer satisfaction. (6 marks)
3. Using the information in the case, evaluate customer satisfaction with Sort-it plc. (8 marks)

Protecting the customer

Getting started...

Customers want to buy goods and services that are safe and of a high quality. They also want information about these goods and services to be correct. When they are not, customers are protected against unfair business practices by government and other agencies.

Case 1

Case 2

Case 3

Case 4

(a) What does the customer need protecting from in each of the examples above?

How are customers protected?

Health and safety laws

Some laws protect customers from harm or illness from goods or services.

- ✪ **The Consumer Safety Act, 1978** prevents the sale of goods which might harm customers. It concentrates mainly upon the safety of goods like children's toys and electrical goods.
- ✪ **The Food and Drugs Act, 1955** makes it illegal to sell food which is not fit to consume. It also lays down minimum standards about what must be contained in food.
- ✪ **The Food Safety Act, 1990** ensures that food is safe and does not mislead the customer in the way it is presented. It is an offence to sell food that does not comply with the Act, for example if it is contaminated, changed so that it becomes harmful or described in a misleading way.
- ✪ **The Food Safety (General Food Hygiene) Regulations, 1995** contains regulations about the preparation and storage of food and equipment.
- ✪ **The Consumer Protection Act, 1987** makes businesses liable if they sell defective goods that injure customers, such as faulty electrical equipment.

Labelling of products

Some laws protect customers against the way businesses label their products.

- ✪ **The Trade Description Act, 1968** states that it is illegal for products to be incorrectly described. For example, a pair of plastic shoes can not be described as being made of leather.
- ✪ **The Food labelling regulations, 1996** state exactly what information should be included on food labels, for example food additives or colourings.
- ✪ **The Sale of Goods Act, 1979** ensures that products do what they say on a label. For example, a waterproof jacket should not leak in the rain.

The sale of products or services

Some laws protect customers when they buy goods or services. These laws are concerned with the quality and quantity of goods and services and the way they are sold to customers.

- ✪ **The Weights and Measures Act, 1951** makes it illegal for a business to sell goods which are underweight or short measured, such as drinks in a bar.
- ✪ **Sales of Goods Act, 1979 and Supply of Goods Act, 1982** state that goods or services should meet certain conditions. They should:
  - be of MERCHANTABLE QUALITY, which means that they must not have any flaws or problems;
  - be fit for the purpose for which they were bought, for example, outdoor paint should not peel off after the first rain shower;
  - have prices that reflect the quality of the product or service, for example, a holiday firm should not charge customers for a four star quality hotel when it only had two stars.
- ✪ **The Sale and Supply of Goods Act, 1994** allows customers to return part of a product. A buyer of a six pack of beer might accept five but return one if there is something wrong with it.
- ✪ **The Consumer Protection Act, 1987** protects customers from defective goods and misleading pricing, for example a statement that a good is '£2 less than the manufacturer's recommended price' when it isn't.
- ✪ **The Unsolicited Goods Act, 1971** prevents businesses from demanding payment from customers for goods they have received but did not order. Unsolicited goods do not need to be paid for and customers can keep them if the seller has not collected them after six months.
- ✪ **The Consumer Credit Act, 1974** gives customers rights when they buy goods on credit. For example, customers must be given a copy of any credit agreement they have signed.

Misuse of information

Customers have to be protected so that information kept on them is accurate and only used for the right purpose. **The Data Protection Act, 1998** sets out rules about how information on consumers is handled, collected and stored as shown in Figure 1.

The use of personal information has many benefits, like improving medical care. But customers might find problems if the information kept on them is wrong, out of date or mixed up with someone else's. For example, a bank might not allow them credit. Also, customers must be asked permission if information gathered on them for one reason, such as paying by credit card, is used for another, such as sending them details of other loans through the post.

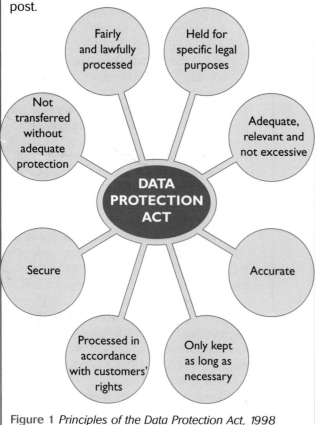

Figure 1 *Principles of the Data Protection Act, 1998*

Codes of practice

Codes of practice are rules which businesses voluntarily agree to keep. For example, the ADVERTISING STANDARDS AUTHORITY (ASA) checks advertising in the UK. It attempts to make sure that advertisers follow the British Code of Advertising and Sales Promotion Practice. This states that advertisements must be legal, decent, honest and truthful and must not cause grave or widespread offence. Other examples of Codes of Practice include the codes of the Association of British Travel Agents and the National House Building Council.

Getting help

Local authorities help to maintain standards. They have Trading Standards Officers who check weights and measures and investigate any businesses where there have been a number of complaints from customers. In serious cases, the business might be taken to court. Environmental Health Officers check on food hygiene and are responsible for enforcing the Food and Drugs Act.

Independent help can also be given by organisations like the Citizens' Advice Bureau. It provides free help and advice to customers about their rights, how to make complaints, getting replacements or taking businesses to the small claims court.

key terms

Advertising Standards Authority (ASA) – monitors advertising in the UK through various codes of practice.
Merchantable quality – where goods and services are fit for sale do not have any serious flaws or problems.

key terms key terms key terms key terms key terms key terms

Quick quiz

1. Match the five statements (a)-(e) to the correct law shown in (i)-(v).

Statement	**Law**

(a) A series of regulations about the preparation and storage of food and equipment.

(b) A law that makes businesses liable for any damage that defective goods may cause its customers.

(c) A law that makes it illegal for a business to sell goods which are underweight.

(d) Laws that state that goods or services should be of merchantable quality.

(e) A law that makes it illegal for products to be incorrectly described.

(i) Trade Description Act.

(ii) Sales of Goods Act and Supply of Goods Act.

(iii) Consumer Protection Act.

(iv) Food Safety (General Food Hygiene) Regulations.

(v) Weights and Measures Act.

2. Name two local authority providers that supply customers with help.

Portfolio practice

Ryan's Sandwich Bar

Tony Ryan has just set up a sandwich bar in the centre of Newcastle, competing with other similar shops in the area. His sandwiches are slightly cheaper than those of other shops and he promises to deliver orders free of charge within 15 minutes of receiving them. Tony advertises that he only uses the best quality fresh ingredients. He also offers a number of special ranges, such as low calorie sandwiches and sandwiches with special vegetarian fillings.

Tony has produced a leaflet advertising his sandwiches and services. He also runs a business website on the Internet.

Joanne is a vegetarian. She sees Ryan's advert and orders a Mediterranean chargrilled vegetable sandwich filled with melted low-fat mozzarella cheese. It is advertised as being suitable for vegetarians.

When the sandwich arrived, she was not impressed. It was 30 minutes late and she was charged for delivery. When she bit into the sandwich, she noticed three things.

- ✪ It had little bits of meat in it from another sandwich.
- ✪ The vegetables in the sandwich came had come from a frozen packet.
- ✪ There was a human hair in it.

She phoned Tony to complain and ask for her money back. But Tony was unwilling to provide a refund.

1. You are working for the Citizens' Advice Bureau. Produce a report for Joanne explaining how you feel Ryan's Sandwich Bar has broken the law. Explain each point and name the laws you think have been broken. (10 marks)

2. How might Joanne pursue her claim against Ryan's Sandwich Bar? (5 marks)

Business documents - buying and supplying goods

Getting started...

When businesses buy goods from suppliers, they use various documents. Some documents record details of the goods they have bought. Others are used to check that the right goods have been ordered and delivered. Documents are also used by the suppliers who are selling their goods. Think about the documents being used by the businesses below.

Case 1 Reynold's furnishings

Jacqui works in the purchasing department of Reynold's Furnishings. Her job is to find suppliers and order materials. She has just received the memo shown below. It is a request for some thread to finish an order for a customer.

Jacqui decides to order the thread from Robertson's Ltd. She writes details of the order - description, quantity, price and date - on an order form. She then posts this document to Robertson's.

> **MEMO**
>
> To: Jacqui
> From: William
> Date: 12.5.03
>
> We need some stronger thread to finish the Thompson's order. We will need it for next week. Could you find a supplier and order three rolls?
> Thank you.

Case 2
Frampton Construction

Jermaine is the stores manager at Frampton Construction. His job is to check all the goods that are delivered to the factory. He checks them off against the delivery document and notices that some are missing.

It is Jermaine's job to tell the supplier that some of the goods are missing. He uses a computer to print out a special form called a goods received note. This lists the goods received in the delivery and also shows any that are missing. Jermaine then posts the document to the supplier.

(a) What documents have Jacqui and Jermaine used?
(b) What are these documents used for?

What documents are used when ordering and delivering business goods?

Business documents

Figure 1 shows the main documents used by Samson's Ltd, a curtain manufacturer, when buying fabric from its supplier, Patel's Ltd. The first three documents are used when ordering and delivering goods. When Samson's wants some fabric, an ORDER FORM is sent to Patel's. When Patel's delivers the fabric, a DELIVERY NOTE is sent with it. When Samson's has checked the order, a GOODS RECEIVED NOTE is sent back to Patel's.

The diagram shows the order in which the documents are used. For example, an order form is sent before a delivery note is issued.

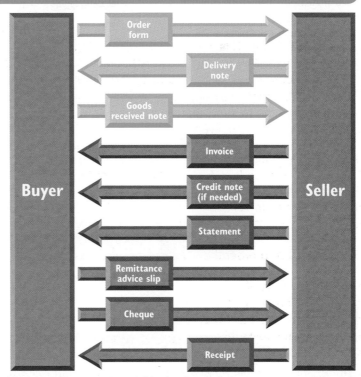

Figure 1 *Documents used by businesses*

Order form

An order form is sent to a supplier. It tells the supplier what goods are wanted and the quantity that should be sent. The information on an order form will include the:

- description of the goods;
- price per unit;
- date of order;
- order number;
- total price of the order;
- address of the supplier;
- address of the business placing the order;
- the date the goods are needed.

The order form shown in Figure 2 is used by Samson's to order fabric from Patel's.

ORDER FORM

Samson's
QUALITY CURTAINS

Samson's Ltd.
42 Luke Street
Uttoxeter
Staffordshire ST4 UX2
Tel: 0800 2378964
Fax: 01377 229876

To: Patel's Ltd.
12 Fox Street
Leicester
LE1 RT6

Purchase order: 038876
Date: 12.4.02

Item	Description	Quantity	Unit Price	Total Price
1	Black chintz	4m	£10.00 per m	£40.00
2	White lace	10m	£12.50 per m	£125.00
3	Blue cotton	8m	£8.00 per m	£64.00

Required by: 19.4.02
Terms: 30 days

Total order value £229.00

Figure 2 *Samson's order form*

Delivery note

Patel's sends a delivery note to Samson's with the goods. Samson's uses this to check that the goods on the note are the same as those delivered. The delivery note contains a description of the goods. It also states that Samson's has 30 days to pay. W Jones, who works for Samson's, has signed the delivery note to show that he has checked the delivery and that the goods on the note are the same as those delivered.

Figure 3 *A delivery note*

DELIVERY NOTE

Patel's Ltd

12 Fox Street, Leicester LEI RT6
Tel: 0600 488931

DELIVERY ADDRESS
Samson's Ltd.
42 Luke Street
Uttoxeter
Staffordshire ST4 UX2

Date: 18.4.03   Order No: 038876

Quantity	Description
4m	Black chintz
10m	White lace
8m	Blue cotton

Dispatch No: 0266
Account No: S290
Terms: 30 days

Checked by and signed on delivery:
W. Jones

Goods received note

This document is signed by the business receiving the goods. It is proof that the goods have been delivered.

Why are documents used in business?

The documents used by businesses are often called paperwork. Paperwork is needed to keep records of business TRANSACTIONS. This helps the business to calculate its total spending and total income for the year. Most of this paperwork can be processed by computer.

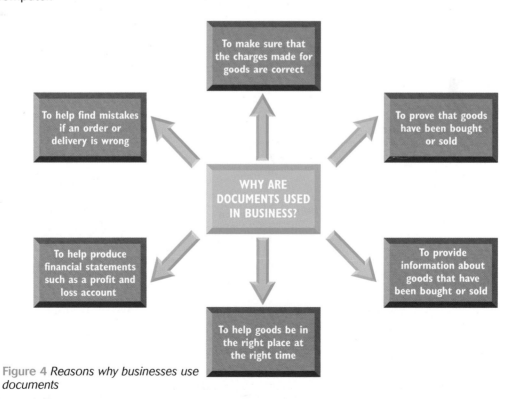

To make sure that the charges made for goods are correct

To help find mistakes if an order or delivery is wrong

To prove that goods have been bought or sold

WHY ARE DOCUMENTS USED IN BUSINESS?

To help produce financial statements such as a profit and loss account

To provide information about goods that have been bought or sold

To help goods be in the right place at the right time

Figure 4 *Reasons why businesses use documents*

key terms

Delivery note - *a document sent by the supplier with the goods so that they can be checked by the purchaser.*

Goods received note - *a document which is signed by the purchaser to prove that the goods have been delivered.*

Order form - *a document used by a purchaser to order goods from a supplier.*

Transactions - *the buying or selling of goods and services.*

Quick quiz

1 Look at Samson's order form.
   (a) What is the unit price of each item?
   (b) What is the total price of the order?
   (c) What is the order number?

2 Look at Figure 1 and decide if the following are true or false.
   (a) A delivery note is sent by the seller.
   (b) A delivery note is sent before an order form.

3 Which of the following is not found on an order form?
   (a) Date of order.
   (b) Order number.
   (c) Cheque number.
   (d) Address of supplier.

Exam practice

Prendergasts

Prendergasts processes and packs fresh vegetables for supermarkets. It buys its supplies from farms and wholesalers. Prendergasts requires 1,500 kilos of potatoes and 400 kilos of swedes from a local supplier. Potatoes cost 12p per kilo and swedes 19p per kilo. The order form below is used.

1. (a) Who will supply the potatoes and swedes? (1 mark)
   (b) When is the order required by? (1 mark)
   (c) How long does Prendergasts have to pay? (1 mark)
2. Prendergasts uses a goods received note, a delivery note and an order form. In what order would they be used? (2 marks)
3. Copy and complete the order form and calculate the total value of the order. (4 marks)
4. Explain 3 reasons why Prendergasts uses documents. (7 marks)

ORDER FORM

PRENDERGASTS
LIMITED

Prendergasts Ltd.
Unit 42
Scunthorpe Ind. Est.
Scunthorpe
ST3 TR4

To: Oldbarn Farm
     Market Rasen
     Lincolnshire

Purchase order: 2445
Date: 21.11.02
Date required: 25.11.02

Quantity	Description	Unit Price	Total Price

Total order value

Terms: 60 days

Figure 5 *Prendergast's order form*

Getting started...

Documents are used by businesses to tell customers how much they owe for the goods they have bought. Think about the documents being used in the cases below.

Case 1 *Techno plc*

Katie works for Techno plc in the finance office. Techno produces keyboards for computers. She has just received a document from Welland Ltd, a company that supplies screws to Techno. The document contains information about some screws bought by Techno a few days earlier. It gives a description of the screws and tells Techno that payment must be made within 30 days.

Case 2 *Conti*

Giovanni and Lorena Conti run a fruit and vegetable wholesaling business in Cardiff. Some of their suppliers deliver goods every day. Giovanni and Lorena do not pay these suppliers after every delivery. Instead, they get a statement each month showing how much they owe.

Case 3 *Helen's Health Store*

Helen runs a health food shop in Bath. She buys stock from a large number of suppliers. Sometimes her orders are short. This means that some of the goods ordered are missing from the delivery. When this happens, the supplier sends Helen a special document. It shows how much she has been over-charged. This amount will be deducted from her next payment.

What is the purpose of the documents received by:
(a) Techno plc
(b) Giovanni and Lorena Conti
(c) Helen's Health Store?

What documents are used to tell customers how much they owe?

Business documents

Figure 1 shows the main documents used by Patel's, a fabric supplier, when supplying fabric to Samson's Ltd, a curtain manfacturer.

The three documents in the centre of Figure 1 are used to tell Samson's about money that is owed. Patel's sends an INVOICE to Samson's to show how much is owed on its last order. The CREDIT NOTE is sent because Samson's has returned some goods and is owed money. Every month, Patel's sends Samson's a STATEMENT OF ACCOUNT to show Samson's how much it owes at the end of the month. The documents are used in this order.

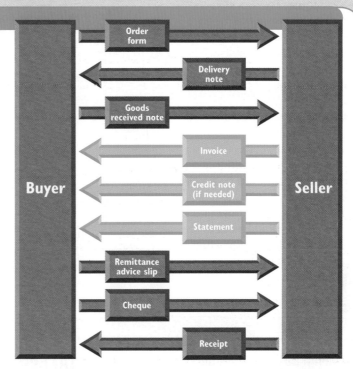

Figure 1 Documents used by businesses

Invoice

An invoice is like a bill. It states what is owed after goods have been delivered. Before making payment, a business will check that the goods on the invoice are the same as those delivered. Invoices show the:

- address of both the supplier and the customer;
- invoice, account and order numbers;
- date of order and date of delivery;
- description of the goods;
- amount of money owed on the order;
- amount of Value Added Tax charged - this is a tax on goods;
- payment terms.

INVOICE

Patel's Ltd
12 Fox Street, Leicester LEI RT6
Tel: 0600 488931 Fax: 01223 388769

To: Samson's Ltd
     42 Luke Street
     Uttoxeter
     Staffordshire
     ST4 UX2

Invoice No:	077665
Order No:	038876
Order Date:	12/4/02
Delivery Date:	18/4/02
Invoice Date:	20/4/02

Item	Description	Quantity	Unit Price	Total Price
1	Black chintz	4m	£10.00 per m	£40.00
2	White lace	10m	£12.50 per m	£125.00
3	Blue cotton	8m	£8.00 per m	£64.00

Dispatch No: 0266
Account No: S290
Terms: 30 days

Goods Total:	£229.00
Plus VAT @ 17.5%	£40.08
Invoice Total	£269.08

Figure 2 An invoice

Credit note

A credit note will be sent to a customer if:

- ☺ the customer has been overcharged;
- ☺ goods have been damaged or lost;
- ☺ goods are returned by the customer;
- ☺ not all the goods ordered were delivered.

A credit note is used to reduce the amount owed by a customer. It looks like an invoice. The one shown here was sent by Patel's Ltd to Samson's Ltd. It shows that the black chintz was returned.

CREDIT NOTE

Patel's Ltd

12 Fox Street, Leicester LE1 RT6
Tel: 0600 488931 Fax: 01223 388769

To: Samson's Ltd
     42 Luke Street
     Uttoxeter
     Staffordshire
     ST4 UX2

	Invoice No:	077665
	Order No:	038876
	Order Date:	12/4/02
	Delivery Date:	18/4/02
	Invoice Date:	20/4/02

Item	Description	Quantity	Unit Price	Total Price
1	Black chintz	4m	£10.00 per m	£40.00

Dispatch No: 0266
Account No: S290

Reason for credit:	Goods Total:	£40.00
Goods returned, colour faded in fabric.	Plus VAT @ 17.5%	£7.00
	Invoice Total	£47.00

Figure 3 *A credit note*

Statement of account

When a business buys goods from the same supplier many times a week or month, the business may arrange to have an account with the supplier. This means that one payment will be made at the end of the month. The supplier sends a statement which lists details of the invoices issued in the debit column.

Credit notes and payments received are shown in the credit column. The statement here is the one sent by Patel's Ltd to Samson's Ltd at the end of April 2002. It shows that Samson's owes Patel's £1,098.58.

STATEMENT OF ACCOUNT

Patel's Ltd

12 Fox Street, Leicester LE1 RT6
Tel: 0600 488931 Fax: 01223 388769

To: Samson's Ltd
    42 Luke Street
    Uttoxeter
    Staffordshire
    ST4 UX2

	Account No:	S290
	Statement No:	165

Date	Reference	Debit (£)	Credit (£)	Balance (£)
				654.00
Apr 1	Balance b/f			818.50
Apr 4	Invoice No.077601	164.50		1,053.50
Apr 6	Invoice No.077631	235.00		453.50
Apr 10	Payment(Thank you)		600.00	722.58
Apr 20	Invoice No.077665	269.08		675.58
Apr 21	Credit note No.115		47.00	1,098.58
Apr 27	Invoice No.077691	423.00		
Amount outstanding:				**£1,098.58**

Figure 4 *A statement of account*

VAT

Some documents will include an amount for VAT. This stands for Value Added Tax. It is calculated by working out 17.5% of the price of the goods. It is added to the price of the goods to arrive at the price inclusive of VAT. The invoice sent by Patel's shows VAT of £40.08. This is worked out as follows:

$$17.5\% \times £229.00 = £40.08$$

The VAT of £40.08 is added to £229.00 to give a total of £269.08. This is the price inclusive of VAT and is the total amount charged by Patel's for the order.

key terms

Credit note - *used to reduce the amount owed by a customer.*
Invoice - *shows how much is owed for an order.*

Statement of account - *shows a list of transactions and the amount owed at the end of the month.*

Quick quiz

1. Name the document that the supplier sends to a business when goods have been returned.
2. Name the document that is used to tell a customer how much is owed for an order.
3. Which of these documents is sent first?
   (a) Invoice. **(b)** Credit note. **(c)** Statement.
4. Look at the invoice sent by Patel's (Figure 2 on page 153). **(i)** Which of the following is the invoice number?
   (a) S290. **(b)** 0266. **(c)** 077665. **(d)** 038876.
   (ii) What is the total amount owed by Samson's?
   (a) £229.00. **(b)** £269.08. **(c)** £40.08. **(d)** £125.00.
   (iii) What is the amount of VAT owed by Samson's?
   (a) £229.00. **(b)** £269.08. **(c)** £40.08. **(d)** £125.00.

Exam practice

Wilkes & Co

Wilkes & Co sells sports and leisure products from its superstore in Coventry. One of its suppliers is Wilson's Ltd. Wilson's makes several deliveries a month to Wilkes.

On 23.5.2002, Wilkes returned some snooker equipment to Wilson's because it was damaged during delivery. Wilson's sent Wilkes a credit note on 26.5.2002 which appears on the monthly statement shown in Figure 5.

1. A credit note was sent for the damaged snooker equipment. State two other reasons why Wilson's might send a credit note to Wilkes & Co. (2 marks)
2. Look at the statement of account.
   (a) How much does Wilkes owe? (1 mark)
   (b) How much did Wilkes pay Wilson's in May? (1 mark)
   (c) What appears in the debit column? (1 mark)
3. Describe the information that a Wilson's invoice might contain. (4 marks)
4. Explain why Wilson's sends both an invoice and a statement to Wilkes. (7 marks)

STATEMENT OF ACCOUNT

Wilson's Ltd

24 Shaw Street, Bradford, Yorkshire
Tel: 0300 239812 Fax: 01478 232175

To: Wilkes & Co
   Unit 17 The Precinct
   Coventry, West Midlands

Account No: 221
Statement No: 211

Date	Reference	Debit (£)	Credit (£)	Balance (£)
May 1	Balance b/f			235.00
May 8	Invoice No.3411	117.50		352.50
May 16	Invoice No.3521	258.50		611.00
May 10	Payment(Thank you)		550.00	61.00
May 21	Invoice No.3641	356.00		417.00
May 26	Credit note No.013		188.00	229.00

Amount outstanding: **£229.00**

Figure 5

Business documents - paying for goods

Getting started...

Businesses use documents when they pay for the goods they have bought. What are these documents for and how do they work? Think about the documents used by the businesses below.

Case 1 Card and small gift shop

Anna Bedford owns a shop that sells greetings cards and small gifts. When she pays her suppliers she uses a special document. The document transfers money from her bank account to the supplier's bank account. It can be used to transfer any amount of money that Anna chooses.

Case 2 Photography studio

Kim So runs a photography studio. He takes high quality photographs at weddings and parties. When he receives a statement from one of his suppliers, there is a slip at the bottom. He tears this off and sends it back with his payment.

Case 3 Singh's Taxis

Amarjit Singh runs a taxi firm. When he buys petrol, he pays in cash. The sales assistant gives him a document that proves he has paid. It shows the amount paid, the date and time of the transaction and the sales assistant's name. Amarjit keeps this document and uses it when doing his bookkeeping.

Case 4 Newspaper printing

Printforce plc prints local newspapers for publishers in the Greater Manchester area. Most of the company's business documents are produced by computer. This saves time. Melissa, who works in the finance department, can process 20 payments in a fraction of the time it would take to do them by hand.

(a) What do (i) Anna Bedford (ii) Kim So and (iii) Amarjit Singh use documents for?
(b) Why does Printforce plc use a computer to produce documents?

How are goods paid for?

Business documents

The final three documents in Figure 1 are used when payment is made by Samson's, a curtain manufacturer, for the goods bought from Patel's, a supplier.

The CHEQUE is used to transfer money from Samson's bank account to Patel's bank account. The cheque is sent to Patel's with a REMITTANCE ADVICE SLIP. This was torn off the bottom of the statement of account sent by Patel's. When Patel's receives the cheque, a RECEIPT is sent to Samson's. The documents are used in this order.

Figure 1 *Documents used by businesses*

Cheques

A cheque is a document that tells a bank to transfer money from one account to another. Money is transferred from the DRAWER'S account to the PAYEE'S account. The drawer is the person or business making the payment. The payee is the person or business receiving the payment. If a cheque is not filled in properly and signed, it cannot be cashed and will be returned by the payee.

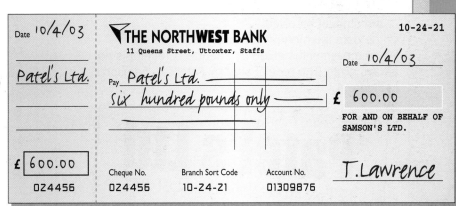

Figure 2 *A cheque used by Samson's (the drawer) to pay Patel's (the payee)*

A cheque used by Samson's to pay Patel's £600 on 10.4.03 is shown in Figure 2.
- The drawer is Samson's Ltd. £600 will be transferred from Samson's account.
- The payee is Patel's Ltd. £600 will be transferred into Patel's account.
- The cheque is dated 10.4.02 which is the date it is written out.
- The cheque is signed by T. Lawrence, an employee of Samson's. This is the AUTHORISED SIGNATORY because this employee has the legal right to sign cheques for Samson's.
- The payment of £600 is written in both words and figures. This gives extra security. A mistake is less likely to be made if the amount is written twice.
- The cheque has a COUNTERFOIL or CHEQUE STUB. This is a record of the cheque details. It stays in the cheque book after the cheque has been torn out.
- The cheque number helps to identify payments. Each cheque has a different number.
- The branch sort code identifies the branch of the bank where the account is held.
- The account number is the drawer's bank account number.

Remittance advice slip

When an invoice or statement is sent to a customer, it sometimes has a slip at the bottom that can be torn off and returned by the customer with the payment. This is called a remittance advice slip. It shows the customer's invoice or statement number so that the payment can be matched up with the correct invoice or statement. This also helps with record keeping. The slip sent by Patel's to Samson's and returned by Samson's is shown in Figure 3.

Please return this advice slip with your payment.

REMITTANCE ADVICE

Statement: No.165
Customer Account No: 5290

Amount paid

£600.00

Remittance Address
Patel's Ltd (Accounts)
12 Fox Street, Leicester LE1 RT6

Figure 3 *A remittance advice slip returned by Samson's to Patel's*

Receipt

When customers have paid, they are given a receipt as proof that payment has been made. Tills often produce a receipt automatically. The receipt shows:
- the supplier's name;
- the amount received;
- the date the money was received.

When a payment is made by cheque, a receipt is not always given. The receipt sent by Patel's to Samson's in Figure 4.

Patel's Ltd
12 Fox Street, Leicester LE1 RT6

RECEIPT

Receipt No: 18887
Total amount paid: £600.00
Method of payment: Cheque
Date Received: 12/4/03

THANK YOU

Figure 4 *A receipt sent by Patel's to Samson's after receiving payment*

Computerised systems

Many businesses use computers to record transactions and produce documents. The use of computers makes paperwork easier.

Advantages of computers
- Transactions are dealt with more quickly.
- They store a large amount of data.
- Fewer staff are needed to do paperwork.
- Information is readily available.
- They are accurate and make fewer mistakes.
- They are easy to use.

Disadvantages of computers
- High cost of equipment and training staff.
- Breakdowns can occur which cause delays and can be costly to repair.
- Jobs can be lost as fewer staff are needed.
- Computers can be infected by viruses and important information lost.

key terms

Authorised signatory - *a person who has the legal right to sign a cheque for a business.*

Cheque - *a document used to transfer money from one bank account to another.*

Counterfoil or cheque stub - *records details of the cheque.*

Drawer - *the person or business who writes out a cheque.*

Payee - *the person or business receiving payment when a cheque is used.*

Receipt - *a document used to confirm that payment has been made.*

Remittance advice slip - *sent with a payment to help match the payment with an invoice or statement.*

quick quiz

1 Fill in the missing words.

**Cheque number   Account number
Sort code**

A cheque contains three numbers. The ...... is the drawer's bank account number. The ...... identifies the branch where the account is held and the ...... helps to identify the payment.

2 True or false?

(a) Only an authorised signatory has the legal right to sign a cheque for a business.

(b) A cheque contains the name and address of the business.

(c) Sometimes, if a payment is made by cheque, a receipt is not given.

3 State three details shown on a receipt.

4 Why is the amount on a cheque written in both words and figures?

Exam practice

Gregson Security

Gregson Security sells security systems to shops and other businesses. Gregson Security buys equipment from a supplier, Tennison's Ltd. Ten days ago, it sent a payment to Tennison's for £670 and returned a remittance advice slip. The cheque is shown in Figure 5.

▼THE NORTHWEST BANK
22 Elm Square, Northampton, N'Hants NN1 2RE

54-23-12

Date 12/7/03

Pay *Tennison's Ltd.*

Six hundred and seventy pounds only

£ 670.00

FOR AND ON BEHALF OF
GREGSON SECURITY

Cheque No.
0005763

Branch Sort Code
54-23-12

Account No.
0146782

Figure 5 *Cheque sent by Gregson Security*

1. State the name of:
   (a) the drawer
   (b) the payee on the cheque. (2 marks)
2. Why has Tennison's Ltd returned the cheque? (2 marks)
3. Explain why Gregson Security has returned a remittance advice slip to Tennison's with its payment. (4 marks)
4. Gregson Security is considering buying a computer to handle its paperwork. What are the advantages and disadvantages to Gregson Security? Do you think this would be a good idea? (7 marks)

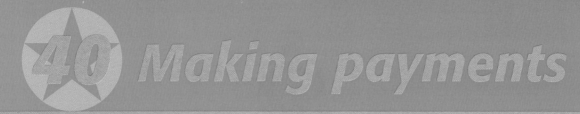

40 Making payments

Getting started...

Businesses make payments for what they buy. They can pay in different ways. They might use cash or cheques. Think about the methods being used by the businesses below.

Case 1 Michael's Hair Salon

I pay most of my bills by cheque. I pay bills such as gas, telephone and business rates by post. It is safe to send cheques in the post. Every month, I get a delivery of hair products. Two weeks later, I get a statement saying how much I owe. I pay this bill by cheque as well.

Case 2 Kim's market stall

I sell clothes from a market stall in Preston. Most of my customers pay in cash, so I often use cash to pay my bills. I buy my clothes from a wholesaler in Manchester. If I pay in cash, I get them cheaper. I employ a young lad to help me at weekends. He likes to be paid in cash. I also use cash to pay my weekly rent of £50.

Case 3 Pressman & Coppock

Pressman & Coppock are partners in a firm of Solicitors. Some of their payments are made directly from the business bank account. The £600 rent on the office is transferred automatically to the landlord's bank account on the first day of each month.

Pressman & Coppock	**N** **North West** Business Account		Sheet No. 103	
Date 31/05/03			Account No. 098755643	
Date	Payment Details	Payments	Receipts	Balance (£)
31 May	Balance brought forward from sheet 102			£115,600
31 May	Direct Debit to Claris Properti	£600		£115,000

Case 4 Wilson Engineering Ltd

Hannatu manages the company's office. She is in charge of making payments for the business. She uses a number of methods. The wages of part-time workers are paid in cash. The wages of full-time staff are paid directly into their bank accounts. Most suppliers are paid by cheque. When Hannatu is travelling, she pays for petrol using a company credit card.

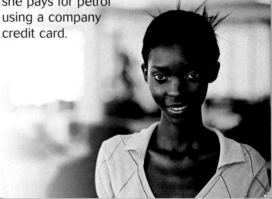

What methods of payment are being used at:
(a) Michael's Hair Salon
(b) Kim's market stall
(c) Pressman & Coppock
(d) Wilson Engineering Ltd?

What payment methods can a business use?

Cash

By cash we mean notes and coins. Cash is used by most businesses. It is best for small payments, such as stamps and stationery. Some businesses still pay their wages using cash. Most businesses also use non-cash methods.

Direct debit

A business can make payments automatically from its bank account by setting up a DIRECT DEBIT. This means that an amount of money is taken from the account at regular intervals. This method is used to pay for gas and electricity bills, where amounts may vary. The business receiving the payment has to apply to the bank for it. Charges made by the bank may be less than for cheques.

A **standing order** is similar. But the business making the payment tells the bank to pay the money. It is used when payments are the same each time.

Cheques

Cheques are often used by businesses. They transfer money from one bank account to another. They can be written for different amounts. It usually takes three days before a cheque is CLEARED. This means that the money does not leave the account for three days. Details of cheque payments are shown on a monthly bank statement.

Cheques are useful for paying bills by post, such as telephone bills. A business has to pay the bank for each cheque it uses. If many cheques are used, the cost to the business can be quite high.

Date 23/3/03

Birmingham Post.

£ 984.00

001298

12-32-91

▼ **THE NORTH**WEST **BANK**
21 New Street, Birmingham, B2 9AH

Date 23/3/03

Pay Birmingham Post

Nine hundred and eighty four pounds only

£ 984.00

FOR AND ON BEHALF OF
GREAT BARR TIMBER LTD.

R.Hayes

Cheque No.	Branch Sort Code	Account No.
001298	12-32-91	37856492

Debit cards

Plastic DEBIT CARDS, such as Switch or Delta, are used by some small businesses, such as sole traders. They might be used to buy materials from suppliers by a small builder, for example. They contain the cardholder's name and sometimes the business name. Unlike credit cards, money is transferred straight from the bank account when a payment is made.

Payments made with a debit card will be shown on a monthly bank statement in the same way as cheques. There is likely to be a limit on the amount that can be paid by debit card.

▼ **THE NORTH**WEST **BANK**
DEBIT CARD

Z10120 Z120Z120Z120

MR RAY HAYES
HAYES BUILDERS

£250

12-Z1-12 3Z3130313Z01 3 10/04
CODE NUMBER   CARD NUMBER   ISSUE EXPIRES END

Credit transfer

A CREDIT TRANSFER is an electronic method of payment. It allows a business to pay money straight into another bank account without using a cheque. It is often used when making a large number of similar types of payment, such as wages.

Details of payments are recorded on a computer and sent directly to the bank for processing. This system is called BACS (Bankers Automated Clearing System).

Unlike direct debits, the business or person receiving the payment does not have to apply to the bank for it.

Credit cards

CREDIT CARDS, such as Visa and Access, allow businesses to buy things and pay for them later. The credit card company makes the payment and then the business pays it back. The card contains information about the owner. This includes the name, signature on the back and account number.

Once a month, a statement is received from the credit card company. It shows all the purchases made and the amount owed. This should be paid by a date shown on the statement. If it isn't, the business will be charged interest. A business is not charged every time it uses a credit card. But it may pay an annual fee.

A credit card is a convenient way of making payment over the phone or the Internet. Payment can be made by reading out or typing in the details. But there is likely to be a limit on the amount that can be paid by credit card.

THE NORTHWEST BANK
CREDIT CARD

ZZZZ 1111 ZZZZ 1111

JOHNSON PETERS LTD

Z1Z1   VALID DATES 10/02-10/04

The advantages and disadvantages of payment methods

	Advantages	Disadvantages
Cash	✪ Quick ✪ Convenient ✪ No charge for use	✪ Can be stolen easily ✪ Payment is immediate
Cheques	✪ Used for postal payments ✪ Record of payment shown on a bank statement	✪ It takes 3 days before money leaves the bank account ✪ Charges made for use can be high
Credit cards	✪ Quick ✪ Convenient ✪ Can be used to get cash ✪ 'Free' credit period before payment is due ✪ Record of payment shown on a statement	✪ High interest rates charged if the amount due is not paid ✪ Not accepted by all businesses ✪ Likely to be a spending limit
Debit cards	✪ Quick ✪ Convenient ✪ Can be used to get cash ✪ Record of payment shown on a bank statement	✪ The money is taken from the bank account immediately ✪ Likely to be a spending limit
Direct debits	✪ Payment is automatic ✪ Useful for regular payments ✪ Record of payment shown on a bank statement ✪ Can be cheaper than cheques	✪ A business might forget a payment is being made and not have enough in its bank account ✪ Charges made for use ✪ Not suitable for single payments
Credit transfers	✪ Quick ✪ Convenient ✪ Record of payment shown on a bank statement	✪ The money is taken from the bank account immediately ✪ Cost of the system and charges for use

key terms

Cleared - *the time it takes to transfer money from one account to another when using a cheque.*
Credit card - *a plastic card which allows the user to buy now and pay later.*
Credit transfer - *the electronic transfer of money from one bank account to another.*
Debit card - *a plastic card used to transfer money from one bank account to another.*
Direct debit - *money taken regularly from a bank account when payment is due. The business receiving the money asks for payment.*

Quick quiz

1 True or false?
(a) Cash would be the best way to buy a machine costing £21,000.
(b) A cheque could be used to pay rent.
(c) A credit card could be used to pay wages.
2 How long does it usually take a cheque to clear?
(a) 4 days. (b) 3 days. (c) 3 weeks. (d) 7. days
3 What information is not contained on a credit card?
(a) Name. (b) Address. (c) Account Number. (d) Signature.
4 Fill in the missing words.

Statement   **Interest**   **Credit card**

A ...... allows a business to buy goods and pay for them later. The cardholder will be sent a ...... each month. This shows how much is owed. If the bill is not paid within a certain period ...... will be charged.

Exam practice

Mitchell's Ltd

Mitchell's bakes speciality bread products. It employs 30 staff at its Luton bakery. It uses a wide range of methods to make payments.

1. Look at Mitchell's bank statement.
    (a) Describe two methods of payment used by Mitchell's. (4 marks)
    (b) Calculate the total of the cheque payments made by Mitchell's. (2 marks)
    (c) Explain two advantages to Mitchell's of using cheques. (4 marks)
2. Mitchell's sometimes uses direct debits and credit cards. Compare these two methods of payment. (7 marks)

THE NORTHWEST BANK

Mitchell's Ltd.
23 Corn Street
Luton LT3 8YT
Tel: 01345 321456

Sheet No. 342

Current Account: Mitchell's Ltd
Statement Date: 27.6.03
Account No: 011762262002

Date	Payment Details	Taken Out	Paid In	Balance(£)
				2,349.80
1 Jun	Balance brought forward from sheet number 341			1,433.80
2 Jun	Direct Debit BRITISH GAS	916.00		142.80
4 Jun	Cheque 014432	1,291.00		4,177.20 OD
5 Jun	Cheque 014433	4,320.00		6,474.79
6 Jun	Credit 001049		10,651.99	6,388.79
6 Jun	Direct Debit BEDS.Council	86.00		856.09
7 Jun	BACS Wages	5,532.70		323.98
8 Jun	Cheque 014434	532.11		
				323.98
9 Jun	Balance carried forward to sheet number 343			

OD = Overdrawn

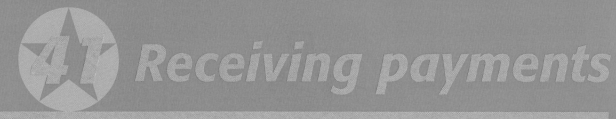
Getting started...

Businesses receive payments from customers in different ways. Think about the methods used in the following businesses.

Case 1 *Ronnie's Antique Cars*

My cars sell for more than £30,000, so I prefer people to pay by cheque. Customers can't drive the cars away immediately. They have to wait a few days until the money is safely in my bank account. I don't like to be paid £30,000 in cash because it is a lot of money to have in the car showroom. But I wouldn't turn it down if I thought I was going to lose a sale.

I WOULD HAVE PREFERRED A CHEQUE.

Case 2 *Play.com*

Play.com sells DVDs over the Internet. It accepts payment by credit card. Customers type in their credit card details onto an order form on the company's website. The DVDs are then sent out by post. Play.com keeps a record of credit card details. This makes it quick and easy to get payment for future orders.

Source: adapted from Play.com website.

Case 3 *Boots*

Boots The Chemist accepts many different types of payment. It might probably prefer you to pay in cash for a small item, such as a packet of energy tablets. Boots might accept cash, a cheque, a debit card or a credit card for a hairdryer. If you had built up enough points on your Boots Advantage Card you could buy a bottle of perfume.

(a) How do the businesses above receive payments?

What payment methods will a business accept from customers?

Cash

Small businesses often like to be paid in cash. They receive payment immediately, so the money can be used to buy other things straight away. Also, there are no charges for depositing cash into a bank.

But it can be risky dealing in cash because it can be stolen or lost. If there is a lot of cash, it may take time to pay it into the bank because it has to be counted.

Most people carry some cash around so businesses will accept it. Notes and certain coins are LEGAL TENDER in the UK. They should not be refused as a method of payment.

Electronic methods

A business may accept payment by electronic methods. Payment is instant and charges can be low.

- A **direct debit** is a way of receiving regular payments. Money is transferred automatically to a business's bank account. But the business must remember to ask the bank for the payment or it will not be paid. A direct debit gives control to the business asking for the payment because, for example, it can ask for different amounts each time a payment is due.
- A **standing order** solves the problem of remembering to ask for the payment. The business paying the money makes the payment. The business receiving the money doesn't have to ask for it. A standing order is used for regular payments of the same amount.
- A **credit transfer** is not used for regular payments. But a business might accept it for large numbers of the same type of payment.

Cheques

Many people have a bank current account which lets them pay for things with a cheque. Businesses may accept payment by cheque as long as the customer has a cheque guarantee card. This tells the business that the bank will guarantee to pay the amount that is shown on the cheque.

Businesses have to wait three working days before a cheque is cleared. Banks also charge businesses for every cheque paid into an account. If hundreds of cheques are paid in each week, the cost can be quite high.

key terms

key terms key terms

★ **Legal tender** - *cash is legal tender in the UK. By law, it should not be refused as payment of a debt.*

Debit cards

There is no time delay with debit cards. Money is transferred instantly. Businesses are charged for debit card transactions. Businesses also need a system to record the payments. Many have a machine that reads the debit card details when the card is 'swiped through'.

A business will only accept payment up to the limit shown on the debit card. This might be £100. The customer's bank will not guarantee payment over this limit. So a business might not accept it for larger payments.

Credit card

Businesses often accept credit card payments for more expensive items. The business is guaranteed payment by the credit card company. They are also useful for making payments over the phone or the Internet. A business records the customer's details and asks the credit card company for payment. Some businesses have their own credit cards, but they can only be used to buy goods from that business. Examples are Marks & Spencer, Burtons and Debenhams.

Credit card companies may charge businesses quite high rates for each transaction. If it was 5%, the charge for accepting a £500 credit card payment would be £25 (5% x £500). Small businesses might refuse to accept payment by credit card because of the high cost. A business is also unlikely to accept payment by credit card for small purchases, such as a newspaper.

Businesses accepting credit card payments may have a machine that reads the credit card details.

Loyalty cards

A shop may accept payment by loyalty card. Customers earn points when they buy goods from a shop. These points are worth an amount of money. When enough points are earned, they can be exchanged for goods sold in that shop. Examples of shops with these cards include Boots and WHSmith. Some cards allow customers to earn points to buy petrol.

These cards are used to retain customers. Shops hope that customers will keep coming back until they earn enough points to exchange them for other goods.

Quick quiz

1 Which one of the following is most likely to be accepted by a shop in payment for a newspaper that costs 30p?
   (a) Cheque.
   (b) Direct debit.
   (c) Cash.
   (d) Credit card.

2 Which of the following methods of payment is unlikely to be accepted for a trolley of goods at a supermarket?
   (a) Cheque.
   (b) Cash.
   (c) Debit card.
   (d) Direct debit.

3 True or false?
   (a) Businesses selling goods on the Internet are most likely to accept payment in cash.
   (b) There is no time delay in receiving payment with a debit card.

4 State two advantages for businesses of receiving payment by direct debit.

Exam practice

Antonelli's

Gina and Roberto Antonelli run a small restaurant in Bristol. Most of their customers are regulars. They usually pay for their meals by cash or cheque.

In the last year more tourists have used the restaurant. They often want to use credit and debit cards to pay for their meals. But this has caused problems because the restaurant doesn't accept them. Gina thinks they should start accepting payments by credit and debit cards in future. Roberto is not so sure.

1. Describe two problems that Antonelli's might have if the business won't accept payment by credit and debit cards. (4 marks)
2. What are the advantages and disadvantages to the business of receiving payments by cash and cheque? (6 marks)
3. Should Antonelli's accept payment by credit and debit card in future? Give reasons for your answer. (7 marks)

Getting started...

> Businesses have to pay for the resources they use. These expenses might include wages, raw materials, rent and insurance. They are called COSTS. Think about the costs of the businesses in the cases below.

Case 1 *Dixons*

Dixons is a national chain store that sells electrical goods. It buys stock such as radios, televisions, CD players, video recorders, video cameras and computer hardware from suppliers. It employs managers and sales assistants in all its stores. Dixons also has to pay quarterly bills such as electricity and telephone. It advertises to attract customers.

Case 2 *Beverley's Dating Agency*

Beverley is planning to set up a dating agency in Birmingham. Before she can start trading, she needs to buy a computer and some special software. She will have to buy some office furniture, a video camera and recorder and a television. She will also have to pay for some questionnaires to be printed so that customer information can be recorded.

Case 3 *Pride Farm*

Pride Farm is owned by Beth and Archie Summers. Unfortunately, the farm is not doing very well. It owes £150,000 to the bank and has to pay £1,125 interest every month. This is on top of everyday expenses such as those shown in the photographs.

> Describe the costs of:
> *(a) Dixons*
> *(b) Beverley's Dating Agency*
> *(c) Pride Farm.*

What costs does a business have?

Start-up costs

Some costs have to be met before a new business can start trading. These are called START-UP COSTS. Start-up costs will differ depending on what sort of business is being set up.

⊗ Retailers may have to buy stock, fixtures and fittings, a cash register and premises.

⊗ Manufacturers will have to buy plant, machinery, equipment, tools, raw materials and parts. The start-up costs for manufacturers are often high.

⊗ Businesses that sell services, such as estate agents, vets and financial services, also have start-up costs. They might include office furniture, computers and equipment.

Existing businesses may also have to meet start-up costs. This is likely when a new product is about to be launched. A business may do market research and buy new equipment before the new product can go into production.

Running costs

Once a business has been set up it will carry on buying resources. It will have to meet its RUNNING COSTS. These are the day-to-day expenses that result from trading. Running costs have to be paid for all the time. Retailers, manufacturers and service providers have many similar running costs. Examples of the running costs of a food manufacturer are shown in Figure 1.

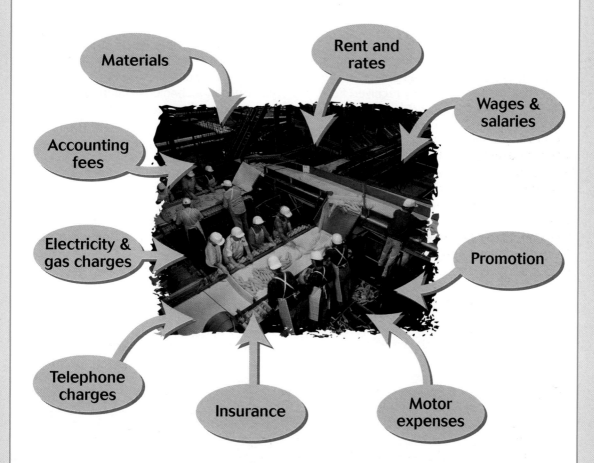

Figure 1 *Examples of the running costs of a food manufacturing business*

Covering start-up costs

When a new business is set up or a new product launched, all the costs must be covered. To begin with, a business must have enough money to meet the start-up costs.

Think about Emma Wright who is going to open a camping equipment shop. She needs £20,000 to cover the cost of stock, rent, fixtures and fittings and other items. Where will this money come from?

Figure 2 shows some possible sources. Emma decides to use £12,000 of her own money (capital). She also borrows £7,000 from the bank. A government grant of £1,000 for a small business like Emma's might also be available.

Businesses launching a new product might use profits from previous years to meet start-up costs.

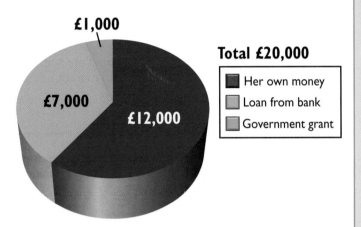

£1,000

£7,000

£12,000

Total £20,000

■ Her own money
■ Loan from bank
■ Government grant

Figure 2 *How Emma's start-up costs can be covered*

Covering running costs

The ongoing running costs also have to be covered. However, most of the money to cover these costs will come from REVENUE. This is the money received from selling goods and services. Emma's revenue will come from selling camping equipment in her shop. Other examples of income might be:
☼ interest from money held in a bank deposit account;
☼ rent from property owned by the business;
☼ income from investments, such as dividends from shares.

Reducing costs

If a business reduces its costs, it can increase its profits. One way of reducing costs is to make more use of IT (information technology). Information can be stored and processed more quickly and accurately using IT. Examples of IT uses in business include the following.
☼ **Word processing.** Standard documents, such as letters, reports, and invoices can be produced professionally.
☼ **Databases.** Electronic filing systems can store huge quantities of information which can be sorted and retrieved instantly.
☼ **Stock control.** Retailers can use computers and bar codes to keep track of stock movements in the store. Computers can be programmed to order stock automatically when required.
☼ **Email.** Messages can be sent more efficiently, cheaper and faster by email than by post.

key terms

Costs – expenses that must be met when setting up and running a business.
Revenue – money a business gets from selling its goods or services.
Running costs – ongoing expenses that result from trading.
Start-up costs – expenses that must be paid before trading can begin.

key terms key terms key terms

Quick quiz

1 Fill in the missing words.   **Bank loan   Machinery   Market research**

After doing some....... Pelham Ltd decided to launch a new type of motorcycle. Its main start-up cost was for...... . It decided to raise most of the money from a ....

2 True or false?

(a) Raw materials are a running cost.

(b) Capital is provided by owners.

(c) Using email is a way of reducing costs.

3 Which of the following would not be used to meet start-up costs?

(a) Capital.   **(c)** Revenue.

(b) Government grant.   **(d)** Bank loan.

4 Which of the following is not a running cost?

(a) Wages.   **(c)** Rates.

(b) Premises.   **(d)** Interest.

Techno Toys UK

Techno Toys UK makes toys and games in its Dudley factory. In 2002 it spent a lot of money developing a new toy - a remote controlled talking bear. The money was spent on market research and building a working model. It took the company four months to complete development and set up a new production line. After six months, 40,000 bears had been produced and the following costs had to be met.

- ✪ Developing the toy   £60,000
- ✪ New production line   £100,000
- ✪ Production wages   £55,000
- ✪ Materials & parts   £23,000
- ✪ Other running costs   £43,000

1. Calculate (a) the total start-up costs (b) the total running costs for Techno Toys UK. (4 marks)
2. Explain the difference between start-up costs and running costs for Techno Toys UK. (6 marks)
3. Explain how Techno Toys UK might cover the start-up and running costs described. (7 marks)

Getting started...

There are different types of business costs. Some costs stay the same when a business produces more output. But other costs go up when more is produced. Think about the costs faced by the following businesses.

Case 1 Powergen

Powergen produces a large amount of the nation's electricity. One of the main costs in electricity generation is constructing a power station. These building costs are not connected with the amount of electricity it produces in the future. In the winter, Powergen has to produce more electricity. This means it has to buy fuel.

Source: adapted from Powergen plc, Annual Review.

Case 2 Kitchenfit

Julie Patterson owns Kitchenfit and rents an office for £1,000 a month in Bromsgrove. She designs and fits kitchens. Once a design has been agreed with a customer, Julie buys the kitchen units and equipment from local suppliers. She then pays Arturo Delgado £400 for fitting each kitchen.

Case 3 Renton's Sportswear

Renton's Sportswear is located in the centre of Portsmouth. Two of its main costs are interest of £900 on a bank loan and rates of £350. These are paid monthly. Other large costs include stock purchases and paying wages to sales assistants. To cope with busy weekends, the owner employs extra part-time staff on Saturday and Sunday.

Identify the costs that increase when output increases for:
(a) Powergen
(b) Kitchenfit
(c) Renton's Sportswear.

How do costs change when a business produces more products?

Fixed costs

Costs that stay the same when a business changes the level of output are called FIXED COSTS. When a manufacturer produces more products in its factory, it does not have to pay more rent to the landlord. Rent and rates are fixed costs. Other examples of fixed costs include:

- ☼ machinery, tools and equipment;
- ☼ premises;
- ☼ insurance;
- ☼ interest payments.

Fixed costs can be shown on a graph. Figure 1 shows the fixed costs for Ruth's ice cream business. She sells ice creams from a van which she rents for £100 per week. The van rental stays at £100 whether Ruth 400 ice creams or 1,000. It is a fixed cost.

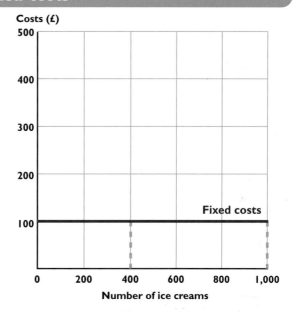

Figure 1 *Fixed costs for Ruth's ice cream business*

Variable costs

Costs that change when the level of output changes are called VARIABLE COSTS. When a manufacturer makes more products, the business will have to buy more raw materials. These raw materials are variable costs. Other examples of variable costs are:

- ☼ packaging;
- ☼ power;
- ☼ factory wages.

Variable costs can also be shown on a graph. Figure 2 shows the variable costs for Ruth's ice cream business. Ruth buys in ice creams from a wholesaler for 50p each. The graph shows that if Ruth buys in 1,000 ice creams a week, total variable costs will be £500 (1,000 x 50p). If she only buys in 400 ice creams, total variable costs fall to £200 (400 x 50p). As the graph shows, when output changes, variable costs also change.

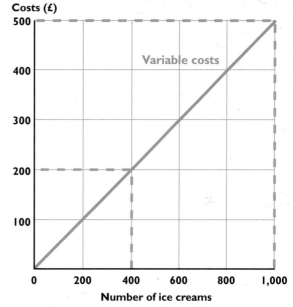

Figure 2 *Variable costs for Ruth's ice cream business*

Total costs

If fixed costs and variable costs are added together, we get TOTAL COSTS.

Total cost = fixed cost + total variable cost

If Ruth buys in 1,000 ice creams a week, total costs will be:

Total cost = £100 + (50p x 1,000)
Total cost = £100 + £500
Total cost = £600

The total cost graph in Figure 3 shows that total costs are £600 when 1,000 ice creams are sold. The graph also shows fixed costs.

Figure 3 *Total costs for Ruth's ice cream business*

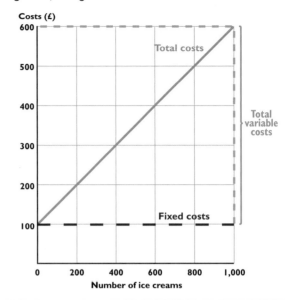

Total revenue

TOTAL REVENUE is the amount of money a business gets from selling its output. It is calculated by multiplying the number of units of output sold by the selling price.

Total revenue = output x price

In the example above, if Ruth sold 1,000 ice creams for £1 each, what would be the value of total revenue?

Total revenue = £1 x 1,000
Total revenue = £1,000

So if Ruth charges £1 each for her ice creams, total revenue will be £1,000. The graph for total revenue is shown in Figure 4. When 400 ice creams are sold, total revenue is £400. When 1,000 ice creams are sold, total revenue is £1,000. But this money is not profit. Ruth still has to cover her costs of £600 out of this £1,000. Profit for 1,000 ice creams is:

Total revenue - total cost = £1,000 - £600 = £400.

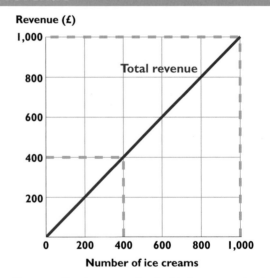

Figure 4 *Total revenue for Ruth's ice cream business*

key terms

- **Fixed costs** – *costs that stay the same at all levels of output.*
- **Total costs** – *fixed costs and variable costs added together.*
- **Total revenue** – *the amount of money a business gets when selling its output.*
- **Variable costs** – *costs that change when output changes. They will go up when output is increased.*

key terms key terms key terms key terms key terms key terms

Quick quiz

1 Which of these is not a fixed cost?
(a) Rent.   **(b)** Wages.
(c) Rates.   **(d)** Machinery.

2 Which of these costs will not increase when output increases?
(a) Wages.   **(b)** Raw materials.
(c) Electricity.   **(d)** Rent.

3 True or false?
(a) Retailers do not have any fixed costs.

(b) Fixed costs = variable costs + total costs.

(c) Variable costs decrease when output is reduced.

4 What is total revenue if 5,000 units are sold for £5.50?

5 If fixed costs are £12,000 and variable costs are £10 per unit, what is total cost if 1,000 units of output are produced?

Exam practice

Nicols Baskets

Joyce Nicols rents a large greenhouse for £100 per month. She produces decorative hanging baskets. As well as her rent, she has other fixed costs of £100 per month.

Variable costs per basket include wire baskets 50p, chains 70p, moss 30p and plants 250p. So they are £4.00 per basket. The total costs, fixed costs and total variable costs are shown in Figure 5.

1. Using examples from the case, explain the difference between fixed costs and variable costs. (4 marks)
2. Using information from Figure 5, complete Table 1. (7 marks)
3. (a) Calculate how much it would cost the business to make 300 hanging baskets in a month. (4 marks).
   (b) Explain what would happen to total costs if the business was shut down for 2 months. (5 marks)

Figure 5 *Costs of Nicols Baskets*

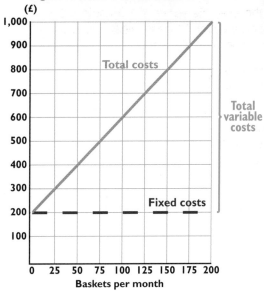

Table 1 *Costs of Nicols Baskets*

No. of Baskets	0	25	50	75	100	125	150	175	200
Fixed costs	£200	£200							
Variable costs	£0	£100							
Total costs	£200	£300							

Getting started...

The flow of money into and out of a business is called **CASH FLOW**. Money flows out of a business when payments are made. Money flows into a business when income is received. Think about the ways money is flowing into and out of the businesses below.

Case 1 *Aston Villa FC*

Aston Villa FC is a Premier League football club. It is also a public limited company. Just before the season starts, it receives money from the sale of season tickets. It also gets money from a Sky TV deal. The club's main costs are the player's wages and the upkeep of the stadium. In August 2002, it sold one of its players to Middlesbrough for £5 million.

Identify the ways in which money is flowing into and out of:
(a) Aston Villa FC
(b) Sally Ryan's Pet Shop
(c) Hedges & Co.

Case 2 *Ryan's Book Shop*

Sally Ryan owns a book shop in Hull. On 31 January 2003, she paid £250 to a supplier for large picture books for young children. On 2 February 2003, she paid an electricity bill of £65.40. At the end of the week, she paid £385 business takings into the bank and paid her part-time helper £60. All payments were made by cheque.

Case 3 *Hedges & Co*

Hedges & Co is a coach company. In May 2003, it received £600 after taking a party of school children to Ireland. However, the business went overdrawn in May. It had to pay for some expensive repairs to one of its coaches along with a large VAT bill, insurance and business rates. In June, the company was charged £140 interest on its bank overdraft, but it did receive £700 from the sale of an old mini bus.

How does cash flow into and out of a business?

Cash inflows

The money coming into a business is often called a CASH INFLOW. Money flows into a business when income is received. Examples of cash inflows could include sales revenue, loans, new capital from the owners, investment income, such as interest or dividends, government grants and cash from the sale of assets. Expected cash inflows for March 2003 for Luptons Ltd, a manufacturer of clothing, are shown in Figure 1.

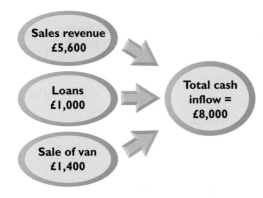

Figure 1 *Expected cash inflows for March 2003 for Luptons Ltd*

Cash outflows

The money going out of a business is often called a CASH OUTFLOW. Money flows out of a business when payments are made. Examples of cash outflows could include payments for materials, wages, telephone, electricity, new machinery, loan repayments and tax payments. Expected cash outflows for March 2003 are shown in Figure 2 for Luptons Ltd.

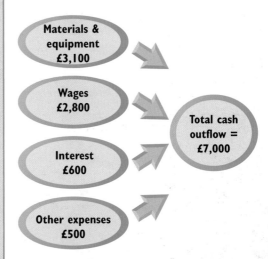

Figure 2 *Expected cash outflows for March 2003 for Luptons Ltd*

Cash flow forecasts

The information on cash inflows and cash outflows from Figures 1 and 2 can be used to prepare a CASH FLOW FORECAST. The cash flow forecast for Luptons Ltd is shown in Figure 3. It is a three month forecast.

The forecast shows that Luptons' cash position is expected to get worse over the next three months. At the end of March, Luptons is expected to have £3,000. However, by the end of May, this falls to only £500. In April and May, the cash outflows are expected to be bigger than the cash inflows. This is why the closing balance falls.

Opening balance
The amount of cash the business has at the start of the month, ie £2,000 at the beginning of March.

Total cash inflow
The total cash Luptons expects to receive during the month, ie £8,000 in March.

Total cash outflow
The total amount of cash Luptons expects to spend during the month, ie £7,000 in March.

Inflow - outflow
The difference between the cash coming in and the cash going out. For March it is £1,000 (£8,000 - £7,000).

Closing balance
The opening balance plus the difference between the cash coming in and the cash going out. For March it is £3,000 (£2,000 + £1,000). The closing balance for March is also the opening balance for April.

Figure 3 *Cash flow forecast for three months for Luptons Ltd*

	March	April	May
			£
Opening balance	2,000	3,000	1,500
Cash inflows			
Sales revenue	5,600	5,800	6,000
Loan	1,000		
Sale of van	1,400		
Total cash inflows	8,000	5,800	6,000
Cash outflows			
Materials & equipment	3,100	3,200	3,300
Wages	2,800	2,800	2,800
Interest	600	600	600
Other expenses	500	700	300
Total cash outflows	7,000	7,300	7,000
Inflow - outflow	1,000	-1,500	-1,000
Closing balance	3,000	1,500	500

key terms

key terms key terms key terms key terms key terms

Quick quiz

1. Which of the following is a cash inflow?
   (a) Wages. **(b)** Interest paid.
   (c) Rent. **(d)** Sales revenue.

2. Which of the following is a cash outflow?
   (a) Bank loan. **(b)** Capital.
   (c) Sales revenue. **(d)** Rates.

3. The opening balance in a cash flow forecast is £23,000. The difference between the cash coming in and the cash going out is £67,000. What is the closing balance?
   (a) £23,000. **(b)** £90,000.
   (c) £67,000. **(d)** £44,000.

4. True or false?
   (a) A dividend received is a cash inflow.
   (b) The purchase of a new lorry would not appear in a cash flow forecast.

5. In a cash flow forecast, the opening balance is £4,500. Total cash inflows are £6,500 and total cash outflows are £13,600. What is the closing balance?

Exam practice

The Wilmslow Music Centre

Mark Robinson owns the Wilmslow Music Centre, a shop selling CDs and music videos. Every three months, he prepares a cash flow forecast to help him check the cash flow in his business. A forecast for the beginning of 2003 is shown in Figure 4, but it is not yet complete.

	Jan	Feb	Mar
Opening balance	1,200	?	?
Cash inflows			
Sales revenue	3,400	3,600	4,100
Interest received	0	200	0
Total cash inflows	3,400	3,800	4,100
Cash outflows			
Stock	2,000	2,400	2,900
Casual labour	500	550	550
Rent	400	400	400
Other expenses	700	1,000	750
Total cash outflows	?	?	?
Inflow - outflow	?	?	?
Closing balance	?	?	?

£

1. Using examples from this case, explain the difference between cash inflows and cash outflows. (4 marks)

2. Complete the cash flow forecast for the Wilmslow Music Centre to show:
   (a) the total cash outflows in each month;
   (b) the closing balance for January, February and March;
   (c) the opening balance for February and March. (8 marks)

3. Is the cash position expected to improve or worsen for the Wilmslow Music Centre? Explain your answer. (4 marks)

Figure 4 *Cash flow forecast for the Wilmslow Music Centre*

Using cash flow forecasts

Getting started...

Cash is often said to be the lifeblood of a business. This means that without cash a business will collapse. Producing a cash flow forecast can help a business control its cash and avoid cash flow problems. Think about the problems faced by the businesses below.

Case 1 The Seafront Hotel

The Seafront Hotel is located near the coast in Cornwall. It is full of guests in the summer, but almost empty in the winter. This is a difficult time for the hotel owner because the bills still have to be paid even though the hotel's receipts are much lower. He is often in danger of running out of cash in the winter.

Case 2 Rainford Ltd

Rainford Ltd builds houses. It is building a house for a customer that will cost £180,000. When building began, it received a deposit of £18,000 from the customer. The company is £15,400 overdrawn at the bank and needs another £31,000 to complete the house. It hopes that the bank will agree to lend this money.

Case 3 Weston Mill

Weston Mill makes fabric for clothes manufacturers. The business has been struggling due to foreign competition, but it has managed to survive by offering good customer service. Unfortunately, an essential machine has broken down and must be replaced. This will cost £25,000 and will use up all the cash of the business.

What problems are faced by:
(a) The Seafront Hotel
(b) Rainford Ltd
(c) Weston Mill?

How do businesses use cash flow forecasts?

Cash flow forecasts

Cash flow forecasts allow businesses to check their cash position. They don't want to run out of cash. A cash flow forecast can also be used to help in planning, for example, to make sure that money is available when it is needed. Cash flow forecasts can also help in making the following decisions.

- Producing new goods or services. When a business launches a new product it must be able to predict the likely cash inflows and outflows. This will help to determine whether it is going to be successful or not.

- Investing in new resources. A cash flow forecast will help determine whether or not a business can afford new equipment. It is best to buy new resources when cash balances are high.

- Carrying out new activities. Many businesses try to sell their products in new markets. Predicting cash inflows and outflows from a new activity can help a business to decide whether it is going to succeed.

Cash flow problems

A business can have a number of cash flow problems. These are shown in Figure 1.

TOO MUCH CASH

Cash does not earn any income for a business. It should be used to buy resources or invested in an account that pays interest.

OUTFLOWS EXCEED INFLOWS

Eventually, the business will run out of cash. This means that it will have to get money from somewhere or close down. Borrowing money is expensive.

UNEXPECTED BILLS

Unexpected bills, such as a tax demand, mean that cash will be used up. This can cause trading difficulties if important resources, such as materials, can't be bought.

Figure 1 *Cash flow problems*

Spreadsheets and cash flow forecasts

Cash flow forecasts can be produced using a computer SPREADSHEET. This can show inflows, outflows and cash balances in a grid. The grid has blank boxes called cells which are arranged in rows and columns. In a cash flow forecast, all the cash inflows and outflows for a particular month are listed in the same column. The type of inflow or outflow makes up each row. Using spreadsheets has benefits.

- It saves time.
- Fewer mistakes are made.
- Totals and balances are calculated automatically by the computer.
- Totals and balances are adjusted automatically when a change is made.
- The computer can draw graphs and charts from the information in the spreadsheet.

Using a spreadsheet

Sam Jarvis runs the Dog and Duck pub. He produced a three month cash flow forecast using a spreadsheet is shown in Figure 2. Sam entered the opening balance, cash inflows and cash outflows. The totals, closing balances and new opening balances were calculated automatically by the computer.

The day after the forecast was produced, he found out that his business rates would go up from £500 to £1,000 per month. He changed the three rates figures in the spreadsheet and the new totals and balances were changed automatically. The amended forecast is shown in Figure 3. The figures in green are the changes made by the spreadsheet programme for January.

	Jan	Feb	Mar £
Opening balance	8,500	13,200	18,600
Cash inflows			
Takings	12,000	13,000	14,000
Rent received	1,000	1,000	1,000
Total cash inflows	13,000	14,000	15,000
Cash outflows			
Stock			
Wages	6,000	6,500	7,000
Rates	1,200	1,300	1,500
Other expenses	500	500	500
	600	300	700
Total cash outflows	8,300	8,600	9,700
Inflow - outflow	4,700	5,400	5,300
Closing balance	13,200	18,600	23,900

Figure 2 *Cash flow forecast for the Dog & Duck*

	Jan	Feb	Mar £
Opening balance	8,500	12,700	17,600
Cash inflows			
Takings	12,000	13,000	14,000
Rent received	1,000	1,000	1,000
Total cash inflows	13,000	14,000	15,000
Cash outflows			
Stock			
Wages	6,000	6,500	7,000
Rates	1,200	1,300	1,500
Other expenses	1,000	1,000	1,000
	600	300	700
Total cash outflows	8,800	9,100	10,200
Inflow - outflow	4,200	4,900	4,800
Closing balance	12,700	17,600	22,400

Figure 3 *Amended cash flow forecast for the Dog & Duck*

Cash and profit

Cash is not the same as profit. A good cash balance is possible even when a business is making a loss. For example, a business would have a lot of cash if it had just taken out a bank loan. Also, a profitable business may have a small cash balance. It might be waiting for a lot of payments from its customers.

key terms

Spreadsheet – a grid made up of cells where figures are entered in columns and rows.

key terms key terms

Quick quiz

1 True or false?

(a) A cash flow forecast might be produced to see whether a new product is likely to be successful.

(b) A business with a good cash flow must be profitable.

(c) An unexpected bill can cause a cash flow problem.

2 Fill in the missing words. **Cells   Computer   Column   Spreadsheet**

A cash flow forecast can be produced on a .... All the figures are entered in .... Figures for the same month will appear in the same .... Totals and balances are calculated automatically by the ....

3 State:

(a) three ways a business might use a cash flow forecast;

(b) three advantages of spreadsheets;

(c) why having too much cash can be a problem for a business.

Exam practice

Amos Motors

Ayalla Amos runs Amos Motors, a motorcycle shop. The business is doing well and she is thinking of expanding by building an extension onto the showroom. This will cost £75,000, but she doesn't want to borrow more than £30,000. Ayalla is hoping that there will be enough cash in the business to pay the rest. Some financial details are given below for the last three months of the year.

1. (a) Produce the three month cash flow forecast for Amos Motors. The opening balance is £11,000. You could use a spreadsheet to do this. (5 marks)
(b) At the beginning of October, an unexpected VAT bill for £3,000 had to be paid. Adjust the cash flow forecast to take this into account. (3 marks)

2. Using the adjusted forecast, explain whether Ayalla will be able to expand her business without borrowing more than £30,000. (4 marks)

3. When Ayalla first set up the business, she experienced cash flow problems. Explain two factors that might have caused her to have cash flow problems. (4 marks)

			£
	October	November	December
Inflows			
Revenue	100,000	120,000	130,000
Outflows			
Stock purchases	75,000	85,000	100,000
Salaries	4,000	4,000	5,000
Motor maintenance	2,000	2,000	3,000
Other expenses	7,000	8,000	12,000

46 Budgets

Getting started...

Planning is important in business. Many businesses forecast their future income and expenditure when planning. These forecasts or plans may be presented in a BUDGET. Think about the forecasts made by the businesses below.

Case 1 *Harpenden Fire Alarms*

Harpenden Fire Alarms makes three types of fire alarm. At the beginning of each quarter, Ricky Jones, the owner, predicts the sales revenue for each alarm. The Standard Alarm sells for £20, the Office Alarm sells for £25 and the Extra Alarm for £40. Ricky uses the sales revenue forecast to help predict the company's income for the quarter.

(£)			
	Jan	Feb	Mar
Standard	10,000	11,000	13,000
Office	2,000	2,000	2,000
Extra	5,000	6,000	7,000
Total revenue	**17,000**	**19,000**	**22,000**

Case 2 *Arnold's Ltd*

Arnold's Ltd produces a range of ladies clothing. Every four months, the production manager is required to prepare a production cost budget. This shows the costs of producing the planned output for the four month period. It helps the purchasing department to plan orders for materials and the finance department to plan the cash needed to meet production costs.

(£)				
	Jan	Feb	Mar	Apr
Silk & cotton	6,000	7,000	8,000	9,000
Other raw materials	3,000	3,500	4,500	5,000
Wages	8,000	8,000	9,000	9,000
Factory overheads	5,000	5,000	5,000	5,000
Total production costs	**22,000**	**23,500**	**26,500**	**28,000**

(a) What do the two businesses above use their budgets for?

What different types of budget do businesses have?

What is a budget?

A budget is a plan. It shows how much money a business plans to spend or receive in the future. Budgets may be presented as a table or on a spreadsheet. Each column represents monthly expenditure or income plans. Budgets are usually prepared for 6 or 12 month periods. Table 1 shows a 6 month overheads budget for Quinn Ceramics. What does it show? It shows that spending is different in each month and the business plans to increase spending on overhead costs over the six months.

Table 1 *Overheads budget for Quinn Ceramics*

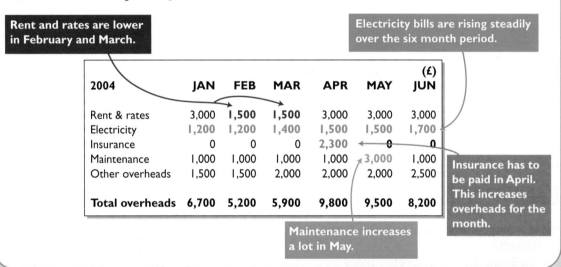

Rent and rates are lower in February and March.

Electricity bills are rising steadily over the six month period.

2004	JAN	FEB	MAR	APR	MAY	JUN (£)
Rent & rates	3,000	1,500	1,500	3,000	3,000	3,000
Electricity	1,200	1,200	1,400	1,500	1,500	1,700
Insurance	0	0	0	2,300	0	0
Maintenance	1,000	1,000	1,000	1,000	3,000	1,000
Other overheads	1,500	1,500	2,000	2,000	2,000	2,500
Total overheads	**6,700**	**5,200**	**5,900**	**9,800**	**9,500**	**8,200**

Insurance has to be paid in April. This increases overheads for the month.

Maintenance increases a lot in May.

Sales budgets

SALES BUDGETS are important because they usually affect all other budgets. For example, if a business plans to increase sales, then it will also have to increase production. The sales budget can show units of output or sales revenue. Table 2 shows the sales revenue plans for Asif Mahood's tent making business.

Table 2 *Sales budget for Asif Mahood's tent business*

2004	JUL	AUG	SEP	OCT	NOV	DEC (£)
Dome	400,000	400,000	300,000	300,000	200,000	100,000
Frame	250,500	250,500	200,000	200,000	200,000	100,000
Ridge	100,000	100,000	50,000	20,000	10,000	10,000

The budget shows that tent sales generally fall as the winter approaches. However, sales of ridge tents are expected to fall more sharply than the other types of tent.

Production budgets

PRODUCTION BUDGETS are used to plan production levels. They show what the business expects to produce in the future. They are influenced by the sales budget. Production budgets can show units of output or production costs. Below is a production budget for Asif Mahood's tent making business. It shows the output that is being planned.

Table 3 *Production budget for Asif Mahood's tent business*

2004						Number of tents
	JUL	**AUG**	**SEP**	**OCT**	**NOV**	**DEC**
Dome	3,000	3,000	3,000	3,000	3,000	3,000
Frame	2,000	2,000	2,000	2,000	2,000	2,000
Ridge	500	500	500	500	500	500

Table 3 shows the planned production levels for the period. Asif plans to produce the same number of tents each month. This makes it easier to organise production. But he must be careful not to produce too many, or too few, using this method. He might find that sales of ridge tents are very low in the new year.

Other types of budget

Many different budgets can be prepared by a business.
- ○ Materials budgets show the types and quantities of materials that the business plans to use.
- ○ Labour budgets show the types and quantities of labour that the business plans to use.
- ○ Departmental budgets show how much each department in a business plans to spend, for example the marketing or human resources department.
- ○ Capital expenditure budgets show the amount to be spent on machinery and equipment.

key terms

Marketing and production departments have to agree on budgets

Quick quiz

1. True or false?
   (a) A budget is a plan.
   (b) Budgets contain predicted financial information.
   (c) Budgets show how much money a business spent last year.
   (d) Budgets can show income or expenditure.
2. Which of the following would not appear in a budget?
   (a) Predicted costs.   (b) Past sales figures.   (c) Forecast sales.
   (d) Planned output levels.
3. State:
   (a) three examples of types of budget that a retailer might produce;
   (b) three things that might appear in a production cost budget for a builder.

Exam practice

Carters Ltd

Carters Ltd manufactures test equipment used in laboratories. The company uses budgets to help manage its finances. Below is a sales budget and a production cost budget for the first 6 months of 2004. Each machine is sold for £500.

Table 4 *Sales budget 2004*

						(£)
	JAN	FEB	MAR	APR	MAY	JUN
No. of machines	40	40	44	44	50	50
Revenue (£)	20,000	20,000	22,000	22,000	25,000	25,000

Table 5 *Production cost budget 2004*

						(£)
	JAN	FEB	MAR	APR	MAY	JUN
Raw materials	2,000	2,000	2,200	2,200	2,500	2,500
Components	3,000	3,000	3,300	3,300	4,000	4,000
Wages	6,000	6,000	6,600	7,000	8,000	8,000
Subcontracting	1,000	1,000	1,200	1,200	2,000	2,000
Overheads	7,000	7,000	7,000	7,000	8,000	8,000
Total	19,000	19,000	20,300	20,700	24,500	24,500

1. Calculate the (a) planned total revenue and (b) planned total cost for the six month period. (2 marks)
2. Using examples in this case, explain the difference between a sales budget and a production costs budget. (6 marks)
3. The company is worried that its costs are rising too fast. Is there any evidence in the budgets to suggest that it is right to be worried? (7 marks)

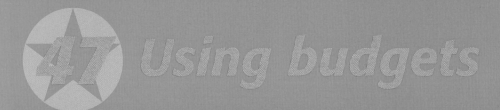

Using budgets

Getting started...

Budgets can help a business to manage its spending and check on its performance. It is possible to control spending by using budgets. For example, if £100,000 is given to the marketing department for its planned spending, the business knows that the department cannot spend more. Think about the way budgets are used by the businesses below.

Case 1 *Matteo's Ltd*

Matteo's Ltd is a small chain of butcher's shops in Yorkshire. Every year, the manager in each shop has to produce an overheads budget. If the spending on overheads is greater than the budgeted amount, the manager has to meet with Laura Matteo, the owner, to explain why more than the agreed amount has been spent.

Case 2 *Quantex plc*

Quantex plc makes a wide range of cloth and fabrics. Budgets are used to check on performance. At the end of each year, the production manager looks at the difference between the budgeted production costs and the actual costs. If the actual costs are higher than the budgeted costs, the manager tries to find out why. This approach helps to keep costs down.

BUDGETED COSTS £20,000

ACTUAL COSTS £50,000

Case 3 *Securance plc*

Securance plc sells life assurance policies. Each year, the sales staff produce a sales budget for their area. This budget is then agreed with the area manager. If sales are the same as those in the budget, a bonus is paid. If sales are greater than the forecast, a bigger bonus is paid. Securance believes that this helps to motivate its staff.

Securance plc

Life Policy

...e plc

...n West Office

SALES TARGETS

APRIL
10,010

MAY
11,288

JUNE
9,765

How are budgets used by:
(a) Matteo's Ltd
(b) Quantex plc
(c) Securance plc?

How are budgets used by businesses?

To plan and control spending

Budgets are used to plan spending. If a business plans what it is going to spend each month in the coming year, it is less likely to overspend. If a business overspends, it could run out of cash and go bankrupt.

A budget will help to keep spending under control. This is because BUDGET HOLDERS are not allowed to spend more than the planned amount. Too much or unnecessary spending will be stopped.

To reduce fraud

Budgets can help reduce fraud in a business. All spending in a business has to be authorised by budget holders. This means that no one else can spend money without the budget holder's permission. This stops staff from spending money fraudulently, such as buying things for their own personal use.

Variances

A VARIANCE occurs when a business spends more or less than its budget. Table 1 below shows budgeted production costs, actual costs and variances for Jenkins & Son, a manufacturer of exhaust systems.

Table 1 *Production cost budget and actual costs for Jenkins & Son (2003)*

						(£000)
	JAN	FEB	MAR	APR	MAY	JUN
Budgeted production costs	140	145	150	150	160	160
Actual costs	139	143	150	151	164	169
Variance	- 1	- 2	0	+ 1	+ 4	+ 9

- means the business underspends
+ means the business overspends

In January, actual costs were £139,000 but budgeted production costs were £140,00. So actual costs were £1,000 lower than budgeted costs. It is good if the business spends less than planned.

In June budgeted costs were £160,000 but actual costs were £169,000. So, actual costs were £9,000 greater than budgeted costs. This is bad because the business has overspent. Jenkins & Son will try to find out why the business has overspent so that they can take steps to avoid this happening again next year.

To motivate staff

Budgets can be used to encourage staff to work harder and be more efficient. It is common to reward staff if they reach targets set in sales forecasts. This encourages them to sell more. Staff can also be rewarded if actual costs are lower than the budgeted costs. This discourages staff from wasting business resources.

MONTHLY BUDGETED SALES TARGET	ACTUAL SALES	BONUS
£10,000	£10,300	YES
£10,000	£8,000	NO

MONTHLY BUDGETED COST TARGET	ACTUAL COSTS	BONUS
£6,000	£8,000	NO
£6,000	£4,300	YES

Quick quiz

1. True or false?
   (a) Budgets can be used to help motivate workers.
   (b) If actual costs are greater than budgeted costs, the business will be happy.
   (c) Budgets help a business not to overspend.

2. Choose the correct word to complete the following sentences.
   Underspent   Overspent   Accountants   Budget holders
   (a) If actual wages are less than budgeted wages, the budget will be ....
   (b) Only ...... are authorised to spend a firm's money.

3. If actual costs are £120,000 and budgeted costs are £140,000, what is the effect?
   (a) £140,000 underspent.   (b) £20,000 overspent.
   (c) £120,000 underspent.   (d) £20,000 underspent.

4. What will budgets help to reduce?
   (a) Sales.   (b) Dividends.
   (c) Fraud.   (d) Staff turnover.

key terms

Budget holder – a person in charge of a budget and authorised to spend money.
Variance – the difference between a budgeted and an actual outcome. This can be overspending or underspending.

key terms key terms key terms key terms key terms key terms ke

Exam practice

Callum Foods

Callum Foods is a large food processing company. It has five departments and each one uses budgets to help improve efficiency. Table 2 below shows budgeted costs, actual costs and variances for the five divisions in 2002.

Table 2 *Budgeted costs for Callum Foods*

(£000)

	Frozen food	Canned food	Dry goods	Drinks	Dairy products
Raw materials	3,900	2,700	4,300	6,200	4,900
Wages	3,000	2,800	5,700	5,000	2,500
Overheads	2,000	2,000	2,000	2,000	2,000
Total costs	8,900	7,500	12,000	13,200	9,400
Actual costs	9,000	7,100	11,100	13,600	9,400
Variances	+ 100	- 400	- 900	+ 400	0

Helen Callum, the financial controller, analyses the variances very carefully at the end of each year. She uses them to identify areas of inefficiency.

1. (a) The variance for the Dairy Products department is 0. What does this mean? (1 mark)
   (b) How is the variance for the Frozen Food department calculated? (1 mark)
2. Did the Dry Goods department spend more or less than expected? Explain your answer. (2 marks)
3. Explain how Helen Callum uses this budget. (4 marks)
4. Discuss other possible uses of budgets for Callum Foods. (7 marks)

Break-even

Getting started...

Businesses have to know how much they need to produce and sell to cover their costs. If their costs are not covered, they will make a LOSS. If revenue is greater than costs, they will make a PROFIT. If costs are exactly the same as revenue, the firm will BREAK-EVEN. What is happening to the businesses below?

Case 1 *Alice's Burgers*

Alice Jones leases a mobile kitchen for £200 a week. She parks it in a lay-by on the busy A40 near Cheltenham. She sells burgers for £1 each. Last week, she sold 400 burgers so her total revenue was £400. Her total costs were £440 made up of £200 for the lease and £240 to make the burgers. Alice wasn't very happy with this.

Case 2 *Harrison's Ltd*

Harrison's Ltd assembles satellite dishes for a major TV broadcaster. Its fixed costs were £500,000 last year. Variable costs were £30 per dish and 25,000 dishes were made. So its total variable costs were £750,000. Its total revenue from sales was £1,250,000.

Case 3 *J Sainsbury plc*

J Sainsbury plc is a large UK and US food retailer. Its activities include Sainsbury's Supermarkets and Sainsbury's Bank in the UK and Shaw's Supermarkets in the US. In 2002 its total revenue was £18,200 million. Its total costs were £17,600 million.

Are:
(a) Alice's Burgers
(b) Harrison's Ltd
(c) J Sainsbury plc
making a loss, a profit or breaking even?

What is meant by breaking even?

The break-even point

A business will break-even when its total cost (TC) is exactly the same as total revenue (TR). This is called the BREAK-EVEN POINT.

For example, if a business produces 5,000 units and sells them for £2 each, total revenue will be £10,000. If total costs are also £10,000, the business is breaking even and 5,000 units is the break-even point. A business does not make a loss or a profit at the break-even point.

Figure 1 shows that a profit (P) is made when TR is greater than TC. A loss (L) is made when TC is greater than TR. The business breaks-even when TR is the same as TC.

Figure 1 *Profit, loss and Break even*

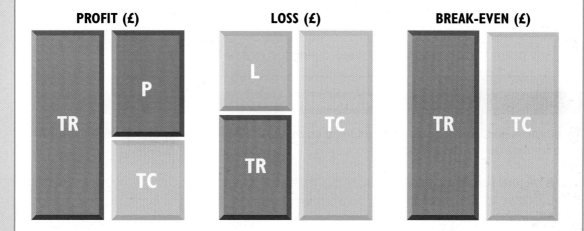

Calculating the break-even point

To calculate the break-even point for a business, we need to know:
- fixed cost;
- variable costs per unit;
- selling price per unit.

The following formula can be used to calculate the break-even point.

$$\text{Break-even point} = \frac{\text{Fixed cost}}{\text{Price per unit} - \text{variable cost per unit}}$$

A worked example

Eric Kerr runs the Salcombe Guest House. His fixed costs are £6,000 a year and variable costs are £20 per room. He charges guests £35 per night for a room.

How many times must he let his rooms during the year for his business to break even?

$$\text{Break-even point} = \frac{\text{Fixed cost}}{\text{Price per unit} - \text{variable cost per unit}}$$

$$= \frac{£6,000}{£35 - £20}$$

$$= \frac{£6,000}{£15}$$

$$= 400 \text{ times}$$

So, Eric needs to let his rooms 400 times during the year to break-even.

Calculating profit

A business can use information about fixed costs, variable costs and prices to calculate profit. The formula below can be used.

Profit = total revenue − total cost

where:
total revenue = price x quantity sold;
total cost = fixed cost + total variable cost

How much profit would the Salcombe Guest House make if the rooms were let 1,000 times during the year?

Total revenue = price per room x quantity let out
Total revenue = £35 x 1,000 = £35,000

Total costs are fixed costs plus total variable costs (variable cost per room x number of rooms)
Total costs = £6,000 + £20,000 (£20 x 1,000) = £26,000

So profit = £35,000 - £26,000 = £9,000

key terms

- **Break-even/break-even point** – *where total costs and total revenue are exactly the same. Neither a profit nor a loss is made.*
- **Loss** – *the amount by which total cost is greater than total revenue.*
- **Profit** – *the amount by which total revenue is greater than total cost.*

key terms key terms key terms key terms key terms key te

Quick quiz

1 True or false?

(a) A business will break even if total revenue is greater than total cost.

(b) If total costs are £4 million and total revenue is £4 million a business will break even.

2 Fill in the missing word in the formula below shown by the (?).

The formula for break-even point is:

$$\frac{\text{Fixed cost}}{\text{price} - (?)}$$

3 **(a)** A business has fixed costs of £10,000 and variable costs of £5 per unit. It sells each unit for £9. Which of the following is the break-even point?

(i) 5,000 units. **(ii)** 2,500 units.

(iii) £2,000. **(iv)** £5,000.

(b) What profit is made if 3,000 units are sold?

4 A business breaks-even when total revenue is £100,000 on the sale of 5,000 units.

(a) What is the total cost?

(b) What is the selling price per unit?

Exam practice

Warrington Caravans

Warrington Caravans Ltd makes caravans. The company rents a factory on an industrial estate in Warrington. The selling price of each caravan is £10,000. The production costs are listed below.

- Rent - £130,000 a year.
- Other fixed costs - £170,000 a year.
- Materials - £1,000 per caravan.
- Labour - £2,000 per caravan.
- Other variable costs - £1,000 per caravan.

1. How much are (a) the fixed costs and (b) the variable costs for Warrington Caravans? (2 marks)
2. How many caravans would Warrington Caravans Ltd need to produce to break-even? (4 marks)
3. How much profit would be made if 80 caravans were sold? (4 marks)
4. What would be the new break-even point if fixed costs rose to £320,000 a year and each caravan was sold for £12,000? (3 marks)
5. Is the business better off when costs and prices are higher? Explain your answer. (4 marks)

Break-even charts

Getting started...

A business can show its costs, revenue and profit on a graph. It is called a BREAK-EVEN CHART. It shows where a business breaks-even. This is where its total revenue is the same as its total costs. Look at the break-even charts for the businesses below.

Case 1 *Riah Watson*

Riah Watson started a business making decorative curtain poles. She sold them to a local dealer for £20 each. Fixed costs were £4,000 and variable costs £10 per pole. Her aim was to break-even and she achieved this after one year. The break-even chart shows this.

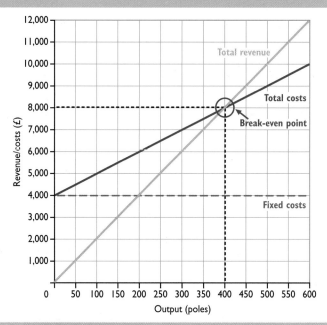

Case 2 *Wozniak Engineering*

Wozniak Engineering has an order for 9,000 circuit boards from a computer manufacturer. The customer has agreed to pay £10 per board. The fixed costs of the business are £30,000 and the total variable costs are £45,000, so total costs are £75,000 to produce 9,000 boards. A break-even chart has been drawn which shows that the order will make £15,000 profit.

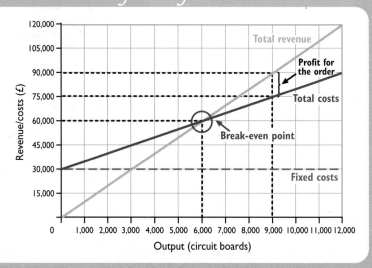

(a) Look at the break-even chart for Riah Watson.
(i) How many poles does she need to make and sell to break-even (where total revenue equals total costs)?
(ii) What are total costs and total revenue at the break-even point?

(b) Look at the break-even chart of Wozniak Engineering.
(i) How many circuit boards does it need to make and sell to break-even?
(ii) Does the business have to produce more or less than the break-even point to meet the order?

What do break-even charts tell a business?

Break-even charts

The break-even chart shows the lines for total costs, total revenue and fixed costs at each level of output. The main purpose of the break-even chart is to show the break-even point. This is where the total revenue and total cost lines cross. Total revenue and total costs are the same at the break-even point.

The break-even chart for Jack Tanner's business is shown in Figure 1. He makes traditional wooden baby chairs which he sells for £100 each. Fixed costs are £20,000. They do not change as output changes. Variable costs are £50 for each chair. Last year, Jack produced and sold 600 chairs.

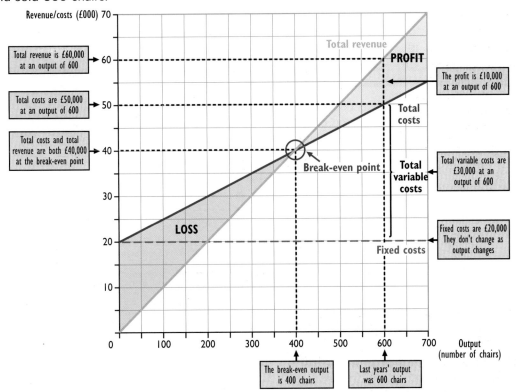

Figure 1

What does the break-even chart for Jack Tanner's business show?
- The horizontal axis measures output. This is the number of chairs that the business makes.
- The vertical axis measures costs and revenue. It also shows profit or loss, which is calculated by revenue - costs.
- Jack Tanner's business breaks-even when 400 chairs are produced and sold. Here total revenue and total costs are the same at £40,000.
  Total revenue = 400 chairs x £100 price = £40,000
  Total costs   = fixed costs of £20,000 + total variable costs of £20,000 (£50 per chair x 400 chairs)
                        = £40,000
- Any output level below the break-even point of 400 chairs leads to a loss.
- Any output above the break-even point gives a profit.
- Jack Tanner's business made a profit when 600 chairs were produced and sold.
  Total revenue =   £100 x 600 = £60,000
  Total costs   =   £20,000 + (£50 x 600) = £20,000 + £30,000 = £50,000
  So profit when 600 chairs are made and sold is:
  Total revenue - total cost = £60,000 - £50,000 = £10,000

Changes in price

What happens when the price is changed?
- ☼ If Jack Tanner raises the price, the total revenue line swings up. This is shown in Figure 2 where the total revenue line is now Total revenue 2. This means that the business needs to make and sell less to break-even. The break-even output falls to 200 chairs. It also means that more profit will be made at every level of output.
- ☼ If price is reduced, the total revenue line swings down. This means that the break-even output is higher.

Figure 2

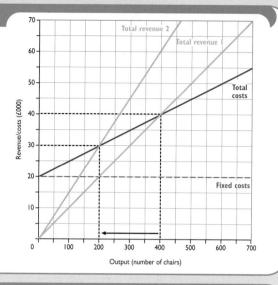

Changes in fixed costs

What happens when fixed costs change?
- ☼ If Jack's fixed costs rise, the fixed cost line moves up to Fixed Costs 2 in Figure 3. The total cost line will also move up to Total costs 2. More needs to made and sold to break-even. The break-even output rises to 600 chairs. Profits are lower at every level of output.
- ☼ If fixed costs are cut, the fixed and total cost lines will move down. This means the break-even output will be lower and the profit higher.

Figure 3

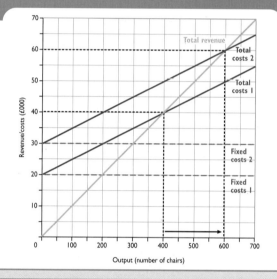

Changes in variable costs

What happens when variable costs change?
- ☼ If Jack's variable costs rise, the total cost line swings up to Total costs 2 in Figure 4. The business will need to make and sell more to break-even. The break-even point rises to 500 chairs. Profits will be lower at every level of output.
- ☼ If variable costs go down, the variable cost line swings down. This means that the break-even output will be lower and the profits higher.

Figure 4

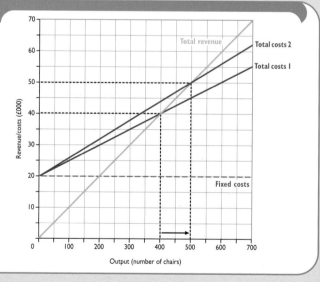

key terms

☼ **Break-even chart** – *a graph showing total cost, total revenue and fixed cost. It shows the break-even point of a business, where total costs equal total revenue.*

key terms key terms key terms key terms key terms key te

Quick quiz

1 True or false?

(a) A break-even chart will show the profit made at different levels of output.

(b) Output is measured on the vertical axis on a break-even chart.

(c) When fixed costs rise, the break-even point falls.

2 Which of these lines is not shown on a break-even chart?

(a) Total cost. (b) Variable cost.
(c) Total revenue.(d) Fixed cost.

3 Which of the following businesses are:
(i) breaking even; (ii) making a profit?

(a) Total revenue is £700 000 and total costs are £500 000.

(b) Total revenue is £100,000. Fixed costs are £20,000 and total variable costs are £80,000.

(c) Total revenue is £20,000. Fixed costs are £5,000, variable costs per product are £5 and the business makes and sells 3,000 products.

(d) A business makes and sells 100 products. The selling price is £500. The fixed costs are £15,000 and the variable costs are £300 for each product.

4 What will cause the break-even point to rise?

(a) Increase in price.

(b) Fall in variable cost.

(c) Fall in fixed cost.

(d) Decrease in price.

Exam practice

Mossock Hall Nursing Home

Mossock Hall Nursing Home has room for up to 40 elderly patients. It currently has 30 patients staying there. Mossock Hall has fixed costs of £100,000 a year and variable costs are £5,000 for each patient. The local authority which pays for the patients is charged £10,000 per patient. The break-even chart for the business is shown in Figure 5.

1. Using the break-even chart, identify:
   (a) the number of patients needed to break-even; (1 mark)
   (b) total costs and revenue at the break-even point; (1 mark)
   (c) total revenue when there are 30 patients; (1 mark)
   (d) profit when there are 30 patients. (1 mark)
2. If Mossock Hall had 40 patients, what would be:
   (a) the total revenue; (1 mark)
   (b) the profit? (2 marks)
3. The owner wants to reduce the break-even point of the business. Explain how this might be done. (6 marks)

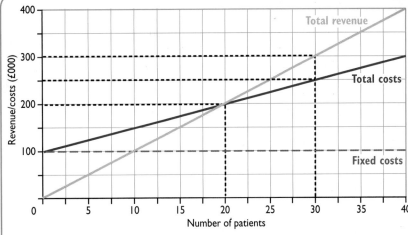

Figure 5

Getting started...

The profit or loss of a business can be calculated by looking at its revenues and its costs over a year. Look at the revenues and costs recorded by the businesses below.

Case 1 *William Carr Associates*

William Carr provides financial advice on tax, pensions, savings and insurance. He receives fees from his clients for giving this advice. He also receives commission from insurance companies for selling their polices. In 2002 he received £128,000 from fees and £175,000 in commissions. His total income was £303,000. He had expenses of £210,000 for his secretary's wages, office expenses, rent and advertising. His profit was therefore £93,000.

Case 2 *Bastian*

Eduard Bastian owns a menswear store. He sells designer label suits, casual wear, shoes and fashion accessories. He calculates his profit by using two steps:
- subtracting the cost of stock purchased from annual sales;
- subtracting overheads from the above figure.

In 2002 his sales were £165,000, stock purchased £75,000 and overheads £53,000. So his profit was £37,000.

Case 3 *Larsen & Son*

Larsen & Son makes jewellery in their factory in Birmingham. In 2002 sales were £467,000. The cost of raw materials, such as precious metals and stones, was £120,000. Employees' wages were £186,000 and general overheads £165,000. Larsen's accountant calculates profit by subtracting wages and raw materials from sales and then subtracting overheads from the answer. In 2002 Larsen & Son made a loss of £4,000.

Explain how the profit or loss was calculated for:
(a) William Carr Associates
(b) Bastian
(c) Larsen & Son.

How can profit and loss be calculated?

Calculating profit and loss

Businesses usually calculate their profit and loss at the end of a FINANCIAL YEAR. This is a 12 month trading period, e.g. from 1 February 2003 to 31 January 2004. To calculate profit, a business needs to know the value of SALES, the COST OF SALES and EXPENSES.

Sales

The total amount of money a business receives from selling goods or services is called sales. It is sometimes called turnover or total revenue.

Cost of sales

For a retailer, cost of sales is the amount paid for stock. This is sometimes called PURCHASES. For a manufacturer, cost of sales is the amount paid for raw materials and components plus the wages paid to factory workers. The amount paid for raw materials and components may also be called purchases.

Expenses

Expenses are the overheads that businesses have to meet. They include all the other miscellaneous costs that have to be paid. Examples of expenses are:
- rent & rates;
- administration costs;
- heating and lighting;
- advertising;
- motor expenses;
- telephone;
- printing and stationery;
- insurance;
- accountancy fees.

Gross profit and net profit

A business normally calculates its profit using two steps. First it calculates GROSS PROFIT. This is profit before expenses and is found by using:

Gross profit = sales – cost of sales

Then it calculates NET PROFIT. This is profit after expenses. Net profit is found by using:

Net profit = gross profit - expenses

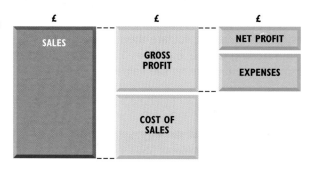

Figure 1 *Calculating gross and net profit*

Sometimes businesses also receive other types of income, such as interest. Net profit is then:

Gross profit - expenses + income

Some of the net profit might be used to pay **taxation**. The rest might be paid to **owners** of the business or **put back** into the business.

Calculating profit for a retailer

Igor Balis owns a toy shop. In 2002 sales were £198,000. Purchases of toys cost £95,000 and his expenses were £64,000. What is the gross profit and net profit?

Gross profit	=	sales - cost of sales
	=	£198,000 - £95,000
	=	£103,000

Net profit	=	gross profit - expenses
	=	£103,000 - £64,000
	=	£39,000

This means that Igor's toy shop made a net profit of £39,000. After tax has been paid on the net profit, Igor can keep what is left or invest it in the business.

Calculating profit for a manufacturer

Castleton Ltd manufactures wheelchairs, adjustable beds, bath lifts and stair lifts. In 2002 sales were £4,231,000. Purchases of raw materials and components were £904,000 and wages paid to production workers were £1,438,000. Expenses for the year were £1,671,000. What is the gross profit and net profit?

Gross profit	=	sales – cost of sales
	=	£4,231,000 - (£904,000 + £1,438,000)
	=	£4,231,00 - £2,342,000
	=	£1,889,000

Net profit	=	gross profit - expenses
	=	£1,889,000 - £1,671,000
	=	£218,000

After tax has been deducted from the £218,000, the remainder can be invested in the business or dividends can be paid to the shareholders.

key terms

Cost of sales – the value of purchases plus wages paid to production workers.
Expenses – general overheads such as rent, rates, heating & lighting.
Financial year – a 12 month trading period.
Gross profit – sales less cost of sales.
Net profit – gross profit less expenses.
Purchases – the amount paid for stock or raw materials and components.
Sales – income from the sale of goods and services.

Quick quiz

1. True or false?
   (a) VAT must not be included in sales.
   (b) Rent and rates are examples of expenses.
   (c) Cost of sales will include motor expenses.

2. How is net profit calculated?
   (a) Sales - cost of sales.   **(b)** Cost of sales - expenses.
   (c) Gross profit - expenses.   **(d)** Sales - expenses.

3. Which is not an example of cost of sales?
   (a) Stock.   **(b)** Production wages.
   (c) Raw materials.   **(d)** Heat & light.

4. A retailer has sales of £95,600, purchases of £43,200 and expenses of £31,700. Calculate the:
   (a) gross profit.   **(b)** net profit.

Exam practice

West Bromwich Steel Products

West Bromwich Steel Products makes parts for pylons and masts. The profit and loss statement for the year ended 31 December 2003 showed the following financial information.

- Sales   £9,560,000

- Raw materials   £1,001,000
- Components   £1,222,000
- Production wages   £2,769,000

- Administration expenses £1,825,000
- Other overheads   £1,555,000

1. Using examples from the case, explain what is meant by cost of sales. (3 marks)
2. (a) Calculate the business's gross profit. (4 marks)
   (b) Calculate the business's net profit. (4 marks)
3. Explain how a business might use its net profit (5 marks)

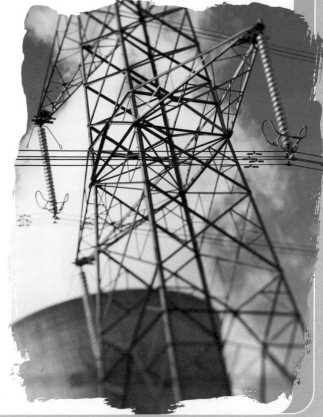

Getting started...

At the end of their financial year, businesses produce financial statements. One of these is a PROFIT AND LOSS ACCOUNT. It shows the income and running costs of a business. It also shows the gross profit and net profit. It is used to see how well a business has performed during the year. Look at the accounts of the businesses below.

Case 1 Corkhill's Garden Centre

Erica Corkhill is a sole trader. She owns a garden centre near Watford. She has been worried recently because her bank overdraft has been increasing. The profit and loss account below helps her to understand why.

Corkhill's Garden Centre
Profit and loss account
Year ended 30.6.03

	£	£
Sales		111,020
Less Cost of sales		53,000
Gross profit		**58,020**
Less expenses:		
Wages	12,300	
Rates	5,600	
Interest	15,800	
Motor expenses	12,400	
Repairs & maintenance	23,300	
		69,400
Net loss		**(11,380)**

Case 2 Sizemore Ltd

Sizemore Ltd is a business that manufactures decorations. At the end of the 2002 financial year, it received a copy of the profit and loss account from the accountant. This is shown below.

Sizemore Ltd
Profit and loss account
year ended 31.12.03

	£	£
Sales		1,754,000
Less Cost of sales		977,000
Gross profit		**777,000**
Less expenses		582,000
Plus interest received		20,000
Net profit		**215,000**
Taxation		45,000
Dividend		30,000
Retained profit		140,000

For (a) Corkhill's Garden Centre and (b) Sizemore Ltd state:
(i) sales revenue
(ii) gross profit
(iii) total expenses
(iv) net profit or net loss
(v) how well you think the business is doing.

What does a profit and loss account show?

The profit and loss account

The profit and loss account provides information on the performance of the business in the last financial year. Some businesses produce profit and loss accounts more often, for example, every month. This helps them to keep an even closer check on performance. The account uses business income and running costs to calculate gross profit and net profit. The layout of the account is important. Information must be presented in a standard way. The account in Figure 1 is for Brian Jennings, a fishmonger who is a sole trader.

What does the statement about profit and loss tell a business? The profit and loss account for Brian Jennings suggests that the fishmonger's business is doing well.
- The gross profit is over half the value of sales. This is quite good.
- Net profit is about half the value of gross profit. This is also quite good.

Figure 1 *Profit and loss account of Brian Jennings, a fishmonger*

Business name, type of account and the date must always be written at the top

Sales, the money from selling goods and services, is the first figure entered

Brian Jennings
Profit and loss account for the year ended 31.8.03

	£	£
Sales		92,300
Less Cost of sales		44,610
Gross profit		**47,690**
Less expenses		
Casual labour	16,000	
Rent & rates	2,100	
Heat & light	1,600	
Advertising	1,740	
Sundry expenses	2,300	
		23,740
Net profit		**23,950**

Expenses are listed and then added up to give a total

Gross profit is calculated by subtracting cost of sales from sales

Sundry expenses include many small costs added together such as postage and stationery

Net profit is calculated by subtracting expenses from gross profit

Preparing a profit and loss account

The following steps are used to prepare the profit and loss account of a sole trader.
- ✪ Write the name of the business and the date on which its financial year ends at the top of the account.
- ✪ Enter the value of sales in the outside column.
- ✪ Enter the cost of sales in the outside column.
- ✪ Calculate the gross profit by subtracting cost of sales from sales. Enter this under cost of sales in the outside column.
- ✪ List all the expenses in the inside column.
- ✪ Add up the expenses and write the total in the outside column.
- ✪ Subtract expenses from gross profit to get net profit.
- ✪ Write net profit in the outside column.

Profit and loss accounts of limited companies

Figure 2 shows the profit and loss account of Abbotsford Ltd, a limited company. It includes figures for gross and net profit, including some other income earned from bank interest. It also shows how the net profit has been used.
- ✪ Part has been paid in taxation to the government.
- ✪ Part has been paid to the shareholders of the company in DIVIDENDS.
- ✪ Part has been retained in the company.

Usually profit and loss statements show figures for two years so that the business can compare figures and judge its performance.

Figure 2 *Profit and loss account for Abbotsford Ltd*

Abbotsford Ltd
Profit and loss account for the year ended 31.8.03

	2002 £m	2003 £m
Sales	3.8	4.6
Less Cost of sales	1.3	1.6
Gross profit	**2.5**	**3.0**
Less expenses	1.7	1.8
Plus other income	0.1	0.1
Net profit	**0.9**	**1.3**
Taxation	0.2	0.3
Dividends	0.1	0.1
Retained profit	0.6	0.9

Sales have increased

Cost of sales have increased

Gross profit has increased because sales have risen more than cost of sales

Expenses have increased

More has been paid in tax

Dividends paid are the same

More profit has been retained

Net profit has increased because gross profit has risen more than expenses

Other income such as interest earned has remained the same

key terms

Profit and loss account – *a financial statement showing the income and costs of a business, which is used to calculate profit.*
Dividend – *a reward paid to shareholders of a company, the owners, for investing in the company.*

key terms key terms key terms key terms key terms key terms

Quick quiz

① True or false?

(a) It is not necessary to show the date on a profit and loss account.

(b) Profit and loss accounts normally have two columns of figures.

(c) The final figure in the profit and loss account is net profit.

② Fill in the missing words.

Net profit   Sales   Expenses   Gross profit   Cost of sales

At the top of a profit and loss account ...... is calculated. This is done by subtracting ...... from .... At the bottom of the account, ... is calculated by subtracting ...... from gross profit.

③ Which of the following would not be found in a profit and loss account?

(a) Loans.   **(b)** Cost of sales.   **(c)** Sales.   **(d)** Expenses.

④ What is the first entry in a profit and loss account?

(a) Gross profit.   **(b)** Sales.   **(c)** Net profit.   **(d)** Expenses.

⑤ What does a profit and loss account measure?

(a) Liquidity.   **(b)** Liabilities.   **(c)** Performance.   **(d)** VAT.

Exam practice

Hereford Office Supplies

Hereford Office Supplies sells office furniture. At the end of its financial year 2003, the following information was gathered.

- ✪ Sales   £156,400
- ✪ Stock purchased   £81,200
  (cost of sales)

- ✪ Business rates   £3,700
- ✪ Wages   £21,200
- ✪ Motor expenses   £8,700
- ✪ Advertising   £2,600
- ✪ Sundry expenses   £5,300

1. What is meant by sundry expenses? (2 marks)
2. Prepare a profit and loss account for Hereford Office Supplies for the year ended 31.12.03. (7 marks)
3. In 2002, gross profit was £79,900 and net profit was £21,900. Explain whether business performance has improved or not. (3 marks)
4. Explain the advantage of showing both this year's and last year's figures on a profit and loss account. (3 marks)

Assets, capital and liabilities

Getting started...

Businesses keep a record of how much money they owe to banks, suppliers, other businesses or individuals, and the owners. They also keep a record of the value of all the resources they own such as plant, machinery, equipment, stock and cash. Look at what is owed and owned by the businesses below.

Case 1 *The Jobsearch Agency*

On 21.5.02, Tirna Pai set up an employment agency in Newcastle. She used £3,000 of her own money and borrowed another £2,000 from a bank.

She bought a computer for £1,000 and a car for £2,500. She spent £400 on stationery and left £1,100 cash in the bank. She also bought some office furniture for £1,600 but has not yet paid for it.

Case 2 *French Ltd*

Lee and Janet French are the owners of French Ltd. They have £80,000 worth of shares. The business makes guitars and violins. It also owes another £50,000 to the bank, £15,500 to its suppliers and a further £36,000 to the shareholders.

On 31.12.02, the factory was valued at £100,000. The company also owns £50,000 of tools and equipment, £25,000 of stock and £6,500 cash in the bank.

Case 3 *JJB Sports*

JJB Sports owns several hundred sports shops around the country. At the end of 2001, it owned £346 million of resources such as stores, fixtures and fittings and £331 million of other resources such as cash and stocks.

However, it owed £408 million to business such as suppliers and £269 million to its shareholders.

Source: adapted from JJB Sports, *Annual Report and Accounts*, 2001.

For cases 1, 2 and 3, calculate:
(a) the total amount owed by each business
(b) the total value of the resources owned by each business.

What are the assets, liabilities and capital of a business?

Assets

The resources owned by a business are called ASSETS. Assets are used by the business to provide goods and services. All business assets fall into one of two categories.

Fixed assets Some assets are bought by a business and used over and over again, often for many years. If an asset is not going to be sold for at least one year, it is called a FIXED ASSET. Examples of fixed assets include:

- ○ land;
- ○ buildings, such as factories and shops;
- ○ plant;
- ○ machinery;
- ○ equipment;
- ○ tools;
- ○ vehicles;
- ○ computers.

A factory and machinery are examples of the fixed assets of a business

Current assets CURRENT ASSETS are the LIQUID ASSETS that a business owns. They are cash or assets that can be turned into cash fairly quickly.

- ○ **Cash.** The money that a business owns is its main liquid asset. This also includes money held at the bank.
- ○ **Debtors.** DEBTORS are the people, other businesses or organisations that owe the business money. For example, a customer who has not paid for the goods he has received is a debtor. Debtors are current assets because the business usually gets the cash it is owed within 90 days.
- ○ **Stocks.** Stocks of raw materials, components and finished goods are current assets. WORK-IN-PROGRESS is also a current asset. This is the value of partly made products, for example, a house under construction.

Stocks are examples of current assets

Liabilities

Liabilities are the debts of the business. This is the money it owes to other businesses or individuals. They are then CREDITORS of the business. Liabilities can be current liabilities or long term liabilities.

Current liabilities Money that a business has to repay within 12 months is called a CURRENT LIABILITY. There are various examples.

- ○ **Trade creditors.** When suppliers are owed money, they are called TRADE CREDITORS. Most businesses have trade creditors. They are usually repaid within 90 days.
- ○ **Taxation.** Limited companies have to pay CORPORATION TAX on their profits. This is paid to the Inland Revenue after the profit has been earned.
- ○ **Dividends.** Limited companies often owe dividends to shareholders. This is a current liability.
- ○ **Bank overdrafts.** If a business has a bank overdraft, the money owed to the bank is a current liability. The bank can demand the money at any time it wishes.

Long term liabilities Money owed for more than 12 months is called a LONG TERM LIABILITY. There are various examples.

- ○ **Long term bank loan.** This is a bank loan taken out for more than one year.
- ○ **Mortgage.** A mortgage is usually a long term loan which uses land or property as security.
- ○ **Debentures.** These are special long term loans to businesses.

Capital, retained profit and shareholders' funds

The money provided by the owners to set up and run a business is called CAPITAL. The capital of limited companies is called share capital. Capital is not usually repaid to the owners unless the business stops trading.

Businesses usually keep some of the profit they make. This is called RETAINED PROFIT. It might be used to buy new assets or invest in new activities. It might also be held as RESERVES and used, for example, to help the business get through a difficult trading period.

Retained profit is added to the business's capital and is owed to the owners of the business. For a limited company, the share capital and reserves added together are called SHAREHOLDERS' FUNDS.

key terms

Assets – *resources owned by a business.*
Capital – *the money put into a business by the owners.*
Corporation tax – *a tax paid by limited companies on their profits.*
Creditors – *people, businesses and other organisations that are owed money.*
Current assets – *the liquid resources owned by a business*
Current liabilities – *money owed by a business that must be repaid within 12 months.*
Debtors – *the money owed to a business by customers and other organisations.*
Fixed assets – *resources that are used over and over again for more than one year.*
Liquid assets – *cash, or assets that can be turned into cash quickly.*
Long term liability – *money owed by a business for more than 12 months.*
Reserves – *money, such as retained profit, owed to the owners of the business.*
Retained profit – *the profit kept by a business in reserve or to invest.*
Shareholders' funds – *the money owed by a limited company to its shareholders.*
Trade creditors – *money owed to suppliers.*
Work-in-progress – *partly finished goods that are still in production.*

key terms key terms key terms key terms key terms key terms ke

Quick quiz

1. True or false?
   (a) Money owed to a business is a liability.
   (b) Fixed assets are liquid assets.
   (c) Stock is a current asset.

2. Which of the following is a current liability?
   (a) Cash.   (b) Debtors.
   (c) Computer.   (d) Trade creditors.

3. Which of the following is a fixed asset?
   (a) Debtors.   (b) Vehicles.
   (c) Bank loan. (d) Debentures.

4. Which of the following is not a liquid asset?
   (a) Stocks.   (b) Cash.
   (c) Land.   (d) Debtors.

5. Fill in the missing words.
   Shareholders' funds   Capital
   Share capital   Limited company

   The money owed to the owners of a business is called .... In the case of ...... it is called .... If the value of reserves is added to the value of share capital the total is called ....

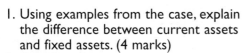

Exam practice

Simmons Ltd

Simmons Ltd is a car hire company operating from premises in Southampton. It owns 20 cars and has struggled in recent years due to competition from large companies like Hertz and Avis. On 31.12.02, the following financial information was provided.

Financial information

Premises	£100,000	Share capital	£50,000
Computer	£2,000	Debtors	£7,000
Cars	£80,000	Mortgage	£80,000
Reserves	£21,000	Bank overdraft	£16,000
Taxation owed	£12,000	Trade creditors	£10,000

1. Using examples from the case, explain the difference between current assets and fixed assets. (4 marks)
2. Calculate the:
   (i) total value of assets;
   (ii) current liabilities;
   (iii) long term liabilities;
   (iv) shareholders' funds. (8 marks)
3. What evidence is there to suggest that Simmons Ltd is struggling? (4 marks)

Getting started...

Businesses prepare a **BALANCE SHEET**. This is a record of the business's assets, liabilities and capital at a certain date. It shows where all the money comes from and how it has been spent. The balance sheet has to balance so the value of the business assets must equal the value of its liabilities and capital added together. In other words, what the business owns must equal what it owes. Look at the two businesses below.

Case 1 *Sherfords*

Sherfords is a restaurant. It is successful and has won a number of local awards for high quality food. On 31.3.03, the following information was provided.

Assets

Premises	£120,000
Fixtures and fittings	£25,000
Van	£4,500
Stock	£7,700
Cash	£11,500

Liabilities

Trade creditors	£4,300
Mortgage	£80,000

Capital

Capital	£25,000
Retained profit	£59,400

Case 2 *Tyre Supplies Ltd*

Tyre Supplies Ltd distributes car tyres in the UK. It rents a warehouse in Warwickshire and a fleet of vans. It employs 45 staff. On 31.12.03, the following information was provided.

Assets

Vans	£130,000
Computers	£7,000
Stocks	£78,000
Debtors	£41,000
Cash	£21,000

Liabilities

Trade creditors	£30,000
Bank loan	£10,000

Capital

Share capital	£150,000
Retained profit	£32,000
Other reserves	£55,000

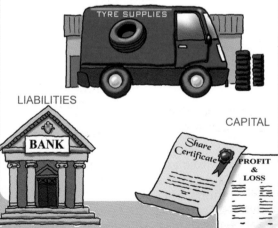

(a) For each business, what is the total value of:
   (i) assets
   (ii) liabilities
   (iii) capital?
(b) What do you notice about the value of assets when compared to the value of liabilities and capital added together?

What does a balance sheet show?

The balance sheet and assets, liabilities and capital

A balance sheet is like a photograph of the financial position of a business at a point in time. It shows the total value of assets, liabilities and capital at the end of the financial year. The balance sheet balances because the value of assets is exactly the same as the value of liabilities and capital added together. M Ball, a sole trader, has assets of £150,000, liabilities of £50,000 and capital of £100,000. This is shown in Figure 1.

Figure 1 Assets, capital and liabilities of M Ball, a sole trader

The structure of a balance sheet

The balance sheet for M Ball is shown in Figure 2. It has two columns. Figures on the outside are total amounts. Figures on the inside are subtotals, which added together make the total amounts.

Balance sheets are presented using a set format. This presentation is slightly different between businesses. The balance sheet of M Ball, a sole trader, will be slightly different from the balance sheet of a limited company.

Figure 2 Balance sheet for M Ball

Name of business and date is shown at the top.

M Ball
Balance sheet as at 31.12.02

	£	£
Fixed assets		
Factory		90,000
Tools & equipment		20,000
		110,000
Current assets		
Stocks	20,000	
Debtors	15,000	
Cash	5,000	
	40,000	
Current liabilities		
Trade creditors	25,000	
Working capital		15,000
Long term liabilities		
Mortgage		(25,000)
Net assets		**100,000**
Capital		
Opening capital	92,000	
Add Profit	38,000	
	130,000	
Less Drawings	30,000	
Closing capital		**100,000**

Fixed assets are listed first. The total is also shown.

Working capital is calculated. It is current assets - current liabilities.

Net assets is assets - liabilities. It can also be calculated as fixed assets + working capital - long term liabilities.

Closing capital is calculated by subtracting drawings from opening capital and profit.

Current assets are listed and totalled.

Current liabilities are listed and totalled.

Long-term liabilities are listed and totalled. They are negative.

Opening capital is the closing balance from the previous year. It is added to this year's profit.

Working capital

If current liabilities are subtracted from current assets, the result is WORKING CAPITAL. This is the amount of liquid resources that a business has available. Working capital is used to pay running costs. If a business is short of working capital, it could have cash flow problems. M Ball's balance sheet shows that he has £15,000 working capital available.

Capital

The bottom of the balance sheet shows the capital. Closing capital is found by adding profit to the opening capital, and then subtracting DRAWINGS. Drawings is the money that the owner takes from the business for personal use. In 2002, M Ball made £38,000 profit and withdrew £30,000 for personal use. The closing capital is £100,000. This means the business owes him £100,000.

Net assets

NET ASSETS is calculated by subtracting all the liabilities from all the assets. M Ball's net assets are calculated by adding fixed assets to working capital and then subtracting long-term liabilities. They are £100,000. Net assets is important because it shows roughly how much the business is worth. The value of net assets is the same figure as closing capital.

Limited company balance sheet

The main difference between sole trader and limited company balance sheets is in the capital section. Limited companies have a shareholders' fund section which shows share capital, retained profit and reserves. The balance sheet for Tomkinson's Ltd in Figure 3 shows this. Another difference is that working capital is called NET CURRENT ASSETS.

Figure 3 *Balance sheet for Tomkinson's Ltd*

Tomkinson's Ltd
Balance sheet as at 31.10.02

	£000	£000
Fixed assets		
Premises		1,000
Fixtures & fittings		670
		1,670
Current assets		
Stocks	450	
Debtors	256	
Cash	76	
	782	
Current liabilities		
Trade creditors	440	
Net current assets		342
Long term liabilities		
Bank loan		(100)
Net assets		**1,912**
Shareholders' funds		
Share capital		1,500
Retained profit		312
Other reserves		100
		1,912

key terms

Balance sheet – *a summary, at a certain point in time, of the assets, liabilities and capital of a business.*
Drawings – *money taken from the business by the owner for personal use.*
Net assets – *total assets less total liabilities. It is a rough guide to the value of a business.*
Net current assets – *current assets minus current liabilities. It is another term for working capital.*
Working capital – *the liquid resources that a business has to cover its running costs. It is calculated by subtracting current liabilities from current assets.*

key terms key terms ke

Quick quiz

① True or false?
   (a) Net current assets is another term for working capital.
   (b) Debtors will be found in the capital section of the balance sheet.
   (c) Net assets is a rough guide to the value of a business.

② Current liabilities for a business are £456,000 and current assets are £782,000. What is working capital?
   (a) £782,000.   **(b)** £1,238,000.
   (c) £326,000.   **(d)** £456,000.

③ Fixed assets for a business are £500,000, current assets are £150,000 and total liabilities are £430,000. What is the net assets?
   (a) £220,000.   **(b)** £650,000.
   (c) £1,080,000.   **(d)** £930,000.

④ Which of the following would not be found under shareholders' funds?
   (a) Retained profit. **(b)** Cash.
   (c) Reserves.   **(d)** Share capital.

⑤ What is the closing capital if opening capital is £65,400, profit is £21,900 and drawings are £25,000?

Exam practice

Soundright Studios

Jacob Miller owns a small recording studio. He produces his own music and records backing tracks and jingles. He sells these on CD. He prints his own CDs and covers at the studio. On 31.12.02, the financial information shown in his balance sheet is:

Machinery	£75,000
Stocks	£12,300
Debtors	£7,800
Cash	£3,600
Total creditors	£8,900
Mortgage	£40,000
Opening capital	£31,000
Profit	£37,800
Drawings	£19,000

1. Using the structure shown in Figure 4, prepare a balance sheet for Sounright Studios as at 31.12.02. Fill in the missing terms and amounts shown by (******). (10 marks)
2. Using the case as an example, explain the meaning of working capital. (4 marks)
3. Jacob has received a £35,000 offer from someone who wants to buy his business. On financial grounds, explain whether he should accept the offer or not. (5 marks).

Soundright Studios
Balance sheet as at 31.12.02

	£	£
Fixed asserts		
******		******
Current assets		
******	******	
******	******	
******	******	
	******	
Current liabilities		
******	******	
Working capital		******
Long term liabilities		
******		******
Net assets		******
Capital		
******	******	
Add ******	******	
	******	
Less ******	******	
Closing capital		******

Figure 4

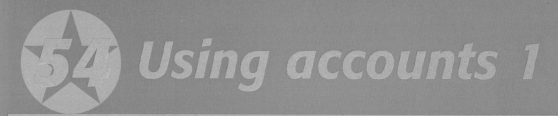
Getting started...

Businesses produce accounts because they provide useful financial information for stakeholders. Different stakeholders will look for different things in the accounts. For example, employees may want to know whether the business can afford to increase their wages. Look at the accounts for the businesses below.

Case 1 *Penny Wilkins*

Penny Wilkins owns an off-licence in Hornchurch. She sells wines, spirits, beers, confectionery and cigarettes. The business has struggled recently due to new competition in the area. If she doesn't make a net profit of £25,000, she may decide to sell up. The profit and loss account for the business is shown below.

Penny Wilkins
Profit and loss account
for the Year ended 31.1.03

	£	£
Sales		134,200
Less Cost of sales		92,300
Gross profit		**41,900**
Less expenses		
Casual labour	5,600	
Heat & light	3,200	
Motor expenses	5,400	
Advertising	3,200	
Sundry expenses	6,500	
		23,900
Net profit		**18,000**

(a) Which items in the accounts will be of most interest to the stakeholders mentioned in each of these businesses?

Case 2 *West End Taxis Ltd*

WESTEND **TAXIS**
call us anytime
02 03 4491

West End Taxis Ltd operates a taxi service in Kidderminster. The business wants to expand its fleet of cabs but it needs to borrow £40,000 from the bank to do so. The company's directors have been asked to provide the bank with the business's last balance sheet. The bank wants to know how much debt the business already has. The balance sheet is shown below.

West End Taxis Ltd
Balance sheet as at 31.3.03

	£	£
Fixed assets		
Premises		120,000
Taxis		110,000
Office furniture		15,000
		245,000
Current assets		
Stock	12,000	
Debtors	6,500	
Cash	12,000	
	30,500	
Current liabilities		
Trade creditors	4,000	
Taxation owed	21,000	
	25,000	
Net current assets		5,500
Long term liabilities		
Mortgage		(100,000)
Net assets		**150,500**
Shareholders' funds		
Share capital		100,000
Retained profit		28,600
Other reserves		21,900
		150,500

How might accounts help stakeholders?

Owners

Sole traders and partners are interested in the performance of their businesses. The profit and loss account may be of most interest. It will show whether:

- sales turnover has improved;
- costs have gone up or down;
- net profit has improved.

Owners are likely to make comparisons with previous years. For example, John Jenkins owns a garage where he services and repairs cars. The figures in Table 1 are taken from from his profit and loss accounts. They show that both his sales and his net profit have increased.

Table 1

	2000	2001	2002
Sales	£214,000	£231,000	£246,000
Net profit	£31,000	£37,000	£49,000

> Sales have increased by £32,000 over 2 years

> Net profit has increased by £11,000 over 2 years

Owners also need the profit and loss account so that they can fill in their tax returns for the Inland Revenue. The tax they pay is based on the business's net profit.

The balance sheet will show how much working capital the business has and how much the business is worth. An owner might want to know how much the business is worth if it is going to be sold, for example.

Shareholders

The owners of limited companies are interested in the business's performance. The dividend that the shareholders receive is usually linked to the amount of profit the business makes.

Also, FINANCIAL ANALYSTS may examine accounts before recommending to investors that they buy or sell shares in plcs. Analysts might also compare the accounts of different companies in the same industry, such as supermarkets for example.

An Annual General Meeting. Shareholders will be interested in the accounts of a company

Banks and other creditors

Creditors are interested in whether a business can pay what it owes. For example, a bank will look at a business's accounts to help it decide whether to give the business a loan. The bank will also look at the balance sheet to see if there is enough working capital. This is because businesses need liquid assets to pay interest and repay loans.

Banks might also be interested in the value of the fixed assets of a business, such as land and property, which may be used as security for loans. The information in Table 2 is for a business that wants a bank loan.

Table 2

Current assets		Current liabilities	
Stock	£56,800	Trade creditors	£51,500
Debtors	£129,000	Taxation owed	£43,000
Cash	£12,000	Other creditors	£9,000
Total	**£197,800**	**Total**	**£103,500**

This business would probably be given a loan. It has plenty of working capital. Working capital is current assests minus current liabilities. Its current assests are £197,800 and its current liabilities are £103,500. So its working capital is £94,300. Its current assets are almost twice as great as its current liabilities.

Quick quiz

1 True or false?
   (a) The Inland Revenue might want to see the accounts of a sole trader.
   (b) Shareholders are likely to be most interested in the current assets owned by a business.
   (c) Banks are most likely to be interested in the gross profit made by a business.

2 Which of the following will tell the owner the value of the business?
   (a) Current liabilities.
   (b) Fixed assets.
   (c) Current assets.
   (d) Net assets.

3 Which of the following could help to tell a creditor whether a firm can pay its debts?
   (a) Fixed assets.
   (b) Working capital.
   (c) Net assets.
   (d) Retained profits.

4 Which of the following would be of most interest to a shareholder?
   (a) Fixed assets.
   (b) Dividends.
   (c) Debtors.
   (d) Long term liabilities.

5 Calculate the value of working capital if stock is £12,000, debtors £17,000, trade creditors £21,000 and cash £16,000.

key terms

Financial analyst – *a person who investigates the financial position of a business when assessing whether to recommend to an investor to buy or sell shares.*

key terms key terms key terms key terms key terms key t

Exam practice

Smithson's Ltd

Smithson's Ltd makes cheese in its own dairy in Stow-on-the-Wold, Gloucestershire. The business has struggled recently due to some unexpected costs. One of the machines broke down and had to be replaced. Smithson's Ltd now needs a £25,000 loan to develop a new type of cheese.

1. Explain why a bank might be interested in the value of Smithson's working capital. (4 marks)
2. Explain why a bank would prefer two years' figures when looking at Smithson's accounts. (4 marks)
3. Has the value of the business fallen or risen between 2001 and 2002? (2 marks)
4. Would a bank be willing to lend Smithson's Ltd the £25,000 it requires? Explain your answer. (7 marks)

Smithson's Ltd
Balance sheet as at 31.1.02

	2002 £	2001 £
Fixed assets		
Premises	80,000	80,000
Equipment	44,000	28,000
Van	10,000	12,000
	134,000	120,000
Current assets		
Stock	12,000	13,400
Debtors	21,500	22,000
Cash in hand	300	3,400
	33,800	38,800
Current liabilities		
Trade creditors	23,000	24,900
Bank overdraft	23,000	0
	46,000	24,900
Net current assets	(12,200)	13,900
Long term liabilities		
Mortgage	80,000	60,000
Net assets	41,800	73,900
Shareholders' funds		
Share capital	40,000	40,000
Retained profit	1,800	33,900
	41,800	73,900

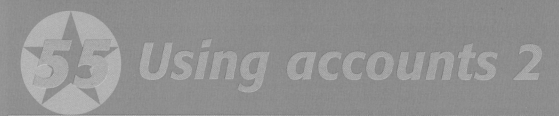

55 Using accounts 2

Getting started...

Owners and creditors are not the only business stakeholders that might be interested in using accounts. Managers, employees and customers may also use the profit and loss account and balance sheet. Think about the stakeholders in the businesses below.

Case 1 Streatham Mouldings

Streatham Mouldings makes plastic products for the building industry. The company believes it is successful because the managers set financial targets that must be met. Every month managers set targets for sales, costs and net profit. Accounts are prepared every month to help with setting targets. The September targets and actual figures are shown below.

	Targets	Actual figures
Sales	£120,000	£124,000
Costs	£85,000	£87,000
Net profit	£35,000	£37,000

Case 2 Purplex plc

Purplex plc employs 500 staff. It supplies security services such as guards, mobile patrols, store detectives and electronic systems. Employees are due to meet managers to discuss next year's pay increase. After looking at an extract from the profit and loss account shown below, the employees want a 6.5% pay rise. They believe that the company can easily afford this increase.

	2001	2002
Sales	£25,400	£28,900
Gross profit	£11,800	£13,900
Net profit	£4,800	£6,100

Case 3 F Gonzalez

Freddie Gonzalez owns a small construction company. He has won a contract to build a factory extension for a local business. However, Freddie requires a £5,000 deposit before he can begin the work. The customer has agreed to this, but wants to see the accounts for Freddie's business for the last three years. He wants to check that the business is financially stable before signing the contract and handing over the £5,000 deposit.

How are stakeholders using the accounts at:
(a) Streatham Mouldings
(b) Purplex plc
(c) F Gonzalez?

How might stakeholders use accounts?

Managers

Managers are responsible for running the business. They make decisions, organise resources, make plans and keep control. Information from the accounts will help managers to see if their targets are being met. Managers may also need to know things such as:

☼ how much cash is available to spend;
☼ what is happening to sales, costs and profit;
☼ whether there is too much debt;
☼ whether the business needs to raise more capital.

Customers

Many businesses sell products to other businesses. These customers may want to look at their accounts to check that the company is financially secure. Customers will not give cash deposits for contracts and orders unless they know the supplier is sound. Customers will also want to be sure that goods can be supplied well into the future.

Accounts may also be used by consumers' groups such as the Consumers' Association to check that consumers are not being overcharged by businesses that make huge profits, for example.

Employees

Employees are mainly concerned with their pay, working conditions and job security. Trade unions may use accounts to see if the business is profitable. If a business is performing well, trade unions are in a stronger position to ask for higher wages. Employees may also decide to look for another job if they think the business is not doing very well.

Other users

Other groups and organisations such as the media, government, competitors, potential investors and the local community might want to look at company accounts. For example, newspapers, magazines, television and radio use financial information when reporting on businesses.

Quick quiz

1 True or false?

(a) Managers might use accounts to set financial targets.

(b) A balance sheet will help employees to determine the profitability of a business.

(c) Customers would use accounts to see how much capital the owners have put in.

2 Which of the following might trade unions be most interested in?

(a) Current assets.

(b) Fixed assets.

(c) Net profit.

(d) Net assets.

3 Who might use accounts to write reports about businesses?

(a) Customers.

(b) Newspapers.

(c) Employees.

(d) Local community.

4 Which of these would be of most interest to a manager controlling cash flow?

(a) Fixed assets.

(b) Gross profit.

(c) Working capital.

(d) Shareholders' funds.

5 State three non-stakeholder groups that might be interested in using accounts.

Exam practice

Brewster & Co

Brewster & Co supplies passenger meals to airlines. The managers are concerned that the performance of the company is worsening. The industry has been hit badly by external factors in the last 2 years.

The managers are also worried by the memo in Figure 3.

Figure 1 Extracts from Brewster & Co's profit & loss account for the year ended 30.9.02

			£000
	2000	2001	2002
Sales	1,833	1,531	1,023
Net profit	381	211	(12)

Figure 3

MEMO

To: Managing Director
From: A. Hargreaves (Union Rep.)
Date: 28.11.02
Subject: Wage negotiations
Could we arrange a meeting fairly urgently to discuss the 7.5% wage claim for 2003?

Figure 2 Extracts from Brewster & Co's balance sheet as at 30.9.02

			£000
	2000	2001	2002
Fixed assets	2,000	1,800	1,900
Working capital	542	109	(875)
Long-term liabilities	(500)	(750)	(1,000)

1. How might airlines respond if they find out that Brewster & Co is struggling? (2 marks)
2. What evidence is there in the accounts to suggest to managers that the business's performance is worsening? (6 marks)
3. How might the information in the accounts affect the outcome of the employees' wage claim? (7 marks)

Sources of finance – short-term

Getting started...

Businesses often need to borrow money to help cover their running costs. The money borrowed for this type of spending is usually repaid quickly. Look at the sources of finance used by the businesses below.

Case 1 *Ella Carter*

Ella Carter set up her travel agency two years ago. Her business has struggled because many people were booking holidays over the Internet. She does not have enough money to pay the rent for her shop and her employees' wages. So she has asked the bank for an overdraft. The bank has agreed to give the business a £1,000 overdraft.

Case 2 *Heath Farm*

Charlie Williams owns Heath Farm in Norfolk, where he grows wheat, barley and oats. The farm is profitable, but he often runs out of cash just before the summer harvest. This year, the farm has had another problem. A tractor caught fire and could not be used any more. Buying another would cost around £20,000. Charlie can't afford this, he has decided to hire one from a local company. He needs it for 4 weeks and it will cost £150 a day.

FOR HIRE £150 per DAY

Case 3 *Floral Tributes*

Floral Tributes is a flower shop owned by Ben Thomas and Judy Flanagan. They buy fresh flowers every day from various suppliers. These cost around £7,000 per month. At the end of the month they get a statement saying how much they owe. Their suppliers give them 30 days to pay.

TODAY

30 DAYS LATER

For each of these businesses:
(a) why was finance needed?
(b) what sources of finance did they use?

What are the short-term sources of funds for a business?

Short-term sources of finance

Short-term finance is money that is borrowed for less than one year. It is mainly used to help a business pay for its day-to-day running costs.

Bank overdraft

A BANK OVERDRAFT is a common type of short-term finance. When an overdraft has been arranged, the bank allows the business to withdraw more money than it has in its current account.

The advantage for the business is that it can use the bank's money whenever it needs to. But the bank will set an overdraft limit which the business must not exceed. A business pays interest only on the amount by which it is overdrawn.

Trade credit

Many businesses buy materials using TRADE CREDIT. This is where a business buys goods and pays for them later. For example, a car manufacturer might buy tyres from a supplier and pay for them 30 days later. Sometimes this can be longer if the supplier agrees.

Trade credit can be a cheap source of finance. But if a business does not pay straight away, it might lose any CASH DISCOUNTS that a supplier is offering. This is where a business reduces the price for prompt payment.

Leasing

Businesses often LEASE property, machinery and vehicles for a short period. This means they pay for using the assets. But they don't actually own them. Leasing or HIRING helps a business because:
- it does not have to find a large amount of money to buy assets outright;
- the assets can be leased for a short time such as a few hours or days;
- the leasing company, not the business, pays the maintenance and repair costs.

Sometimes assets are leased for a long time. However, this can be very expensive.

Businesses can lease machinery and equipment

Short-term bank loans

A short-term bank loan, say for six months, might be used to help boost working capital when a business is short of money. A bank loan is an amount of money given to a business by a bank, for example, which must be repaid in total by a given date. Interest is charged on the full amount of the loan yet to be repaid.

Credit cards

Credit cards are often used to pay for resources such as petrol, raw materials and hotel bills. The advantage of using a credit card for a business is that if the credit card bill is settled within a certain time, no interest is paid.

NatWest

Loans

Of all shapes and sizes

key terms

- **Bank overdraft** – *a flexible loan which allows a business to spend more money than it has in its bank account.*
- **Cash discounts** – *a deduction from a bill if it is settled quickly.*
- **Hiring/leasing** – *paying for the use of assets without actually owning them.*
- **Trade credit** – *buying goods or services and paying for them at a later date.*

key terms key terms key terms key terms key terms key terms

Quick quiz

1. True or false?
   (a) A mortgage is an example of short-term finance.
   (b) Short-term finance is often used to increase working capital.
   (c) Credit cards can be used to obtain interest free credit for a short period.

2. Which of these is not an example of short-term finance?
   (a) Overdraft.
   (b) Share capital.
   (c) Leasing.
   (d) Trade credit.

3. Which of these would not be used to buy raw materials?
   (a) Mortgage.   (b) Trade credit.
   (c) Credit card.   (d) Overdraft.

4. Which of these organisations would lend money under a hire purchase agreement?
   (a) Building society.
   (b) Discount house.
   (c) Bank of England.
   (d) Finance house.

5. State one advantage and one disadvantage of using trade credit.

Exam practice

Formalwear Ltd

Formalwear Ltd produces men's suits which are sold to retailers around the country. It has recently received a large order from a regular customer, which will be profitable.

To complete the order £3,500 of materials will have to be bought. The business will also need a special sewing machine. The machine would cost £4,500 to buy, but is only needed for two weeks. At the moment there is not enough money in the company's bank account to pay for the machine or the materials.

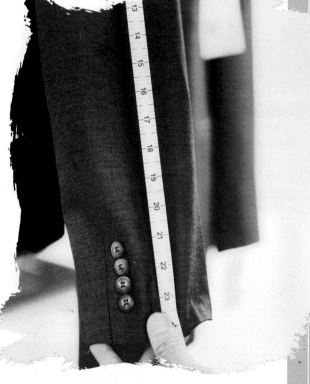

1. The business is thinking of using its bank overdraft facility to buy the materials. Explain why a bank overdraft is a flexible source of finance. (4 marks)
2. Explain one other suitable source of finance that the business might use to buy the materials. (4 marks)
3. Do you think that the business should lease the special sewing machine or take out a short term loan to buy it? (8 marks)

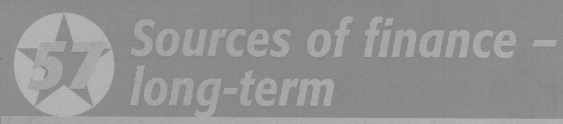

Sources of finance – long-term

Getting started...

When a business is set up, it needs money to buy resources. Some of this money comes from the owner and some comes from other sources. Even when a business is running, it often needs to raise more money. For example, a business may need finance to expand or buy new fixed assets. Look at the sources of finance used by the businesses below.

Case 1 Brenda Sullivan

Brenda is about to start her own business selling trophies and commemorative plaques. She will also offer other services, such as computerised engineering and glass engraving. Brenda has worked out that she needs £20,000 to buy equipment and and other resources. She is going to use £12,000 of her own savings and an £8,000 bank loan.

Case 2 Welling Games Ltd

Welling Games Ltd designs and sells board games to toy distributors. It has an idea for a new board game, but it will cost about £100,000 to develop. The company can't raise this money on its own. The bank has refused to give it a loan. So it is thinking of asking a specialist company which provides funds for growing businesses.

Case 3 Fast Despatch Ltd

Fast Despatch Ltd operates a courier service in Devon. It guarantees to deliver small parcels and packages anywhere in the country within 19 hours. The company is doing well and wants to expand. To do this, it needs to buy transit vans costing £30,000. The finance could come from a bank loan or retained profit. Using hire purchase is also a possibility.

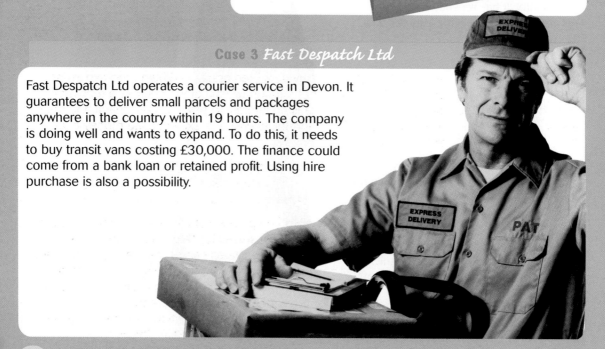

For each of these businesses, describe:
(a) the sources of finance
(b) what the finance was used for.

What are the sources of long-term finance for a business?

Long-term finance

Money borrowed for more than one year is called long-term finance. Long-term finance is used to set up a business, to buy more expensive fixed assets or to fund expansion. There are many different sources of long-term finance.

Figure 1

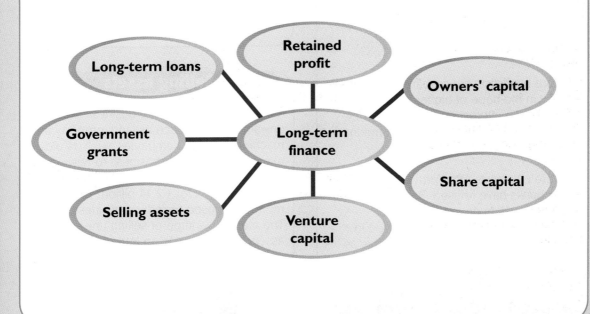

Retained profit

Businesses often keep some of their profit to buy new fixed assets and help fund expansion. Retained profit might also help a business to get through difficult times, such as a recession. The advantages of retained profit are that there is no interest to pay, it is convenient and there are no administration costs. But, there is an opportunity cost. For example, the money could have been given back to the owners.

Owner's capital

Owners usually risk their own money when setting up a business. They might use savings, the proceeds from redundancy or money raised from friends and relatives. Once this money is put into the business, it is not likely to be taken out.

Share capital

When limited companies want to raise capital, they might do this by issuing shares for sale. The amount of money raised from issuing shares can be very large, sometimes, millions of pounds. When limited companies are formed, shares are issued to help set up the business. However, established companies might decide to issue more shares in the future to raise additional money. They can do this by making a RIGHTS ISSUE. This is where existing shareholders are given the right to buy some new shares at a discount. It is a cheap and easy way of issuing shares.

Venture capital

Finance can be provided by VENTURE CAPITALISTS. These are wealthy individuals or companies who specialise in investing in growing businesses, usually small limited companies. This type of finance is sometimes called risk capital because the lenders risk losing their money if the business fails. Venture capitalist companies, such as 3i or PruVen, specialise in lending money to businesses. In return for their investment, lenders usually get a stake in the business and a share in its profits. This means that they may be involved in decision making.

Venture capitalists are prepared to risk their money in the hope of higher returns. For example, the interest on the money they have lent will be higher than from putting it into a bank deposit account.

Venture capitalists often provide money when banks have refused. But some business owners do not like venture capitalists because they are involved in business decisions. They may see this as interference in the running of the business.

Long-term loans

Banks and building societies provide two types of long-term finance.
- MORTGAGES are loans usually for up to 25 years which are secured on a property. This means that a bank can take away a business's property if it fails to repay the interest or the loan. Mortgages are a cheap source of long-term finance.
- An unsecured loan is one without any assets used as security. The interest on this type of loan is very high.

Selling assets

Money can be raised if a business sells unwanted assets such as land, property and machinery. Large companies, such as plcs, may sell part of their business to raise cash. For example, in 2001 BT sold its *Yellow Pages* business for £2.14 billion. The money was used to reduce business debts. The main advantage of selling unwanted assets is that there is no interest to pay.

Government grants

Local Authorities get money from the government and the European Union (EU) to help businesses in their area. Businesses can apply for loans and grants from local authorities if they locate their premises in areas suffering from high unemployment. Government grants are used to attract businesses to these areas so that they create jobs. The grants and loans are very attractive but the paperwork needed to get them is complicated and can be off-putting for local authorities businesses.

Hire purchase

HIRE PURCHASE might be used to buy assets. This is where a business borrows money from a finance house to buy a machine or piece of equipment, for example. The machine can be used by a business and paid back over a longer period of time. The business only owns the machine or equipment when the final payment is made. Sometimes hire purchase can be over a period of less than a year. Then it is a short-term source of finance.

key terms

- **Hire purchase** – *buying assets using a loan from a finance house.*
- **Mortgage** – *a long-term loan secured with land or property.*
- **Rights issue** – *a method of issuing shares to existing shareholders at a discount.*
- **Venture capitalists** – *financial institutions and individuals that provide money for growing businesses.*

key terms key terms key terms key terms key terms key terms key te

Quick quiz

1. True or false?
   (a) A mortgage is taken out for about a year.
   (b) Retained profit has zero opportunity cost.
   (c) Venture capitalists may take a stake in a business.

2. Which of these provide venture capital?
   (a) Banks.   (b) Venture capitalists.
   (c) Owners.   (d) Government.

3. Which of these could buy a rights issue of shares?
   (a) Venture capitalists. (b) Shareholders.
   (c) Government.   (d) Building society.

4. What must a business do to qualify for government loans or grants?
   (a) Operate as a manufacturer.
   (b) Make a profit.
   (c) Create jobs.
   (d) Pay interest to banks.

5. Fill in the missing words.
   Large   Limited companies
   Shares   Share capital

   The money raised from selling …… is called …… . Only …… can use this method to raise finance. The amount raised is often …… .

Exam practice

Kid's Clobber

Kids' Clobber is owned by Michelle Porter. She has two shops in Southampton selling children's clothes. The business is doing very well so she wants to expand by opening more shops along the South coast. She has found three new sites. Two are in Portsmouth and one is in Bournemouth. The expansion will cost £90,000. She plans to use £20,000 retained profit but she needs to borrow the rest.

Banks have refused to lend her any money because all the stores are rented and Michelle has no assets to provide any security for a loan. She has talked to a venture capitalist who will lend her £70,000. But, in return, this business wants 30% of the future profits made by all her shops.

1. What is the main advantage to Michelle of using retained profit to fund the expansion of Kids' Clobber? (2 marks)
2. Explain why banks often need security for loans. (6 marks)
3. What are the advantages and disadvantages to Michelle of using a venture capitalist to help fund the expansion of Kids' Clobber? Do you think she should raise the money in this way? (7 marks).

Getting started...

It is important that businesses plan their future activities carefully. They need to plan how much they are going to spend and they must also ensure that there is enough money to cover their spending. Without careful financial planning, businesses might get into difficulties. For example, they could run out of cash. Look at the plans being made by the businesses below.

Case 1 *Harpers Ltd*

Harpers Ltd is a manufacturer of electrical motors which are fitted into refrigerators and washing machines. Jeff Harper, the managing director, does a lot of planning for the business. For example, he:
- produces cash flow forecasts;
- prepares budgets;
- sets targets for sales and profits;
- has a plan in case there is any unexpected expenditure.

Jeff has found that careful planning has improved the performance of the business.

Case 2 *Carl Roberts*

Carl Roberts owns a garage in Maidstone. He plans to expand the business by setting up an automatic car wash. The car wash unit will cost £12,000. Carl plans to borrow £4,000 from the bank, use £4,000 of his own savings and £4,000 from retained profits. Carl has calculated that if the car wash is successful, it will pay for itself in 20 months.

Case 3 *Perkins plc*

Perkins plc produces canned foods for dogs and cats. The company wants to increase sales by 30% over the next 3 years and it plans to launch an advertising campaign to achieve this target. The company plans to spend £2.5 million, £3 million and £3.5 million in 2003, 2004 and 2005 respectively. The company has calculated that if sales increase by the planned 30%, profits will rise by 50%.

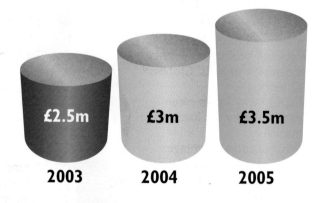

£2.5m	£3m	£3.5m
2003	**2004**	**2005**

Describe the financial planning being done by:
(a) Harpers Ltd
(b) Carl Roberts
(c) Perkins plc.

How does a business plan its finance?

The importance of planning

Everyone makes plans. Planning is important because it helps things to run more smoothly. What would happen if your holiday abroad wasn't planned properly? You might not get into the country if you didn't have a visa or there may be nowhere to stay because all the hotels are full. Money might run out because the prices are higher than you thought. Planning will help to avoid problems like these.

Financial planning helps businesses to:
- avoid running out of cash;
- meet financial targets;
- make the best use of resources;
- deal with financial problems, such as unexpected costs;
- keep stakeholders informed about the progress and future of the business.

Planning income and expenditure

Most businesses spend some time planning how much they expect to spend in the next year and how much income they expect to get. Cash flow forecasts may be used to do this. If a cash flow forecast shows that a business will run out of cash in six months time, it will have to plan where to get some money from, for example from a bank loan.

Setting targets

Financial planning often involves setting targets. Setting targets helps a business to achieve its objectives. A business might set targets for:
- sales units;
- sales revenue;
- profit;
- costs.

Profit and loss accounts might be used when setting targets. For example, if the net profit was £150,000 last year, the business might set a target of £175,000 for the next year.

Planning new activities

Businesses may need to plan when they get involved in new activities. New activities might include a confectionery manufacturer, such as Cadbury Schweppes, launching a new chocolate bar. New activities might need planning for:
- new sources of funds
- new staff recruitment;
- a special marketing campaign;
- the construction of a new building.

Businesses are also likely to estimate how long it will take new activities to make a profit or to break-even.

Planning and stakeholders

Financial plans may be useful to business stakeholders. For example:
- managers will want to know how much money they are going to get to run their departments;
- owners will want to know what profits have been forecast;
- creditors will want to know if the business looks financially secure;
- investors will want to know whether future plans will give a high enough return on their investment.

A business plan

It is common for a business to write a BUSINESS PLAN showing how its objectives will be achieved. It may be written when a new business is set up or when a new activity is planned. It might include:

- ✪ name and address of the business;
- ✪ business objectives;
- ✪ product or service being produced;
- ✪ details about the market;
- ✪ types and numbers of staff needed;
- ✪ resources needed, such as equipment;
- ✪ estimated costs;
- ✪ sources of finance;
- ✪ a cash flow forecast.

Banks and other financial organisations often give help to businesses when drawing up a business plan when they first set up.

Contingency planning

CONTINGENCY PLANS are the plans made by a business to deal with serious problems such as a fire, flood, strike, legal claims against the business or a large bad debt. Such problems may mean that a business runs out of cash or has to stop production. Contingency plans may involve:

- ✪ having emergency funds ready;
- ✪ special training for managers and staff;
- ✪ having access to alternative premises;
- ✪ holding emergency stocks of products;
- ✪ having effective communication systems.

key terms

✪ Business plan – *a document showing how a business plans to meet its objectives.*
✪ Contingency plans – *plans made by a business to deal with serious problems.*

key terms key terms key terms key terms key terms key t

Quick quiz

1 True or false?

(a) A cash flow forecast may be used when making financial plans.

(b) Contingency plans are most likely to be made when setting up a small business.

(c) Financial plans will be of interest to the local council.

2 Which of these would not appear in a business plan?

(a) Staffing numbers.

(b) Cash flow forecast.

(c) Staff records.

(d) Estimated costs.

3 Which of these stakeholders would not be interested in financial plans?

(a) Government.

(b) Owners.

(c) Creditors.

(d) Managers.

4 State three financial targets that a business might set when planning.

5 State three serious problems for which a business may have contingency plans.

Exam practice

Sandersons

Michelle Sanderson runs a health food shop in Cheltenham. It is very successful and Michelle now wants to set up a web site selling health food by mail order. This new activity will involve buying new resources and going into debt. Michelle reckons that the following setting up costs will have to be met:

- IT costs £12,000
- New stock £15,000
- Advertising £5,000
- Other set-up costs £8,000

To fund the new activity Michelle plans to use £14,000 retained profit and £8,000 of her own money. She hopes that her bank will provide the rest.

1. Calculate how much Michelle must plan to borrow for the new activity. (2 marks)
2. Before granting a loan, the bank has asked Michelle to produce a business plan for the new venture. Explain what Michelle might include in this business plan. (6 marks)
3. Use examples to explain how financial planning might help Michelle when running her business. (7 marks)

Index

References in colour are defined in the key terms sections of the book.

A

ACAS 122
accountants 34
accounts 34
   defined 34
   and customers 221
   and employees 221
   and managers 221
   and stakeholders 217, 218, 221
   and their uses 216-219
administration and IT support 36-39
administration 37
advertising 53
   defined 53, 54
advertising agency 53
   defined 53, 54
advertising media 53
   defined 53, 54
Advertising Standards Authority (ASA) 146
   defined 146
after-sales service 57
   defined 57, 58
aims of business 4-7
   defined 5,6
Alternative Investment Market (AIM) 14
aims (see business aims)
Annual General Meeting 13
anti-virus software 66
   defined 66
application forms 129
application letter 130
appraisal 134
   defined 134, 135
arbitration 122
   defined 122
assets 209
   defined 209,210
   and balance sheet 213
assisted areas 21
authorised signatory 157
   defined 157, 159

B

balance sheet 212-215
   defined 212,214
   structure 213
   and sole traders 213
   and limited companies 214
bank loan 226, 230
bank overdraft 225
   defined 225, 226
batch production 42
   defined 42
BBC 18
board of directors 102
bonus 110
bookkeeping 34
   defined 34
brand 50
   defined 50
break-even 192-195
   defined 192, 194
break-even charts 196
   defined 196, 198
break-even point 193
   defined 193, 194
brownfield sites 21
   defined 21, 22
budgets 184-187, 188-191
   defined 184,186
   and fraud 189
   and motivation 190
   and their use 189, 190
budget holders 189
   defined 189, 190
business activity 24-27
business communications 68-75
business documents 148-151, 149, 152-155, 156-159
   and computerised systems 158
business functions 101
   defined 101, 102
business objectives 4-7
   defined 6
business ownership 8-11, 12-15, 16-19
business rates 21
   defined 21, 22
business transactions 34
   defined 34

C

calculating profit and loss 200-203
capital 210
   defined 210
   and balance sheet 213,21
capital expenditure budget 86
capital goods 25
   defined 25, 26
capital intensive 41
   defined 41, 42
cash 161, 165
   and profit 182
   as current asset 209
cash flow 176-179
   defined 176, 178
cash flow forecasts 178, 180-183, 181
   defined 178
cash flow problems 181
cash inflow 177
   defined 177, 178
cash outflow 177
   defined 177, 178
cashier 33
cheque 157, 161, 165
   defined 157, 159
Citizens Advice Bureau 146
cleaning and maintenance 38
cleared (cheque) 161
   defined 161, 163
clerical work 37
client services 26
   defined 26
coaching 133
codes of practice 146
commission 110
communications 68-71
   defined 69
communication methods 72-75
communication problems 70
competition 76-79, 77
   defined 77, 78
   and benefits 77
   and technology 78
competition policies 90
   defined 90
competitors 80-83
computer aided design (CAD) 46
   defined 46
computer aided manufacturing (CAM) 46
   defined 46
consumer co-operative 18
   defined 18
Consumer Credit Act 1974 145
consumer goods 25
   defined 25, 26
consumer protection 144-147
Consumer Protection Act 1987 145